MÉLANGES

SUR LA

VIE PRIVÉE ET PUBLIQUE

DU

MARQUIS DE LABRADOR

ÉCRITS PAR LUI-MÊME

ET RENFERMANT UNE REVUE DE LA POLITIQUE DE L'EUROPE
DEPUIS 1798 JUSQU'AU MOIS D'OCTOBRE 1849
ET DES RÉVÉLATIONS TRÈS-IMPORTANTES
SUR LE CONGRÈS DE VIENNE.

Bueno de rogar,
Malo de forzar.

Precibus non vi flectendus.

PARIS

IMPRIMÉ PAR E. THUNOT ET Cⁱᵉ

RUE RACINE, 26, PRÈS DE L'ODÉON

1849

MÉLANGES

SUR LA

VIE PRIVÉE ET PUBLIQUE

DU

MARQUIS DE LABRADOR

AVANT-PROPOS.

Le marquis de Labrador fut le seul plénipotentiaire chargé de représenter l'Espagne au congrès de Vienne. Chaque jour, il écrivait le procès-verbal des séances, et il l'envoyait au ministre des affaires étrangères à Madrid ; mais il conservait avec soin par devers lui le double de cette correspondance, ayant, dès le commencement du congrès, formé le projet d'en écrire l'histoire. Le seul style qui eût pu convenir à un pareil sujet, c'est celui que Tacite a employé pour dévoiler et stigmatiser la politique des maîtres de Rome dégénérée. Ce grand historien est le modèle que M. de Labrador se serait efforcé d'imiter.

La révolution d'Espagne, en 1820, empêcha M. de Labrador de mettre son projet à exécution ; mais il conserva les matériaux de son travail, et les transporta à

Rome en 1828 , lorsqu'il s'y rendit en qualité d'ambassadeur. Malheureusement M. de Labrador, ayant, après
dix-huit ans d'absence , désiré faire un voyage en Espagne et étant parti pour Madrid en 1831, laissa ces manuscrits dans son cabinet. Le secrétaire de l'ambassade, qui
resta comme chargé d'affaires, était un homme d'esprit et
d'honneur, et on ne peut concevoir dans quel but il envoya
à Madrid une liste détaillée de ces manuscrits. On ne conçoit
pas non plus dans quelle intention le ministre ordonna que
tous ces papiers lui fussent envoyés. Pour rendre cette affaire
plus inexplicable encore, jamais le ministre des affaires étrangères n'en parla à M. de Labrador, qui était alors à Madrid,
de façon que M. de Labrador, de retour à Rome en 1832,
fut fort surpris de n'y plus trouver ses notes particulières et les
documents qui devaient lui servir pour écrire l'histoire qu'il
préparait. La mort du roi Ferdinand compliqua les affaires,
et M. de Labrador fut forcé de renoncer à son projet. Ne
pouvant pas écrire sur le congrès de Vienne selon le plan
qu'il avait conçu, il s'est contenté de recueillir les faits les
plus marquants de l'époque dont il s'agit, et il les a réunis au
récit de sa longue carrière politique, à dater de 1798, de
sorte qu'à compter de cette époque, ces mémoires seront une
histoire fidèle de la politique de l'Europe. Le congrès de
Vienne occupera naturellement dans ce récit une place pro-
portionnée à son importance; d'autant plus que M. de Labrador est le seul qui puisse faire des révélations curieuses
sur cette réunion diplomatique, qui, destinée à mettre fin
aux usurpations et aux abus commis depuis la révolution de

France, ne fit, au contraire, que les confirmer, portant ainsi le coup de grâce à ce que l'on appelait le droit de la nature et des gens, c'est-à-dire aux principes d'après lesquels se réglaient les rapports entre les différents gouvernements de l'Europe. Le congrès de Vienne, en disposant de Gênes, de Venise, de Parme et d'une partie de la Saxe, a introduit dans l'Europe politique le système suivi dans le grand empire de Neptune, où les gros poissons dévorent les petits (*). C'est fort triste et fort dur à dire ; mais c'est l'exacte vérité, et ceux qui pourraient en douter seront forcés d'en convenir lorsqu'ils auront lu ces mélanges.

(*) Pour augmenter encore, s'il était possible, l'état de désordre dans lequel se trouvent les relations entre les différents gouvernements de l'Europe, des publicistes de beaucoup d'esprit, d'une vaste érudition et, j'aime à le croire, d'une entière bonne foi, ont donné le titre de grandes puissances ou de puissances de premier ordre à quelques gouvernements de l'Europe, et ils ont placé l'Espagne parmi les puissances de second ordre. Ces estimables écrivains n'ont manqué que d'une chose, de données exactes et vraies sur la force des puissances qu'ils se sont ainsi permis de classer à leur guise ; sans cela, il serait impossible de concevoir le rang subalterne qu'ils ont assigné à l'Espagne, et cela dans un temps où plusieurs de ces grandes puissances, qu'ils ont tant vantées, s'écroulent comme ces vastes et magnifiques édifices qui ont été construits à la hâte et sans autre règle pour le choix des matériaux que celle de prendre tout ce qu'on a trouvé sous la main. Les personnes qui vivront encore vingt ou trente ans pourront dire combien de ces prétendues grandes puissances seront restées debout, et se trouveront en mesure de se comparer à l'Espagne.

MÉLANGES

SUR LA

VIE PRIVÉE ET PUBLIQUE

DU

MARQUIS DE LABRADOR.

———◆◈◆———

Don Pedro Gomez Havela, marquis de Labrador, naquit à Valencia de Alcantara, petite ville forte de la province d'Estramadure. Il eut pour père don Diego Gomez Patiño et pour mère doña Catalina Havela Alvarado. Son grand-père fut don Bartolomé Gomez Labrador et sa grand'mère, doña Maria Josefa Patiño. Après qu'il eut fait ses premières études dans sa ville natale, ses parents l'envoyèrent, à l'âge de douze ans, à Salamanque pour y compléter son éducation sous la direction de don Justo Garcia, professeur de mathématiques, qui a laissé des ouvrages très-estimés sur cette science. Il était en outre fort remarquable comme latiniste, et savait l'hébreu, l'anglais et le français (1). M. de Labrador étudia sous lui pendant deux ans les mathématiques et il assistait en même temps aux cours de philosophie. Pour la poésie, il fut l'élève de Mélendez, qui, né comme lui en Estramadure, fut le premier à relever la poésie espagnole de la décadence dans laquelle elle était tombée depuis les premières années du XVIIIe siècle. M. de Labrador a conservé toute sa vie un goût très-vif pour la poésie; mais ses occupations l'ont empêché de s'y adonner.

Il étudia le droit de la nature et des gens (2) sous la direction du professeur Caballero, qui devint par la suite ministre de la justice du roi Charles IV, et qui, sous le titre de marquis Caballero, joua un grand rôle dans le mouvement d'Aranjuez, en 1808. Il passa plus de huit années à Salamanque, se préparant par de longues et sérieuses études à la carrière diplomatique, à laquelle ses parents le destinaient.

La première place diplomatique qu'obtint M. de Labrador fut celle de chargé d'affaires à Florence, en 1798.

Le pape Pie VI, chassé de Rome par ordre du

Directoire exécutif, résidait à Sienne, et il avait auprès de lui le cardinal espagnol Lorenzana, archevêque de Tolède, chargé par la cour d'Espagne de résider auprès du saint-père comme ambassadeur, et de pourvoir à tout ce dont il pourrait avoir besoin, ainsi que sa suite.

Le tremblement de terre qui avait fait de grands ravages à Sienne, et les préparatifs de l'Autriche et de la Russie pour envahir l'Italie décidèrent le gouvernement français à faire partir le pape pour Parme. A Florence, le général français qui commandait dans cette ville s'opposa à ce que le cardinal Lorenzana accompagnât plus loin le saint-père, et le retint malgré lui dans la capitale de la Toscane. Quelque temps après, la cour d'Espagne envoya à M. de Labrador l'ordre d'aller rejoindre Pie VI et de rester auprès de lui si on le laissait en Italie. Le pape, à qui on avait désigné Turin pour sa résidence, invita M. de Labrador à s'y rendre; mais, lorsque M. de Labrador arriva à Turin, le général Grouchy, qui commandait dans cette ville, venait de faire partir Sa Sainteté pour Briançon. Alors M. de Labrador retourna à Florence, où lui arriva, quelque temps après, l'ordre d'aller rejoindre Sa Sainteté en France. M. de Labrador trouva à Grenoble la suite du saint-père, notamment les prélats Spina et Caracciolo, qui furent plus tard cardinaux. Le pape était resté à Briançon avec deux domestiques et dans un complet dénûment.

Le vénérable pontife fut si touché de l'arrivée de M. de Labrador que, dans une bulle qu'il expédia quelque temps après, il lui donnait le titre d'Ange envoyé par le ciel à son secours. M. de Labrador fit les démarches les plus actives auprès du général qui commandait en Dauphiné, pour obtenir que Sa Sainteté, qui avait quatre-vingt-trois ans et des infirmités, fût transférée à Grenoble et réunie aux personnes de sa suite, parmi lesquelles se trouvait son médecin. Le général, malgré sa bonne volonté, ne crut pas pouvoir accéder à cette demande, et il fallut attendre un ordre de Paris, que M. de Labrador obtint en écrivant à M. Azara, alors ambassadeur auprès du gouvernement français. On fit donc venir le pape à Grenoble; mais on ne tarda pas à le conduire avec sa suite à la citadelle de Valence en Dauphiné. M. de Labrador se rendit dans la même ville, et il était la seule personne qui, sans faire partie de la suite du pape, pût approcher de Sa Sainteté, ce qu'il faisait tous les jours. Ce n'était pas à cela que se bornaient les attentions de M. de Labrador; tout ce que le vénérable captif pouvait souhaiter lui était à l'instant procuré, et la cour d'Espagne payait aux quinze personnes de sa suite les mêmes appointements que le pape leur donnait auparavant à Rome.

C'est à Valence que Pie VI termina sa carrière, le 29 août 1799. Après ce triste événement, le gouvernement français refusa aux Italiens de la suite du pontife des passe-ports pour retourner dans leur patrie, et ils étaient encore à Valence lorsque le général Bonaparte y passa pour se rendre à Paris, à son retour d'Égypte. Il avait remarqué, avant d'entrer dans la ville, des prêtres italiens et, pendant qu'il changeait de chevaux, il voulut savoir pour quelles raisons ils se trouvaient en Dauphiné. Le prélat Spina, qui était celui de ces Italiens qui parlait le mieux le français, expliqua à Bonaparte la cause de leur séjour et le pria de faire, à son arrivée à Paris, des démarches pour leur obtenir l'autorisation de retourner en Italie. Bonaparte le promit et tint parole; des passe-ports leur furent aussitôt délivrés. M. de Labrador, de son côté, fut autorisé à passer par Paris, et il s'y trouvait encore lorsque les cardinaux qui s'étaient réfugiés dans les pays non occupés par les armées françaises, formèrent le projet de se réunir en conclave à Venise pour choisir un successeur à Pie VI. M. de Labrador reçut l'ordre de son gouvernement d'aller à Venise et de se présenter aux cardinaux comme ministre d'Espagne. Il devait passer par Vienne et il avait déjà reçu ses passe-ports, lorsque la nouvelle de la bataille de Marengo parvint à Paris. On dit d'abord que l'armée française avait été repoussée et battue, et les deux consuls et les ministres se réunirent pour nommer un successeur à Bonaparte comme premier consul. Le choix tomba sur le général Carnot; mais, le lendemain, tout changea d'aspect. M. de Labrabor, qui habitait l'hôtel du Carrousel, tout près des Tuileries, fut réveillé à six heures du matin par son valet de chambre, qui lui annonça la visite de l'évêque constitutionnel de Blois, l'abbé Grégoire. L'abbé Grégoire fut introduit chez M. de Labrador, et il lui dit que le troisième consul, qu'il venait de quitter, lui avait appris que, par un courrier extraordinaire, on savait que, non-seulement les Autrichiens avaient été mis en déroute, mais que Bonaparte s'était rendu maître de treize forteresses. Par suite de cette grande nouvelle, M. de Talleyrand, ministre des affaires étrangères, écrivit un petit billet à M. de Labrador, l'invitant à dîner à sa maison de campagne de Passy, et le priant de suspendre son départ pour Venise. M. de Talleyrand dit, à cette occasion, à M. de Labrador que le premier consul voulait faire par son moyen des ouvertures au pape qui serait élu à Venise, et qu'il lui donnait rendez-vous à Milan. M. de Labrador partit sans délai, mais il se croisa à Lyon avec le premier consul et ne put communiquer avec lui sur les ouvertures que celui-ci voulait faire au saint-siége. M. de Talleyrand, de son côté, avait borné ses instructions à quatre mots. C'était de dire au nouveau pape que le premier consul serait très-libéral envers le saint-siége en ce qui regardait les affaires temporelles, si le saint-père l'était envers la France pour ce qui regardait les affaires spirituelles.

Lorsque M. de Labrador arriva en Italie, on avait élu le cardinal Chiaramonti, qui prit le nom de Pie VII. Il fit part au nouveau pape du désir qu'avait Bonaparte de faire un concordat avec le saint-siége. Ensuite il s'occupa des affaires de son gouvernement, et spécialement de la demande que faisait l'Espagne de prélever en faveur du trésor royal, pour la liquidation de la dette nationale, la neuvième partie du produit de la dîme, ce qui, selon les calculs des ministres espagnols, devait donner à l'État une somme annuelle de quinze millions de francs. On avait déjà exigé tant de sacrifices du clergé, qu'il paraissait difficile qu'on accordât une demande aussi exorbitante. On le fit cependant, mais les cardinaux et les prélats déclarèrent, depuis ce moment, la guerre à M. de Labrador, et, malgré l'estime et même l'amitié que Pie VII avait pour lui, on fit savoir à la cour d'Espagne que sa personne n'était pas agréable à Rome. On lui donna comme successeur M. Vargas Laguna, et il fut rappelé en Espagne; mais, en route, il reçut une mission pour Florence, où se trouvait le général Murat avec son quartier général.

La reine Marie-Louise, épouse de Charles IV, avait marié sa fille aînée à l'héritier présomptif de la couronne de Portugal (3), et la troisième à celui du royaume des Deux-Siciles; quant à la seconde, qui était pourtant celle qu'elle préférait, elle lui avait fait faire un mariage bien moins avantageux : elle lui avait donné pour époux le prince de Parme. Or elle souhaitait ardemment que cette princesse eût aussi une couronne. En conséquence de ses désirs, exprimés à l'ambassadeur de France à Madrid, on forma le projet d'ériger en royaume le grand-duché de Toscane et de le céder à l'Espagne en faveur du duc de Parme, en échange des trois duchés de Parme, Plaisance et Guastalla. Mais, comme ces trois duchés n'avaient pas la moitié de la population de la Toscane, on demanda et on obtint que l'Espagne cédât la Louisiane et remit six vaisseaux de ligne armés, et 30 millions de francs. Ces négociations furent conduites à Paris par M. Yzquierdo, directeur du Musée d'histoire naturelle de Madrid, que le tout-puissant Godoy avait investi de ses pleins pouvoirs. M. de Labrador n'eut donc aucune part dans cette négociation. Lorsque le nouveau roi d'Étrurie vint à Florence avec l'Infante d'Espagne, sa femme, et son fils aîné, M. de Labrador fut accrédité comme ministre plénipotentiaire, poste qu'il conserva jusqu'à ce que Bonaparte, qui avait vendu si cher la Toscane à l'Espagne, jugea à propos de la reprendre, en donnant à la reine d'Étrurie, qui avait perdu son mari, la ville d'Oporto et un territoire habité par trois cent mille âmes, en échange de la Toscane, qui en avait plus d'un million.

Bonaparte se trouvait alors à Milan. Il écrivit à la reine douairière d'Étrurie que le traité d'échange entre la Toscane et le territoire d'Oporto pour Sa Majesté, et celui de la province des Algarves pour le prince de la Paix, n'aurait dû s'effectuer qu'à la paix générale, mais qu'une imprudence de M. de Beauharnais avait rendu ce traité public; que dès lors la reine ne pouvait plus rester à Florence, et qu'il la priait de se rendre à Milan. M. de Labrador accompagna la princesse et son enfant, qui avait été reconnu comme roi d'Étrurie par Napoléon et par toutes les puissances soumises à son influence, comme l'Autriche, la Hollande et la république Cisalpine. A son arrivée à Milan, M. de Labrador reçut un billet de M. de Champagny, ministre des affaires étrangères, dans lequel il lui disait que Sa Majesté Impériale l'attendait dans la matinée du lendemain. Dans cette audience, Bonaparte tâcha de persuader à M. de Labrador que c'était à sa protection que le prince des Asturies avait dû sa liberté lorsqu'il avait été arrêté comme complice de la conspiration contre son père.

Napoléon faisait alors fortifier Alexandrie en Piémont, et il avait défendu de donner à personne des chevaux de poste jusqu'à ce qu'il eût quitté Milan. M. de Labrador resta donc pendant huit jours à Milan avec la reine d'Étrurie, dont Napoléon avait décidé le voyage pour Madrid. Pendant son séjour à Milan, Bonaparte allait presque tous les jours faire de longues visites à M. de Melcy, alors duc de Lodi. M. de Melcy avait des parents en Espagne, et il avait habité Saragosse; il possédait en outre en Catalogne le comté de Héril. On croyait que les longues visites de Napoléon avaient pour but les affaires d'Italie, mais il ne faisait que prendre quelques livres et surtout examiner la carte d'Espagne, ce qui fit penser à MM. de Melcy et de Labrador, et au général O'Farril, qui était aussi de la suite de la reine d'Étrurie, que Bonaparte avait des vues sur la Péninsule. Ce qui n'était qu'un soupçon devint bientôt une certitude ; car, un jour, le roi de Bavière dit à MM. de Labrador et O'Farril qu'il était l'allié de Napoléon, mais qu'avant tout il était l'ami et le parent du roi d'Espagne ; qu'il leur disait donc en confidence que, se promenant en voiture avec Bonaparte, celui-ci avait demandé au général Berthier quand les cent mille hommes seraient prêts à passer les monts. Comme toute l'Italie était alors occupée par les troupes françaises, par ces cent mille hommes prêts à passer les monts, on ne pouvait entendre qu'une armée française s'apprêtant à franchir les Pyrénées.

M. de Labrador informa sa cour de ces propos par un courrier extraordinaire. Mais l'aveuglement de la reine Marie-Louise et de Godoy était tel qu'on lui répondit que jamais le cabinet espagnol n'avait reçu autant de preuves de la bienveillance de Bonaparte, à qui on donnait le titre d'intime ami et d'allié. L'avant-garde de l'armée française qui devait occuper l'Espagne arriva bientôt à Perpignan, et, parmi les généraux, il s'en trouvait un, appelé Nicolas, Dalmate d'origine, lequel disait publiquement qu'il allait avec ses soldats s'emparer de l'Espagne. Le comte de Santa-Clara, capitaine général de la Catalogne, étant venu au-devant de la reine d'Étrurie et de son fils, avait entendu ces propos; il en fit part à la cour, qui, dans son incurable aveuglement, persista à regarder Napoléon comme son intime ami et allié.

A son arrivée à Aranjuez, M. de Labrador fut très-bien reçu par le roi Charles IV et par la reine, mais non pas par don Manuel Godoy. Ce fut en vain que tous les hommes de bon sens se déclarèrent contre l'avis de ce puissant favori, qui, en qualité de généralissime des armées espagnoles, envoya aux commandants des frontières l'ordre de ne mettre aucun obstacle au passage des Français et de les recevoir partout en amis et en alliés. Par suite de ces ordres, les Français qui pénétrèrent en Catalogne par Figuières furent admis à Barcelone, de même que ceux qui entrèrent par Irun le furent à Pampelune.

La division qui occupait Pampelune recevait tous les jours le pain dans la citadelle, où était le magasin du fournisseur. Il était tombé beaucoup de neige, et les soldats français qui portaient des sacs pour

mettre le pain furent poursuivis par d'autres soldats,
qui leur jetaient des boules de neige. Ils franchirent
ainsi les portes de la citadelle, suivis par leurs camarades, et, lorsqu'ils se trouvèrent en nombre suffi-
sant, les premiers tirèrent des armes de leurs sacs,
désarmèrent les sentinelles et s'emparèrent de la
citadelle. Au moment où cette comédie se jouait à
Pampelune, les troupes françaises qui occupaient
Barcelone manœuvraient sur la place près de la citadelle, dont les portes étaient ouvertes, et, simu-
lant un mouvement sur un autre point, elles se
portèrent à l'improviste sur la citadelle, dont elles
s'emparèrent en laissant les deux sentinelles ébahies
de cette manœuvre fort inattendue.

C'est ainsi que Napoléon se rendit maître de ces
deux places fortes. On ne peut contester qu'il ait été
l'un des premiers génies militaires des temps modernes; il a été aussi très-remarquable dans le choix
des hommes qu'il employait, surtout depuis que
l'expérience lui eut appris à bien distinguer les talents
et les aptitudes. Mais, malgré son génie et ses victoires, Napoléon ne pourra jamais être placé parmi les
grands hommes, parce que la ruse et la perfidie ont
quelque chose de bas et de dégradant. Il y a loin
d'ailleurs du génie de Napoléon à celui d'Alexandre

et de César, qui, avec peu de ressources, faisaient de grandes choses, et qui ont imposé aux siècles leurs institutions militaires, dont les nôtres ne sont en partie que la copie.

Depuis que M. de Labrador était arrivé à Aranjuez avec la reine d'Étrurie, l'horizon politique de l'Espagne continuait à se rembrunir de plus en plus. Il avait trouvé à Perpignan l'avant-garde de l'armée française, et cette avant-garde était déjà maîtresse de Barcelone et des autres places de Catalogne qu'il lui avait plu d'occuper; en même temps, Murat et Dupont se rapprochaient de Madrid, l'un par la route de Valladolid, et l'autre par celle de Ségovie.

Lorsque Bonaparte avait formé le projet de s'emparer du Portugal, il avait envoyé le général Junot avec une grande armée, à laquelle il avait demandé à l'Espagne de réunir deux corps d'armée espagnols; ce qui lui avait été accordé comme tout ce qu'il demandait, et sans que le général qui commandait toutes ces forces fît connaître le but de cette invasion du Portugal. On fit marcher ces troupes sur Lisbonne et sur Oporto. La cour de Portugal, intimidée, prit la résolution d'abandonner son royaume, et s'embarqua pour Rio-Janeiro. C'était le but que Bona-

parte s'était proposé, et, une fois que la cour de
Portugal eut perdu de vue les côtes de son royaume,
il fit publier une proclamation dans laquelle il disait
aux Portugais que, puisque leur souverain les avait
abandonnés, ils n'avaient pas d'autre ressource que
celle de se jeter dans ses bras. Ce plan avait si bien
réussi à Bonaparte qu'il voulut le suivre également
en Espagne, en forçant la famille royale à
partir pour Cadix, et de là pour l'Amérique espagnole.

M. Yzquierdo arriva de Paris à Aranjuez, et fit
part à don Manuel Godoy d'une conférence qu'il
avait eue avec le prince de Talleyrand, dans laquelle
celui-ci s'était montré très-courroucé contre le
prince de la Paix, et avait donné à entendre que le
mouvement de l'armée française sur Madrid n'avait
d'autre but que l'éloignement de ce favori. Aussitôt
que le roi et la reine eurent connaissance de cette
communication, on prit la résolution de partir pour
Cadix. On fit aposter sur la route tous les chevaux
et les mulets des écuries du roi, et cette mesure fit
connaître la détermination que l'on avait prise, et
que l'on avait eu grand soin jusque-là de tenir se-
crète. L'exécution du projet de fuite fut empêchée par
l'émeute qui eut lieu à Aranjuez le 18 mars 1808.

M. de Labrador était alors à Madrid, et il ne s'étendra pas sur cet événement, assez connu d'ailleurs par les relations détaillées qu'en ont publiées d'autres personnes (4). Depuis ce mouvement du 18 mars, il n'arriva aucun événement digne d'être remarqué jusqu'au 9 avril, que M. de Labrador partit avec le roi.

Pendant que les troupes françaises s'avançaient vers Madrid, l'ambassadeur Beauharnais annonçait la prochaine arrivée de Napoléon. On lui prépara un appartement au palais royal, et aussitôt l'ambassadeur fit déposer sur une table du salon le petit chapeau et les autres attributs inséparables de son maître. Le général Savary, qui le précédait, demanda s'il ne serait pas convenable que le prince des Asturies, nom que l'on donnait au roi Ferdinand, allât au-devant de Sa Majesté Impériale. Le duc de San-Carlos, grand maître de la maison du roi, le duc de l'Infantado, ami de Sa Majesté, et le chanoine Escoiquiz, qui avait été son précepteur, décidèrent facilement le roi Ferdinand à se porter jusqu'à Buitrago pour y recevoir son hôte auguste. Outre ces trois personnages, le roi Ferdinand choisit pour l'accompagner son ministre des affaires étrangères Cevallos, le marquis de Muzquiz, qui avait été ambassadeur à Paris, et le marquis de Labrador.

La monarchie espagnole n'était plus, en 1808, ce qu'elle avait été sous Charles-Quint et Philippe II. La guerre de succession avait mis l'Europe en feu ; les Espagnols, au lieu de se tenir unis et d'empêcher les autres nations de se mêler de leurs affaires, s'étaient déclarés, les uns pour un prince français, les autres pour un Autrichien (5). Aucun de ces prétendants n'avait réellement droit à la couronne d'Espagne, puisque les infantes dont ils tenaient leurs droits y avaient renoncé en leur nom et en celui de leurs successeurs. Mais la cour de Versailles et celle de Vienne prétendirent que les infantes pouvaient bien renoncer pour elles, mais non pas pour leurs descendants. Si cette doctrine des casuistes politiques était appliquée aux traités de paix, elle remplirait l'Europe d'une confusion encore plus grande que celle qui existe actuellement ; si on l'appliquait aux transactions particulières, les enfants de ceux qui auraient cédé leurs biens pourraient dire aussi que leurs pères ou leurs devanciers avaient le droit de le faire pour eux, mais qu'ils ne pouvaient pas compromettre l'avenir de leurs descendants.

La guerre de succession se termina au préjudice

de la monarchie espagnole, en faisant asseoir sur le trône de Charles-Quint un petit-fils de Louis XIV, et en donnant à l'Autriche Naples, la Sicile, le Milanais, toutes les possessions en Italie et ce que l'on nomme maintenant la Belgique. La Savoie eut aussi sa part : on lui céda la Sardaigne, que l'on érigea en royaume. L'Angleterre eut Gibraltar, pour être un des boulevards de sa puissance navale. On s'est beaucoup récrié et on se récrie tous les jours contre le partage de la malheureuse Pologne ; mais on ne dit pas un mot de ce partage plus ancien et non moins inique. Malgré tant de pertes, en 1808, le soleil ne se couchait pas sur les pays où flottait le drapeau espagnol, et le roi d'une si vaste monarchie allait au-devant d'un pauvre gentilhomme corse, qui n'avait pu recevoir une éducation convenable que grâce à la générosité de la cour de France.

Quoiqu'il eût été formellement stipulé que le roi Ferdinand reviendrait avec sa suite passer la nuit à Madrid, l'envoyé de Napoléon obtint que l'on poursuivît jusqu'à Burgos, sur l'assurance qu'il donna que l'empereur des Français viendrait dans cette ville embrasser le roi Ferdinand. Le marquis de Murquiz et M. de Labrador firent tout ce qui dépendait d'eux pour empêcher cette funeste résolution ;

mais les trois conseillers du roi disaient que l'Espagne n'avait pas assez de baïonnettes pour s'opposer
à la volonté de Bonaparte. On partit donc pour
Burgos, où Savary répéta le même manége, et il fut
décidé qu'on irait jusqu'à Vitoria parce que, disait
Savary, l'aspect que présentaient les affaires du Nord
ne permettait pas à Napoléon de venir jusqu'à Burgos. A Vitoria, le peuple montra plus de bon sens
que les conseillers du roi, et il s'opposa au départ de
Sa Majesté, en coupant les harnais des mulets atte-
lés à la voiture. Mais on fit venir des troupes et
on trompa les habitants de Vitoria en faisant pla-
carder une proclamation au nom du roi, dans laquelle on déclarait que tous les différends qui exis-
taient étaient aplanis, que Sa Majesté n'allait que
pour embrasser son ami l'empereur et qu'il reviendrait de suite à Madrid. On partit donc de Vitoria
pour Irun, que l'on ne devait pas dépasser. La voiture où se trouvait le marquis de Murquiz et M. de
Labrador se cassa près de Vergara et on dut passer
la nuit à la réparer; lorsque ces deux diplomates
arrivèrent à Irun, le roi était déjà à Bayonne,
où devait s'accomplir l'acte de perfidie le plus ré-
voltant que l'on ait jamais osé commettre dans
l'Europe civilisée.

Bonaparte déclara de vive voix au roi Ferdinand qu'il le regardait comme rebelle envers son père et son roi, et en même temps il lui signifia qu'il eût à nommer une personne chargée de traiter avec son ministre Champagny pour réparer les torts de l'Espagne à l'égard de l'empereur. Le principal grief était une proclamation du généralissime Godoy, qui avait été publiée en 1 06, pour annoncer à l'armée espagnole qu'il allait se mettre à sa tête, qu'il fallait se préparer à une longue route, et qu'il espérait qu'elle se conduirait toujours avec son courage habituel. Pour satisfaire à cette prétention si extraordinaire, le roi Ferdinand nomma son ministre des affaires étrangères M. Cevallos ; mais Bonaparte le refusa en disant qu'il le regardait comme traître au roi Charles IV, et ce fut alors que le roi désigna M. de Labrador, qui fut accepté, non sans objections, par Bonaparte. Celui-ci occupant alors la petite maison de campagne de Marrac, M. de Labrador s'y rendit pour avoir sa première conférence avec M. de Champagny. La chambre où avait lieu cette conférence n'était séparée du salon où se tenait Napoléon que par un rideau, de façon qu'il entendait ce que les deux plénipotentiaires se disaient.

M. de Champagny commença par dire à M. de La-

brador qu'il le considérait comme un homme trop
éclairé pour pouvoir se faire illusion sur l'état de
l'Espagne ; que l'empereur, malgré son génie, sa
renommée et ses armées constamment victorieuses,
ne pouvait être tranquille sur son trône tant que
celui d'Espagne serait occupé par un Bourbon, qui
aurait toujours la pensée de venger ses parents de la
branche aînée ; qu'ainsi le sort de l'Espagne était
irrévocablement fixé ; que Napoléon avait décidé de
placer sur le trône d'Espagne son frère Joseph ; que
l'on choisirait pour ministres du nouveau roi les Espagnols les plus capables, et que ceux qui s'oppo-
seraient aux desseins de l'empereur devaient craindre
sa toute-puissance.

M. de Labrador répondit à M. de Champagny que
ni lui ni l'empereur son maître ne connaissaient
l'Espagne ni les Espagnols ; que lui, comme plénipotentiaire de Ferdinand VII, roi d'Espagne, il
étendrait son bras droit sur la table et se le laisserait
couper plutôt que d'apposer une signature qui le
déshonorerait aux yeux de l'Espagne et du monde
entier. Cette réponse fut connue du général Berthier,
et ce fut à cette occasion qu'il dit que M. de Labrador était le plus féroce de tous les Espagnols. Le général Berthier se trompait : la guerre de Napoléon

contre l'Espagne a dû le persuader que, lorsqu'il s'agissait d'indépendance, tous les Espagnols partageaient l'opinion de M. de Labrador, excepté un petit nombre qui se croyaient plus civilisés que la généralité de leurs compatriotes, et qui en réalité n'étaient que vicieux et corrompus.

Lorsqu'on reçut la nouvelle de ce qui s'était passé à Madrid le 2 mai, on fit partir le roi Ferdinand pour Valençay, sans le séparer pour le moment, ni du duc de San-Carlos ni du chanoine Escoiquiz. Toutes les autres personnes qui avaient accompagné le roi jusqu'à Bayonne reçurent des passe-ports pour retourner en Espagne; mais on les refusa à M. de Labrador, à qui on donna la commission d'aller à Florence pour faire la séparation des effets mobiliers appartenant au roi d'Étrurie, comme souverain de la Toscane, de ceux qui avaient appartenu à son père, et que l'on y avait apportés de Parme. M. de Labrador se rendit donc à Florence, où commandait le général Menou, celui-là même qui, dans l'expédition d'Égypte, s'était fait mahométan et avait épousé la fille d'un propriétaire de bains du Caire. Ce général envoya dire un soir, à dix heures, à M. de Labrador, qu'il le priait de se rendre chez lui pour recevoir une communication très-importante. M. de Labrador se rendit à cette invitation, et il fut reçu par un aide de camp qui lui intima l'ordre de reconnaître Joseph Bonaparte. La même intimation fut faite au secrétaire de légation Argumosa, et à quatre autres Espagnols qui résidaient à Florence, savoir : un ancien pensionnaire de l'École de peinture à Rome, un employé à la Bibliothèque royale de Madrid et deux jeunes graveurs.

A des époques que l'on nomme barbares, lorsqu'on envahissait un pays, on se contentait de demander le serment de fidélité aux municipalités. Bonaparte étendit cette injonction à tous ceux dont il craignait les opinions contraires à son ambition. M. de Labrador, son secrétaire de légation, un courrier de cabinet et les artistes mentionnés, ayant refusé de prêter serment, furent conduits à la forteresse de Florence, où l'on enferma ensemble dans une petite chambre M. de Labrador, M. Argumosa et le courrier de cabinet. Ils y passèrent la nuit sur des chaises, car on ne leur donna pas même de matelas. Malgré cela, on prétend que, depuis la première révolution de France, la civilisation a fait de grands progrès. Si par civilisation on entend les nouvelles découvertes dans les sciences et dans la construction des machines, on a raison de s'applaudir des progrès de l'esprit humain ; mais, pour ce qui est de la vraie liberté des nations, du bien-être des individus et des égards dus à tout homme, quelles que soient ses opinions, on se trompe énormément. M de Labrador, M. Argumosa et le courrier de cabinet furent ensuite transportés à Dijon. Les quatre artistes reçurent l'ordre de s'y rendre aussi, et, comme ils n'avaient pas les moyens de se faire conduire en voiture, ils auraient été forcés d'y aller à pied escortés par des gendarmes, si M. de Labrador n'eût payé pour eux une voiture ainsi que le voyage et le retour des gendarmes chargés de les conduire. On mit vingt jours pour se rendre de Florence à Dijon, et dans les auberges on plaçait un gendarme à la porte de la chambre de M. de Labrador.

M. de Labrador resta à Dijon depuis la fin d'octobre 1808 jusqu'au mois de mai 1811, époque à laquelle on lui accorda la permission de choisir un meilleur climat ; il se décida pour Nîmes. Il resta dans cette ville jusqu'au mois de mai 1812. A cette époque, il s'échappa, et, traversant le Roussillon et la Catalogne, occupés alors par les Français, il se rendit, partie à cheval partie à pied, à Villanueva de Sitches en Catalogne ; de là il s'embarqua pour Palma, capitale de Majorque, où il ne s'arrêta que le temps nécessaire pour admirer la douceur du climat de cette île et l'abondance de ses productions. Les mœurs des habitants de Majorque sont entièrement patriarcales, et c'est peut-être le seul pays d'Europe où l'on trouve encore des hommes que notre fausse civilisation n'a nullement atteints.

M. de Labrador partit de Majorque à bord de la frégate espagnole *la Esmeralda*, chargée de prendre la correspondance de la partie de l'Espagne qui n'était pas occupée par les Français. On se rendit d'abord à Alicante et de là à Carthagène, où le capitaine de la frégate ne voulut pas débarquer à cause de la fièvre jaune qui y sévissait. Les autorités de cette place prétendaient que c'était un bruit calomnieux, et, pour se venger du refus du capitaine, ils écrivirent à la régence de Cadix que cette frégate était atteinte du fléau. On ordonna donc au capitaine de se rendre à Algéciras pour y faire quarantaine. La frégate avait à bord deux cents recrues; pendant les vingt-quatre jours de quarantaine, au mois d'août, et dans un climat aussi chaud que celui d'Algéciras, il y avait tout sujet de craindre que des maladies ne se déclarassent en effet sur le navire; heureusement ces craintes ne se réalisèrent pas, et, à peine la quarantaine était-elle terminée, qu'on reçut la nouvelle de la levée du siége de Cadix par les Français. On se rendit donc à ce port, où M. de Labrador fut reçu avec beaucoup de joie par ses amis qui siégeaient aux cortès. Une des places de la régence qui avait été occupée par le général O'Donell, était alors vacante par suite de la démission de ce général. Les amis de M. de Labrador voulaient l'y porter; mais il s'y refusa, parce qu'à son avis, il était impossible de gouverner avec la Constitution de 1812. On nomma M. Villamil, magistrat au conseil de la guerre, un des hommes les plus instruits de la magistrature, et d'une modestie et d'une probité extraordinaires. Il était privé de ses propriétés, situées dans les Asturies, et cependant il n'accepta la place de régent qu'à la condition de n'avoir point d'appointements. Il s'établit dans un petit appartement à la douane de Cadix, et, quoiqu'il fût un des régents de l'Espagne et des Indes, il n'avait pour tout ameublement qu'une table et quelques chaises de paille. M. de Labrador fut de son côté nommé ministre des affaires étrangères, place où il n'y avait presque rien à faire, puisque la régence n'était reconnue que par le roi de Naples, alors réfugié en Sicile. Quelque temps après, la Suède se détacha de la France, reconnut la régence, et fit un traité, qui fut signé par M. de Labrador, et dans lequel on s'offrait réciproquement amitié et rétablissement des anciennes relations.

M. de Labrador avait quitté son pays en 1798, et il avait laissé l'Espagne sous le gouvernement absolu de Charles IV, ou, pour mieux dire, de Marie-Louise et de Manuel Godoy, qui, simple garde du corps, sachant à peine signer son nom à vingt ans, avait été nommé ministre des affaires étrangères, généralissime et grand amiral. N'ayant pas su faire la guerre à la République française, il fit avec elle une paix humiliante qui lui valut le titre de prince de la Paix et celui d'altesse, chose toute nouvelle en Espagne, où on ne donnait le titre de prince qu'à l'héritier de la couronne. Du reste, à la fin de 1812, avec une régence, des cortès et une constitution, M. de Labrador trouva le même gouvernement arbitraire, exercé par quelques avocats et quelques prêtres, qui dominaient dans les cortès. Ceux-ci ne regardaient la régence et les ministres que comme de simples commis, obligés d'accorder les places qu'ils demandaient pour eux ou pour leurs parents. Parmi les députés, se trouvait alors le jeune Toréno, rempli de vanité et désireux de s'enrichir, ce qu'il a réalisé par la suite. Les prêtres Muñoz-Torrero et Oliveros étaient deux hommes vertueux et instruits sur les théories du gouvernement représentatif, mais fort étrangers à la connaissance du cœur humain et ne se doutant pas de ce que c'était que conduire des hommes. Pour s'en convaincre, il suffit de lire la Constitution de 1812, qui n'est qu'un recueil de maximes morales. On y lit que tous les Espagnols doivent être justes et bienfaisants. On pourrait se demander pourquoi on n'a pas écrit aussi dans la Constitution que toutes les femmes espagnoles seraient sages et fidèles. Je ne sais pas si Toréno, Martinez de la Rosa, Calatrava et autres députés croyaient possible de gouverner une grande nation avec des aphorismes et des lieux communs.

M. de Labrador eut le tort envers les cortès de ne pouvoir donner ni des ambassades, ni des places ambitionnées par les amis et les parents des députés influents. Il fut donc remplacé au ministère des affaires étrangères, qu'il quitta sans regret, l'ayant accepté avec répugnance.

Fort peu de temps après, le général Vénégas, qu venait de pacifier le Mexique, où il avait exercé les fonctions de vice-roi, arriva à Cadix. Lorsque le vaisseau à bord duquel il était avait quitté Vera-Cruz, la fièvre jaune y sévissait. Malgré cela, on le dispensa

de la quarantaine, d'abord parce l'on prétendait que
les deux seules personnes qui avaient succombé pendant la traversée n'avaient pas été atteintes de la
contagion , et ensuite parce que l'opinion générale
des médecins était que la fièvre jaune n'était pas
contagieuse. La vérité était qu'un matelot qu'on
disait mort d'un crachement de sang avait succombé
réellement avec les vomissements caractéristiques de
l'épidémie. Cette cruelle maladie régnait depuis des
siècles en Amérique, et jamais elle ne s'était commu-
niquée à l'Espagne, malgré les centaines de vaisseaux
qui entraient chaque année dans les ports de la Péninsule sans être soumis à la quarantaine. Pourtant,
depuis quelques années, la maladie avait fait des ap-
paritions sur plusieurs points du littoral. On transporta les bagages du général Vénégas chez un commis des affaires étrangères qui avait des relations
d'amitié avec lui, et qui fut une des premières vic-
times. Cependant les cortès et la régence, d'après
l'avis de plusieurs médecins, soutinrent qu'il ne s'a-
gissait que de fièvres de la saison. Les particuliers
ne furent pas aussi aveugles que le gouvernement,
et ils s'empressèrent de s'éloigner de Cadix. Ce fut
à cette occasion que M. de Labrador partit pour Madrid, où il arriva dans le mois de septembre 1813.

Il ne restait plus de l'ancienne population de
Madrid que quelques centaines de familles pauvres ;
les hôtels étaient fermés, les places et les rues rem-
plies d'immondices et de ruines, que la municipalité
ne pouvait pas faire enlever faute de fonds. La tournure des affaires dans le nord de l'Europe ayant
forcé Napoléon de rendre la liberté au roi et aux
princes espagnols dans le printemps de 1814, M. de
Labrador partit de Madrid au mois d'avril pour aller
rejoindre le roi à Valence ; mais il n'y trouva que
l'infant don Antonio, parce que le général Palafox
avait persuadé à S. M. d'aller visiter Saragosse. Le général, assis à côté du roi dans une voiture découverte, fut salué par ses compatriotes les Aragonais
comme le sauveur de la monarchie. M. de Labrador quitta Valence pour se rendre à Saragosse ; mais
il rencontra le roi en chemin et le suivit à Valence.
Outre le général Palafox, Sa Majesté avait avec elle le
duc de San-Carlos, ministre de la justice, et le chanoine Escoiquiz, conseiller d'État. En arrivant à Valence, cette suite s'augmenta du duc de l'Infantado
et d'autres personnes venues de Madrid. Les cortès
avaient déclaré qu'avant de prendre possession du
palais de Madrid, le roi Ferdinand devait se rendre
à la salle où elles tenaient leurs séances et prêter

serment à une constitution qu'il ne connaissait pas.
On avait décrété en même temps l'augmentation de
la garde nationale, et pris d'autres mesures qui an-
nonçaient la résolution de faire prévaloir le pouvoir
législatif sur celui du roi. Pour rendre nuls ces efforts
d'une minorité turbulente, les conseillers du roi décidèrent que l'on publierait en son nom un manifeste,
dont la rédaction fut confiée à M. de Labrador. La
pensée dominante dans ce manifeste était que le roi,
se voyant transporté de la prison de Valençay au milieu de ses sujets, s'était trouvé saisi d'admiration
lorsqu'il avait été instruit des efforts surhumains
que ce miracle avait coûté. Pour exprimer cette pensée, le roi, empruntant l'expression d'un grand poëte
espagnol, disait que le titre de roi d'un tel peuple lui
paraissait plus grand et plus glorieux que le titre de
souverain de tout le reste du monde. On ajoutait que,
s'il y avait eu de la part d'un petit nombre d'Espagnols des fautes commises, Sa Majesté éloignait la
vue de ces misères de la faiblesse humaine, qu'il se
regardait comme le père de tous ses sujets, et qu'il
mettrait à conserver leurs droits la même ardeur et
la même constance qu'ils avaient mises à conserver
ceux de la royauté. Cette phrase ne plut pas aux
conseillers du roi, qui n'avaient, pour la plupart, ni

instruction ni expérience, sauf toutefois MM. Villamil et Lardizabal, que le roi avait fait venir de Madrid
pour les consulter.

On résolut donc, à la majorité des voix, de s'abs-
tenir dans ce manifeste de parler des droits des sujets,
comme si un prince pouvait demander à son pays
des secours en hommes et en argent sans contracter
l'obligation de les employer pour la défense et le bien-
être de celui-ci. On retrancha donc du manifeste les
paragraphes qui avaient déplu, et on le publia ainsi
mutilé.

Aucun peuple d'Europe n'a eu un aussi mauvais
gouvernement que celui de l'Espagne, depuis la mort
de Charles III jusqu'à la guerre d'invasion. Malgré
cela, le nom du roi était encore un vrai talisman, et,
quand on eût publié le manifeste, tout rentra dans
l'ordre. On aurait pu tirer un immense parti de cette
vénération de la nation espagnole pour la royauté.
Le voyage du roi à Madrid fut une véritable ovation ;
les habitants des villes éloignées de la route accou-
raient en foule de plusieurs lieues au-devant de Ferdinand VII, et on voyait souvent des groupes de paysans qui, tenant leurs enfants par la main, criaient
qu'ils en avaient perdu deux ou trois au service de
Sa Majesté, mais que, si elle n'était pas encore con-

tente, ils étaient disposés à aller avec le reste de leurs familles combattre ceux qui avaient tenu Sa Majesté captive.

M. de Labrador quitta Madrid dix jours après l'entrée du roi, pour aller conclure le traité de paix avec la France. Tandis qu'il se rendait à Paris, les anciens courtisans de Charles IV et un de ses ministres (6) allaient tous les jours au palais pendant le dîner de Sa Majesté, et ils ne cessaient de répéter qu'il fallait persuader au roi de tout rétablir comme en 1808. C'est alors que commença la persécution contre ceux à qui on attribuait les idées qu'on appelait en France libérales. Parmi les persécutés, se trouvèrent Martinez de la Rosa et d'autres députés, qui furent envoyés en Afrique. Cette mesure injuste était en même temps on ne peut plus contraire à toute vraie politique.

A son arrivée à Paris, M. de Labrador se présenta à M. de Talleyrand, ministre des affaires étrangères, qui prétendit que l'on n'avait pas besoin de faire un traité avec l'Espagne, puisqu'on avait traité avec ses alliés. (7).

Louis XVIII ne fut pas de l'avis de son ministre, et il lui ordonna de traiter avec M. de Labrador. La seule difficulté à vaincre, c'était de décider sur quel-

3

pied on rétablirait les relations entre les deux pays. Napoléon, abusant de sa toute-puissance, avait établi des droits énormes d'ancrage sur les bâtiments espagnols, forcés de payer même lorsqu'ils étaient contraints par le mauvais temps d'entrer dans un port français, sans y avoir vendu ni acheté aucune marchandise. Ces droits étaient surtout onéreux pour les bâtiments catalans qui faisaient le commerce avec l'Italie. On pourrait dire, sans exagération, que le droit d'ancrage était souvent supérieur à la valeur des denrées de bas prix qui faisaient le fond du commerce entre l'Espagne et l'Italie; et il était arrivé que, pour ne pas payer des droits si forts, les bâtiments espagnols qui traversaient le golfe du Lion préféraient courir les risques d'un naufrage. Après quelques conférences, le ministre français et le plénipotentiaire espagnol se mirent d'accord, et stipulèrent qu'à compter de la date de la convention qu'on aller signer, les relations entre la France et l'Espagne seraient rétablies sur le pied où elles étaient au 1er janvier 1792, et on remit à un autre moment les autres stipulations qu'il pouvait y avoir à faire.

M. de Labrador se rendit à Vienne dans le mois de septembre, pour prendre part aux délibérations du congrès, composé seulement des représentants des six puissances qui avaient signé le traité de paix.

Les plénipotentiaires étaient réunis depuis fort peu de jours, lorsque M. de Labrador découvrit que l'Angleterre, la Russie, la Prusse et l'Autriche avaient signé entre elles une convention amicale, dans laquelle on stipulait que, pour ce qui avait rapport aux affaires générales ; on ne ferait aucune attention aux réclamations de la France et de l'Espagne. Cette démarche était si ignoble et si perfide que, lorsque M. de Labrador en fit part à M. de Talleyrand, celui-ci prétendit que la bonne foi de M. de Labrador avait été surprise, et que sans doute il avait payé fort cher une pure invention, qui ne méritait aucun crédit. Mais, par un hasard singulier, M. de Labrador avait l'original de cette convention, signé par les chefs des quatre cabinets désignés. M. de Labrador fit voir à M. de Talleyrand cet étrange document, et le laissa maître d'en prendre copie. De son côté, il en envoya un exemplaire à son gouvernement, et fit rendre l'original à la personne qui le lui avait procuré.

Dans cet état de choses, les plénipotentiaires de France et d'Espagne se trouvaient deux contre quatre ; et, comme seule ressource qui leur restât, ils deman-

dèrent que ceux de la Suède et du Portugal fussent
admis au congrès de Vienne, ces puissances ayant
adhéré au traité de Paris. Mais cet expédient ne fut
d'aucune utilité; car le Portugal se laissa dominer
par l'Angleterre, et la Suède par la Russie.

Les premiers travaux du congrès eurent pour but
l'abolition de la traite des noirs. Lord Castlereagh,
qui portait la parole au nom de l'Angleterre, avait un
grand intérêt à faire prononcer cette abolition par
le congrès. L'Angleterre s'était préparée pendant plus
de trente ans à la mesure de l'abolition, qu'elle avait
prononcée, et, pendant ce temps, les propriétaires
anglais avaient acheté un si grand nombre d'esclaves,
qu'ils avaient formé une population capable de suffire
à tous les travaux. C'était pour l'Angleterre un point
d'honneur que l'abolition de la traite chez les autres
nations, et les Anglais se sont toujours distingués
pour faire marcher de front l'honneur et l'utilité.
La France, l'Espagne et le Portugal se trouvaient
dans une situation toute différente, parce que, dans
leurs possessions, il n'y avait pas autant de nègres
qu'à la Jamaïque, et que jamais on n'avait importé
autant de négresses que de nègres. Les ministres qui
représentaient au congrès ces gouvernements étaient
d'accord sur le principe, mais ils demandaient huit

ans pour prononcer l'abolition. Lord Castlereagh
faisait tenir souvent deux séances par jour pour dé-
velopper son thème favori de l'abolition, qu'il voulait
faire prononcer immédiatement. Comme mesure pré-
paratoire, on décida de faire une déclaration au nom
de toutes les puissances réunies au congrès, et la
rédaction en fut confiée à M. Gentz, premier secrétaire du congrès. M. Gentz était un de ces publicistes
allemands très-féconds en paroles et en phrases et
visant toujours à l'effet. La déclaration qu'il rédigea
n'était qu'une emphatique déclamation. Après en avoir
entendu la lecture, M. de Labrador, prenant la parole, dit que tous les ministres étaient d'accord sur
l'injustice de la traite, mais qu'on ne pouvait pas
laisser passer une phrase où l'on disait que la traite
était illégitime. Cette remarque de M. de Labrador
n'était pas une dispute de mots; en effet, si on laissait
subsister la phrase qui déclarait la traite illégitime,
il fallait la condamner à l'instant, sans laisser passer
les huit ans jugés nécessaires, et les nègres, étant
le produit d'un trafic illégitime, devaient être affran-
chis sur-le-champ. Cette remarque parut juste, et on
adopta une autre déclaration.

M. de Lowenhielm, ministre plénipotent iaire de
Suède, proposa un jour au congrès que l'on deman-

dât à l'Espagne la cession de l'île de Minorque, pour
y établir l'ordre de Malte. M. de Lowenhielm est un
homme modéré et de très-bon sens, et il était très-
facile de comprendre que cette proposition ne venait
point de lui. M. de Labrador eut beaucoup de peine
à se contenir ; mais, affectant une grande froideur,
il répondit qu'il ne croyait pas possible la restaura-
tion ou, pour mieux dire, la résurrection de l'ordre
de Malte, mort ignominieusement lorsque les chevaliers qui tenaient garnison dans l'imprenable forteresse de leur île la cédèrent, sans tirer un coup de
canon, à Bonaparte, qui ne faisait que passer par là
pour se rendre en Égypte, et qui n'avait ni le temps
ni les moyens de les attaquer. Que cet acte eût été la
conséquence d'une lâcheté ou d'une trahison, l'ordre
de chevalerie qui s'en était rendu coupable ne pouvait
jamais prétendre à être rétabli. Si cependant les
puisssances principales de l'Europe croyaient possible le rétablissement de l'ordre de Malte, l'île de
Minorque ne serait point convenable, à cause de sa
petitesse et de la nature de son territoire, puisque
ce n'est presque qu'un rocher. Que la meilleure
manière de rétablir l'ordre de Malte serait de lui
rendre l'île de Malte, qui lui avait été donnée par
l'empereur Charles-Quint, comme roi d'Espagne,

puisque c'était à l'Espagne qu'appartenait alors cette île comme dépendance de la Sicile, laquelle faisait elle-même partie des possessions du roi catholique. L'Angleterre s'étant emparée de cette île, on ne ferait qu'un acte de justice en la restituant aux propriétaires ; mais, comme il était difficile que l'Angleterre voulût se dessaisir d'une possession précieuse pour elle, elle pourrait donner pour le rétablissement des chevaliers de Malte un bon port de l'Irlande avec un terrain assez vaste et assez fertile pour qu'ils pussent s'y établir convenablement. Le seul moyen de traiter une semblable question était de la tourner ainsi en plaisanterie. Si quelqu'un s'étonne qu'on ait eu la hardiesse de proposer à l'Espagne la cession de Minorque, il suffira de lui dire que, si la Russie, la France ou l'Angleterre avaient eu le malheur de passer une vingtaine d'années sous un gouvernement comme celui de l'Espagne depuis la mort de Charles III jusqu'en 1808, et de souffrir ensuite l'invasion de Bonaparte, la Russie, la France ou l'Angleterre seraient tombées dans un état plus humiliant encore que celui auquel on a voulu réduire l'Espagne dans le congrès de Vienne.

Pendant qu'on perdait le temps en fêtes et en dîners, Bonaparte débarqua en France, où il trouva, comme c'était naturel, un grand nombre de ses partisans prêts à le soutenir. Lorsque cette nouvelle arriva à Vienne, les ministres du congrès, les rois et les princes se trouvaient réunis au palais impérial. Les princes allemands qui, sous le patronage de Napoléon, avaient obtenu des couronnes et des agrandissements de territoire, parurent les plus affectés.

A cette nouvelle, la première réunion du congrès eut pour objet la publication d'une déclaration qui mettait Bonaparte au ban de l'Europe, pour avoir manqué au traité conclu avec lui après son abdication de Fontainebleau. Par ce traité, il avait été stipulé qu'on lui conserverait le titre d'empereur et le domaine de l'île d'Elbe. Il est inconcevable qu'un homme qui avait gagné tant d'éclatantes victoires, et qui pendant tant d'années avait exercé une si grande influence sur toute l'Europe, ait eu la mesquine ambition de conserver un vain titre et le pouvoir sur une petite île. Mais tel est le cœur humain, grand et petit d'un jour à l'autre. Les plénipotentiaires anglais s'opposèrent à la déclaration qui, pour ainsi dire, mettait Bonaparte hors de la loi, et ils prétendaient qu'il n'était pas justiciable des membres du congrès. A la rigueur, ils pouvaient avoir raison, si on se bornait à la teneur de la déclaration; mais leur scrupule était extraordinaire, venant des plénipotentiaires d'un gouvernement qui a exterminé les dynasties qui régnaient sur trois cents millions d'Indiens, pour les remplacer par les officiers ou les commis d'une compagnie de marchands.

La déclaration eut un grand retentissement en France; et plus tard, dans le mois de mai, Fouché et les autres partisans de Napoléon expédièrent à Vienne M. de Montrond, chargé de s'entendre avec M. de Talleyrand, afin d'obtenir une seconde déclaration qui, annulant la première, laisserait à la France la liberté de choisir le gouvernement qui lui conviendrait. Un soir, M. de Labrador reçut de la part de M. de Talleyrand l'invitation de se rendre chez lui pour une affaire très-importante. M. de Talleyrand, qui se trouvait au milieu d'une nombreuse société, le pria de passer dans le cabinet de M. de La Benardière, chef des travaux politiques de son ministère. M. de La Benardière était un homme d'une rare instruction, et qui savait donner aux notes diplomatiques et à toute sa correspondance une tournure énergique et agréable. Il avait en outre l'avantage d'être très-laborieux, et, se croyant malade, il n'acceptait jamais de dîners, n'assistait

à aucune réunion et ne quittait jamais son appartement. Il était vraiment l'homme aux travaux diplomatiques. Aussitôt qu'il aperçut M. de Labrador, il
lui dit qu'en attendant l'arrivée de M. de Talleyrand,
il devait lui faire voir les épreuves d'une seconde
déclaration, modifiant la première. Ces épreuves,
qui sortaient de l'imprimerie, étaient signées par les
ministres de Russie, d'Autriche, de Prusse, de
France et d'Angleterre. M. de La Benardière avoua
à M. de Labrador que son opinion personnelle était
que le congrès ne devait point faire une seconde
déclaration, ou que ce ne devait être que pour confirmer la première et non pour l'affaiblir. Mais il
ajouta que, selon M. de Talleyrand, l'empereur
Alexandre avait dit que, si on ne faisait pas une seconde déclaration, il ne ferait pas marcher un seul
soldat en faveur des Bourbons, parce qu'il ne voulait
pas avoir à soutenir en France une guerre nationale
comme celle que Bonaparte avait soutenue en Espagne. Les personnes qui entouraient M. de Talleyrand s'étant enfin retirées, celui-ci vint dans le
cabinet de M. de La Benardière. Il prétendit que, si
on n'avait pas appelé M. de Labrador pour discuter
la nouvelle déclaration à faire, c'était parce que le
temps pressait et que l'on n'était pas sûr de le trou-

ver au moment où les autres plénipotentiaires
s'étaient réunis. Du reste, il croyait qu'il était urgent de faire cette nouvelle déclaration, et il ne
doutait pas que M. de Labrador ne se rendît à l'é-
vidence, et ne mît de côté tout amour-propre.
M. de Labrador répondit qu'il ne songeait jamais à
son amour-propre lorsqu'il s'agissait d'un devoir;
mais qu'il croyait qu'il était contraire à la dignité du
congrès de se contredire et d'annuler un de ses
actes. Il ajouta qu'en même temps que la dignité du
congrès serait blessée, celle de l'Espagne recevrait
une atteinte mortelle, puisqu'elle avait au congrès
un plénipotentiaire qui y siégeait avec les mêmes
droits que les cinq autres, qui avaient signé l'épreuve
de la contre-déclaration. Il ajouta que l'Espagne
n'avait jamais été sous la tutelle d'aucune puissance; qu'il voyait l'affectation avec laquelle quelques puissances se donnaient le titre de grandes;
mais qu'il croyait qu'il n'y en avait aucune aussi
grande que l'Espagne, et qu'il doutait qu'aucune
autre eût pu, comme elle l'avait fait, résister à
l'armée française, lorsque Napoléon possédait, avec
l'ancien territoire de la France, la Belgique, la Hollande, le Rhin et toute l'Italie; que l'Espagne, pour
s'opposer à des forces aussi formidables, n'avait ni

armée ni gouvernement, et que, seule, sans autre
secours que trente mille Anglais, elle avait ré-
sisté (8). M. de Labrador ajouta que, si on publiait
cette seconde déclaration, lui, de son côté, publierait une protestation. Là-dessus, M. de Talleyrand
termina la conférence en disant que plus tard on
verrait ce que l'on aurait à faire. M. de Labrador
alla trouver le comte de Palmella, qui dit qu'on ne
l'avait pas averti non plus, et que, s'il se faisait une
protestation, il la signerait. Il fit la même démarche
auprès de M. de Lowenhielm, de qui il obtint la même
promesse. Il crut ensuite opportun de voir le comte
de Munster, qui n'était pas membre du congrès, mais
qui, comme ministre d'Angleterre pour le royaume
de Hanovre, avait une grande influence, méritée
d'ailleurs par ses talents. M. de Labrador alla en
outre faire une visite à lord Clancarty, qui, après le
départ de lord Castlereagh, était resté à la tête de la
légation anglaise. Lord Clancarty, homme de bonne
foi, avoua qu'il avait vu avec peine l'obstination de
quelques membres du congrès, qui voulaient affaiblir l'effet produit par la première déclaration, mais
qu'il avait dû céder; du reste, que si M. de Labrador
protestait, il dirait franchement son avis. Par ce
moyen, on mit fin à la ténébreuse intrigue ourdie à

Paris par Fouché. M. de Talleyrand écrivit un billet à M. de Labrador, en lui disant que leur but était le même, c'est-à-dire le rétablissement de l'autorité des Bourbons en France ; que M. de Labrador croyait que le moyen direct était le meilleur, mais que lui, qui connaissait l'amour-propre de ses compatriotes, était persuadé qu'en les laissant libres, ils choisiraient Louis XVIII. Ce billet faisait partie des papiers que M. de Labrador avait fait transporter à Rome pendant son ambassade. Cette affaire finit là, sans que M. de Talleyrand en reparlât jamais. Une des qualités de cet homme d'État, c'était de se dominer si parfaitement, qu'au milieu de la discussion la plus vive, lorsqu'il voyait qu'il ne pouvait avoir l'avantage, il se résignait et s'endormait. Ce fait s'est répété plusieurs fois pendant les séances du congrès, surtout dans les discussions avec lord Castlereagh.

Débarrassés du projet de la seconde déclaration, les plénipotentiaires, au lieu de mettre fin aux usurpations de territoire qui avaient eu lieu en Europe depuis la révolution de France, s'occupèrent de les confirmer ou d'en commettre d'autres.

Les deux républiques de Gênes et de Venise, qui avaient rendu de si grands services à l'Europe contre les Turcs, avaient été anéanties : leur rétablisse-

ment aurait été d'une rigoureuse justice. Pour ce qui
concernait Gênes., l'Angleterre donna ordre à lord
Bentinck, qui commandait huit mille hommes en Sicile, de venir faire le siége de cette ville par terre, pendant que la flotte anglaise la bloquerait par mer. A
peine arrivé, lord Bentinck publia une proclamation
dans laquelle il se donnait le titre de plénipotentiaire. En cette qualité, il exhortait les Génois à
s'unir à lui, et il promettait, au nom de son gouvernement, le rétablissement de la république. Dès
lors, les habitants des campagnes et tous ceux qui
approvisionnaient la ville, cessèrent d'apporter des
vivres et firent cause commune avec la division anglaise. Comme la flotte anglaise empêchait le ravi-
taillement par mer, la garnison française se vit
forcée d'évacuer la ville, et lord Bentinck fit élire un
doge de Gênes, et prononça le rétablissement de
l'ancienne République, ce qui n'empêcha pas le
congrès de Vienne d'ordonner la réunion de ce pays
à la Sardaigne. Cette réunion était si contraire aux
vœux des Génois, qu'ils envoyèrent à Vienne le marquis de Brignolle, si remarquable par son talent,
son instruction et ses qualités vraiment chevale-
resques. Sa mission était de dire aux ministres du
congrès que, si le nom de république leur déplaisait,

ils demandaient la réunion de Gênes au duché de
Parme, sous la souveraineté de l'héritier des trois
duchés. Ce fut en vain que le marquis de Brignolle
et M. de Labrador firent dans ce but toutes sortes de
démarches; il était décidé que Gênes ferait partie
de la Sardaigne. Il en fut de même pour Venise;
et, comme s'il n'eût pas suffi de confirmer les anciennes usurpations, on en commit une nouvelle et
plus criante, en donnant à Marie-Louise les États que
le duc de Parme possédait comme héritier de la
maison Farnèse, dont il descendait. Le cardinal
Maury et deux autres évêques français avaient déclaré, lors du couronnement de Napoléon, que son
mariage avec Madame Joséphine de la Pagerie avait
été célébré selon le rite de l'Église catholique. Si ce
certificat était exact, Marie-Louise ne pouvait être la
femme de Napoléon, du vivant de l'impératrice Joséphine. En tout cas, ni comme archiduchesse, ni
comme impératrice, Marie-Louise n'avait aucun
droit. M. de Labrador fit toutes les protestations pos-
sibles; mais il fallait ajouter à tous les autres scan-
dales ce scandale encore plus grand, et Marie-Louise,
avec les trois ou quatre maris qu'elle a eus succes-
sivement, a joui des revenus des trois duchés, pendant que l'héritier légitime a dû se contenter du

duché de Lucques. La cession d'une partie de la Saxe à la Prusse fut une œuvre non moins contraire à la justice et au droit des gens. M. de Labrador n'eut pas même la satisfaction de pouvoir la censurer, puisque les puissances qui se sont donné le titre de grandes avaient décidé que l'Espagne n'interviendrait pas dans les affaires d'Allemagne, ce qui ne les empêchait pas d'intervenir elles dans les affaires de la Péninsule. La Prusse, l'Autriche et la Russie avaient découvert qu'elles étaient moins loin de l'Espagne que l'Espagne ne l'est de l'Allemagne.

Les hommes d'État qui sont tombés dans de si graves erreurs, non-seulement ont manqué à toutes les règles de la justice, mais encore ils ont montré qu'ils avaient la vue très-basse en politique. L'Espagne, qu'ils ont tâché d'anéantir, est plus nécessaire à l'équilibre européen qu'aucune des puissances du Nord. Il ne sera jamais possible à aucune d'elles, ni peut-être à toutes ensemble, de vaincre le penchant que de tout temps la France a eu de dominer en Italie et de s'agrandir en Belgique et en Allemagne. Or l'Espagne, même privée de ses colonies, peut mettre sur pied une armée de deux cent mille hommes, puisque la Prusse, avec moins de ressources et de population, en entretient une de quatre cent mille; et il suffit de jeter un coup d'œil sur une carte pour voir que deux cent mille Espagnols menaçant la France sur la longue ligne qui s'étend de Perpignan à Bayonne, seraient plus utiles pour préserver l'Italie de toute tentative de la part de la France, que les armées quatre fois plus nombreuses des princes d'Allemagne et même de la Russie.

Du reste, si le plénipotentiaire espagnol n'eut pas l'occasion de dire son avis sur le démembrement de la Saxe, le plénipotentiaire français en parla avec énergie, et il employa toutes les ressources de son esprit pour empêcher ce nouveau scandale, qui malheureusement entrait dans les vues des puissances du Nord.

Relativement aux dispositions à prendre pour faire échouer les projets de Napoléon, les plénipotentiaires décidèrent que la Russie, l'Autriche et la Prusse enverraient chacune cent cinquante mille hommes, et que ce serait à celles qui pourraient fournir ce contingent qu'il appartiendrait de déterminer le plan d'opérations. On décida en même temps que, bien que l'Angleterre ne fût pas dans la possibilité de fournir cent cinquante mille hommes, elle serait admise à discuter le plan de campagne, parce qu'elle fournirait en argent ce qu'elle ne pouvait donner en hommes. On fit savoir au plénipotentiaire espagnol que l'Espagne ne pouvait pas prendre part à la direction de la guerre parce qu'elle ne pouvait fournir cent cinquante mille hommes. C'est alors que l'on commença à donner à la Russie, à l'Autriche, à la Prusse et à l'Angleterre le nom de grandes puissances. A ces quatre on ajouta la France, et certes il n'y a rien à dire sur cette dernière détermination. La vérité pourtant est qu'une de ces grandes puissances perdit, dans une bataille qui ne dura qu'une heure et demie, sa capitale et une partie de son territoire, et qu'elle aurait perdu son existence politique sans l'insistance de ses alliés.

Avant de s'engager dans la guerre contre Napoléon, les plénipotentiaires voulurent régler l'étiquette à observer entre les différentes puissances d'Europe. Dans les siècles précédents, il n'y avait presque aucune discussion sur ce point, puisque toutes les puissances cédaient le pas à l'empereur d'Allemagne, comme successeur de ceux de Rome; et les différends qui avaient existé entre la France et l'Espagne, on les avait réglés en attribuant la préséance au titre d'ambassadeur, et ensuite à celui de ministre plénipotentiaire, et, à rang égal, à celui dont les lettres de créance auraient été les premières présentées. La Russie ne pesait pas alors autant dans la balance de l'Europe, et l'Angleterre était loin d'avoir la même importance que de nos jours. Au congrès de Vienne, ces deux puissances avaient des prétentions contraires à celles de la France et de l'Espagne, et il était urgent de régler un point qui aurait facilement donné lieu à des complications diplomatiques. Ce fut M. de Labrador qui fut choisi pour présider cette commission; et, à la satisfaction de tous, il fut établi comme règle générale que l'ambassadeur de n'importe quelle puissance aurait le pas sur le ministre plénipotentiaire, de même que le miministre plénipotentiaire l'aurait sur le ministre résident, et qu'à égalité de rang, la préséance appartiendrait à celui qui aurait présenté plus anciennement ses lettres de créance. On fit à cette règle générale une exception en faveur du nonce du pape, et, chose digne de remarque, ni la Russie, ni l'Angleterre, ni la Prusse ne s'opposèrent à cette marque de considération en faveur du chef spirituel de tant de millions de catholiques, tandis que le ministre de Portugal, dont le roi porte le titre de Très-Fidèle, voulut réclamer contre.

On aurait voulu régler par cette même commission l'affaire des saluts des bâtiments de guerre dans les ports étrangers, et ceux de ces mêmes bâtiments envers ceux de commerce. Dans l'état actuel, il y a des difficultés continuelles sur les saluts que les vaisseaux doivent au pavillon du souverain des ports dans lesquels ils entrent. L'Angleterre commet sur ce point un grand abus de force, puisqu'il n'y a point de mer ni de rivière navigable où l'on ne trouve quelque vaisseau anglais, qui oblige, non-seulement les bâtiments de commerce, mais ceux de guerre, à répondre à l'appel qu'il leur fait à coups de canon. Le président de la commission fit la motion de régler ces deux points, et il fut soutenu par tous les membres; mais le ministre anglais opposa la plus vive résistance, et il prétendit qu'il n'avait pas de pouvoirs pour régler cette affaire. Les exorbitantes prétentions de l'Angleterre ne sont basées que sur l'immense force maritime qu'elle possède depuis que la marine espagnole a été anéantie au service de la France, et celle de la France diminuée par les guerres de la révolution.

Lorsque le congrès eut terminé sa tâche, le plénipotentiaire espagnol refusa de signer le protocole, se fondant sur les usurpations de pouvoirs des puissances soi-disant grandes, et sur l'injustice des anciennes usurpations que l'on avait maintenues, et des nouvelles que l'on avait commises. Le gouver-

nement espagnol approuva la résolution de son plénipotentiaire, et celui-ci refusa l'invitation que lui
faisait M. de Talleyrand de se rendre à Gand, où se
trouvait Louis XVIII, parce qu'il aurait fallu pour
cela une autorisation de son gouvernement. Il se
rendit donc à Paris, où s'établit une commission de
plénipotentiaires qui avaient assisté au congrès, pour
traiter les affaires pendantes. Dans cette commission, on agitait la question des forteresses que l'on
devait construire en Belgique pour les opposer au
triple rang que la France possède. Le plénipotentiaire espagnol ne faisait pas partie de cette commission ; mais il s'y présenta un jour pour demander
que l'on accordât à son gouvernement une somme
pour rétablir les fortifications d'Hostalrich, de Gi-
rone, de Roses et de Berga, qui toutes avaient été
détruites pendant la guerre de l'invasion, tandis que
toutes les forteresses françaises de ce côté étaient in-
tactes. La commission accorda 36 millions de francs,
qui furent exactement payés par la France ; mais pas
un sou ne fut employé à la réparation des forteresses : la plus grande partie de cet argent fut dé-
pensée par le ministre des finances pour d'autres
objets, et 9 millions furent la proie d'un agent infi-
dèle, au nom duquel on avait fait faire les inscrip-

tions, qui auraient dû l'être au nom du trésorier de la couronne. Le ministre des affaires étrangères qui avait commis cette faute était libéral et un des fondateurs de la constitution de 1812. En attendant, on continuait à Paris les négociations pour s'entendre sur la signature du protocole par l'Espagne, et le ministre des affaires étrangères de cette cour était pressé de terminer l'affaire pour avoir l'occasion de recevoir des décorations et des tabatières ornées de brillants.

On nomma donc M. de Labrador ambassadeur à Naples, et on fit venir à Paris le comte de Fernan Nuñez, avec l'ordre de signer le protocole dans l'état où M. de Labrador l'avait laissé. Ce fut à cette occasion que le comte de Fernan Nuñez fut créé duc, sans que ce changement de titre lui fût d'aucune utilité, parce qu'étant grand d'Espagne, il jouissait des mêmes honneurs. Mais, dans ces derniers temps, on a préféré le titre de duc, et un grand nombre de grands d'Espagne et d'individus qui ne l'étaient pas ont demandé le titre de duc, sans avoir le revenu de 40,000 ducats, exigé par la loi. De cette manière, ce titre est devenu très-commun, et la plupart de ceux qui le portent sont obligés de demander des pensions pour soutenir leur nouvelle dignité (9).

M. de Labrador se rendit à Naples en octobre. Il avait été chargé au congrès de Vienne des intérêts de cette cour, et ce fut par suite des services qu'il lui avait rendus qu'il obtint le grand cordon de Saint-Ferdinand. Pendant son séjour à Vienne, il avait été informé que le roi de Naples, alors réfugié en Sicile, sans avoir aucun sujet de mauvaise intelligence avec la cour d'Espagne, s'était emparé de tous les biens appartenant aux Espagnols dans la Sicile. Parmi ces propriétés, se trouvaient celles du conquérant de la Sicile, Cabréra, dont l'héritage était tombé dans la maison d'Albe, devenue elle-même par les femmes majorat des ducs de Berwick; celles du marquis de Villafranca, qui est la branche aînée masculine de la maison d'Albe; celles du comte de Fuentes et de plusieurs autres grands seigneurs espagnols. C'était en vain que le ministre d'Espagne en Sicile avait réclamé contre cet attentat, commis au préjudice d'une puissance amie, qui, pendant tant de siècles avait été souveraine de la Sicile.

Parmi les personnes qui avaient accompagné à Vienne l'archiduchesse d'Autriche, reine des Deux-Siciles, se trouvait le chevalier de Médicis, qui jouissait d'une grande faveur à cette cour. M. de Labrador s'adressa à lui pour obtenir réparation d'une injustice aussi criante, et fit entendre que, si on ne levait le séquestre, il porterait plainte au congrès. Le séquestre fut en effet levé, mais on ne rendit pas les revenus que l'on avait touchés pendant plusieurs années, tandis que l'on faisait tomber sur les propriétaires les charges qui pesaient sur les biens pour les églises ou les hôpitaux. Lorsqu'on avait séparé les Deux-Siciles de l'Espagne, on avait stipulé que les Espagnols jouiraient en Sicile des mêmes droits que les Siciliens, et réciproquement. Malgré cette promesse solennelle, en levant le séquestre, on conserva un droit de 15 pour 100 sur les revenus de ces biens, au profit du trésor des Deux-Siciles. M. de Labrador eut à commencer son ambassade par réclamer contre cette usurpation. Quoiqu'elle fût évidente, il ne réussit qu'à faire diminuer de moitié cette exaction, parce que le roi de Naples, tout en cédant aux raisons de M. de Labrador, soutenait que, pour la sécurité de sa conscience, il devait adopter l'opinion de la majorité de ses ministres. Or cette majorité se bornait au chevalier de Médicis, puisque le ministre des affaires étrangères, un respectable vieillard, et le ministre de la justice, un avocat, étaient toujours de l'avis du chevalier de Médicis. Celui-ci était, on ne sait pas pourquoi, l'ennemi acharné de la cour d'Espagne, et tout ce qu'il pouvait usurper sur les sujets de cette puissance lui paraissait de bonne prise. Un des vice-rois de Naples, de la maison Alvarez de Tolède, avait fondé à Naples, à ses frais, un magnifique hôpital pour les Espagnols. Il y avait dans cet hôpital une église, où l'on avait érigé un monument en marbre en l'honneur du fondateur. C'était le principal ouvrage de sculpture moderne à Naples. Le chevalier de Médicis s'empara de cet hôpital pour y installer son ministère des finances, et il en destina une partie pour la bourse de commerce. En vain le chargé d'affaires avait-il réclamé; la cour d'Espagne recommandait toujours d'user de grands ménagements, et de ne pas donner des motifs de plainte dans ses réclamations.

Ce fut pendant le temps de l'ambassade de M. de Labrador à Naples que fut traité le mariage de l'infant don François de Paule avec la fille aînée du duc de Calabre, héritier de la couronne des Deux-Siciles. M. de Labrador ayant parlé au roi de ce projet de mariage, Sa Majesté lui dit que, comme il n'était que le grand-père, il fallait que M. de Labrador se rendît à Palerme pour en faire la demande au père de la princesse. On mit à la disposition de M. de Labrador pour son voyage une frégate napolitaine, et, après avoir fait avec toute la pompe usitée la demande de la princesse, il resta une vingtaine de jours à Palerme, où le duc de Calabre et l'infante d'Espagne, sa femme, lui firent l'honneur de l'inviter à dîner presque tous les jours. On le plaçait à table entre la princesse Louise-Charlotte et la seconde fille du duc de Calabre, la princesse Marie-Christine. Celle-ci, qui pouvait avoir dix à douze ans, était si jolie et si bien élevée, qu'un jour que M. de Labrador s'entretenait avec sa mère, la princese étant venue à passer, l'ambassadeur ne put s'empêcher de dire qu'il regrettait qu'elle fût si jeune, car il aurait désiré la demander pour un autre prince de la famille royale.

Pendant cette même ambassade, Charles IV, qui n'avait pas revu Naples depuis l'âge de neuf ans, y vint de Rome, où il s'était établi. Son entrevue avec son frère, le roi des Deux-Siciles, fut extrêmement touchante (10). Après quelques mois de séjour à Naples, Charles IV retourna à Rome pour être le témoin muet de ce qu'il plaisait à Marie-Louise et à Godoy de faire chez Sa Majesté. Le séjour de Naples lui avait été si agréable, qu'il y revint bientôt et y mourut, quelques jours après avoir reçu la nouvelle du trépas de la reine à Rome.

Lorsque Charles IV et sa femme s'étaient rendus
d'Aranjuez à Bayonne, le roi n'avait pour son usage
que quelques bijoux, consistant en une ganse de
brillants pour le chapeau, une garniture de boutons
d'habit, une poignée d'épée et d'autres petits objets.
Tout cela avait été vendu à Marseille, parce que Napoléon ne donna pas la somme promise tant qu'il
sut que le roi avait quelques valeurs à sa disposition.
Quant à la reine Marie-Louise, elle avait rapporté
pour 6 millions de pierreries, et elle avait remis ces
objets à madame Tudo, qui, à la mort de la reine,
épousa Godoy. M. Vargas Laguna, ministre d'Espagne
à Rome, qui devait sa fortune à Godoy, mais qui
était un de ces hommes qui ne transigent pas avec
leur devoir, parla si fermement à Charles IV de l'obligation où il était de faire rendre à la couronne d'Espagne ce qui lui appartenait, qu'il finit par l'obtenir,
et ces bijoux furent envoyés en Espagne; mais, au
lieu d'être conservés comme trésor de la couronne,
ils furent partagés entre les princesses, parce que l'infante Louise-Charlotte le voulut ainsi. Cette infante
avait pris une influence telle que personne ne lui
résistait, et elle ne devait nullement cette influence
à la supériorité de son jugement ou de son esprit,
mais à une violence de caractère, qui faisait trembler

jusqu'à Ferdinand lui-même. Ce fut elle qui, malgré l'étiquette de la cour, obtint de donner des
bals au palais de Madrid. L'étiquette défendait aussi
de donner le grand cordon de Charles III aux ministres plénipotentiaires ; l'infante napolitaine l'obtint
pour un chargé d'affaires de Naples, et, le jour de
sa fête, elle fit attendre pendant plus d'une heure
les grands seigneurs, pour recevoir en audience
particulière ce même chargé d'affaires qu'elle venait
de faire décorer.

Les autres trésors que la cour avait en diamants
avaient été enlevés par Murat le 2 mai 1808. Un Pié-
montais, ministre de Napoléon à Naples pendant le
règne de Murat, assurait que les diamants apportés
d'Espagne avaient été estimés 43 millions. Cette
somme paraîtra un peu forte ; mais on sait que l'Espagne était très-riche en joyaux.

Lorsque le roi Ferdinand VII prêta serment à la
Constitution de 1812, M. de Labrador présenta au roi
de Naples ses lettres de rappel. Le jour même où
M. de Labrador devait partir de Naples, il reçut une
invitation du roi Ferdinand pour dîner à Sessa. Parmi
les personnes qui, ce jour-là, se trouvaient à la table
de Sa Majesté, était l'héritier de la couronne de Da-
nemark ; et, en sa présence, le vieux roi Ferdinand

dit à M. de Labrador qu'à son avis il faisait mal
d'aller en Espagne ; qu'il l'engageait à rester à Naples, où rien ne lui manquerait, et où il serait traité
comme l'ami le plus intime de Sa Majesté. Le vieux
roi était un homme de cœur, et il ne lui a manqué
que de bons ministres et un meilleur entourage.
M. de Labrador remercia Sa Majesté, et, traversant
l'Italie et la France, il alla passer quelque temps en
Belgique et en Suisse. Il était de retour à Paris lorsque
le roi d'Espagne, trouvant qu'il ne pouvait gouverner avec la Constitution de 1812, au lieu de tâcher
de la réformer d'accord avec les cortès, ou bien de
se mettre à la tête de ses troupes fidèles, s'adressa à
la cour de France pour obtenir l'envoi de cent mille
hommes dans son royaume. Cette détermination aurait paru dans d'autres temps impossible, puisque
les soldats que le roi d'Espagne faisait venir contre
ses sujets étaient les mêmes qui avaient naguère en-
vahi l'Espagne, et dont les chefs avaient proclamé
que la seule armée espagnole était celle de Joseph,
et que ceux qui reconnaîtraient un autre souverain
seraient regardés comme des brigands et fusillés ;
proclamations qui, du reste, n'avaient point été de
simples menaces ; mais qui avaient été mises à exécution avec une dureté à laquelle on s'était vu forcé de

répondre par de sanglantes représailles. Aussitôt que l'on eut décidé l'envoi des troupes françaises, M. de Labrador quitta Paris, ne pouvant concevoir qu'il fût digne d'un Espagnol de rester dans un pays dont l'armée faisait la guerre à ses compatriotes. Lorsque le roi Ferdinand se décida à appeler à son secours l'armée française, il fit perdre à sa couronne son indépendance, sa dignité et l'éclat que lui avaient valu tant de siècles d'une glorieuse indépendance.

M. de Labrador paya cher la manifestation de ses opinions ; lorsque le roi Ferdinand sortit de Cadix et remonta sur son trône, il nomma un nouveau conseil d'État, et, bien que M. de Labrador fût membre de ce conseil depuis 1814 et que cette place fût à vie, il la lui retira, et le laissa sans place ni appointements jusqu'en 1827, époque à laquelle on le nomma ambassadeur à Rome. Mais sa santé ne lui permit pas de s'y rendre avant l'année 1828.

Dans l'espace de fort peu de temps, le trône pontifical se trouva deux fois vacant, par la mort du pape Léon XII et par celle de son successeur Pie VIII. On s'occupa du choix d'un nouveau pape, et l'Espagne et la France protégeaient le cardinal de Gregorio, pendant que l'Autriche portait le cardinal Capellari, qui fut élu. Il y avait, à cette époque, à Rome, six ou sept cardinaux français; mais l'ambassadeur, M. de Châteaubriand, ne put jamais disposer de trois voix, qu'il aurait fallu pour que le cardinal Gregorio fût élu (11).

Pendant que l'auteur de ces mélanges était ambassadeur à Rome. il reçut, en 1829, l'ordre de se rendre à Naples pour demander la princesse Marie-Christine, seconde fille du duc de Calabre, pour son oncle le roi d'Espagne, Ferdinand VII. Ces commissions étaient fort enviées par les plus grands seigneurs de l'Espagne, d'abord par l'honneur qu'ils en recevaient, et ensuite parce qu'on avait introduit la mauvaise habitude de faire à cette occasion des comptes de dépenses fort élevés, dans lesquels figuraient une grande quantité de vaisselle plate, des porcelaines, des cristaux, du linge de table le plus recherché, des voitures, des livrées de gala et des chevaux. On y ajoutait une somme considérable pour les illuminations et les dîners (12).

M. de Labrador n'eut d'autres dispositions à faire, avant de quitter Rome, que de faire partir ses domestiques, ses chevaux et ses voitures. Il fit son entrée à Naples avec la pompe usitée en pareil cas. On lui fixa le jour de la présentation solennelle pour la demande, et ce jour-là il adressa au roi de Naples, entouré de toute sa cour, un discours en espagnol pour lui demander la main de sa fille. Le roi la fit venir, et, après qu'elle eut exprimé son consentement, l'ambassadeur s'avança, lui baisa la main, la considérant déjà comme sa reine, et lui présenta le portrait du roi, entouré d'un triple rang de gros diamants. On avait oublié d'expédier ce portrait de Madrid, et il fallut le faire faire et le donner à monter à Naples. Lorsque l'ambassadeur s'approcha de la princesse, il s'aperçut que, depuis 1818 qu'il l'avait vue à Palerme, elle avait encore gagné en beauté et qu'elle était une jeune personne accomplie. C'était une chose remarquable qu'étant née à Naples, elle eût la physionomie et la démarche d'une Espagnole. Elle avait même su s'approprier ce regard et ce sourire dont le secret n'est connu que des jeunes filles et des femmes de l'Espagne, sourire et regard qu'elles tiennent de l'heureux climat de ce pays. On sait qu'aux plus beaux jours de l'empire romain, lorsqu'il dominait la plus grande partie du monde connu, les femmes qui faisaient les délices du peuple-roi dans ses festins étaient des Espagnoles, et surtout des femmes de Cadix.

Après avoir donné les fêtes et les dîners d'usage dans de pareilles occasions, l'ambassadeur retourna à Rome, et il envoya ses comptes des dépenses, qui, ne comprenant pas le portrait garni de brillants, ne dépassa pas la somme de 100,000 francs. Il avait cru donner un bon exemple à ceux qui auraient après lui de pareilles commissions; mais il se trompa, car les courtisans de Madrid ne virent dans sa noble conduite qu'un trait de fierté. Avouons pourtant que l'Espagne serait heureuse si tous ses enfants avaient cette espèce d'orgueil.

Après la mort de Ferdinand VII, M. de Labrador reçut l'ordre de reconnaître comme sa souveraine la fille aînée de ce roi. Il répondit que, selon son opinion, la couronne appartenait à Don Carlos. Par suite de cette réponse, on le déclara déchu de toutes ses dignités, places et décorations, pour s'être refusé à reconnaître le gouvernement de la fille du roi. Ce gouvernement avait sans doute le droit de l'exclure de toutes les places qui dépendaient de lui; mais, quant au collier de la Toison d'or, on ne peut en être privé, selon la loi fondamentale de l'ordre, qu'après avoir été jugé par ses pairs, c'est-à-dire par les autres chevaliers de la Toison d'or, qui, réunis en chapitre, et après avoir entendu l'accusé, l'auraient déclaré félon. Quand même, au lieu du chapitre des chevaliers de la Toison d'or, on aurait formé un jury composé de tout ce qu'il

5

y a de plus avili parmi les galériens, M. de Labrador est sûr que ces jurés ne l'auraient pas déclaré
félon, pourvu qu'on n'eût pas acheté leurs votes; car
la conscience du genre humain, même parmi les galériens, se refuse à déclarer félon celui qui n'a fait
qu'être constamment fidèle à sa parole. Lorsque
Bonaparte se fit nommer consul à vie, les généraux
Carnot, Miaulis et autres se refusèrent à le reconnaître en cette qualité, et, malgré ce refus, il ne les
priva point de leurs places, et, lorsque plus tard Bonaparte se fit proclamer empereur et qu'ils se refusèrent également à le reconnaître, il leur conserva
cependant sa confiance. Malheureusement, en Espagne, on imite toujours ce qu'il y a de puéril dans les
pays étrangers, mais jamais ce qu'il y a de noble et
de généreux (13).

En 1831, M. de Labrador revit à Madrid la reine
Christine, qui, depuis ce temps-là, a éprouvé bien des
pertes, a eu bien des chagrins et a couru assez de
dangers. Grâce à la Providence, elle est à présent à
Madrid, dans la force de l'âge, et elle a eu le bonheur
ou le malheur de placer sa fille aînée sur le trône. En
s'exprimant ainsi, M. de Labrador n'entend attaquer
en aucune sorte ni la reine-mère ni sa postérité. Il a
trop de vénération pour celle qui fut l'épouse de son

roi et pour ses filles, pour qu'on puisse avoir aucun doute sur sa pensée. M. de Labrador a été toute sa vie grand admirateur d'Isabelle la Catholique et de Marie-Thérèse d'Autriche, et, sans s'occuper des défauts de Catherine II, il a rendu justice à ses talents. Il sait que Sixte V, qui se connaissait en politique et en gouvernement, disait qu'Élisabeth d'Angleterre, qui fit tant de mal à l'Espagne, était une grande tête de princesse. Mais, en général, M. de Labrador ne croit pas que le gouvernement d'une femme puisse convenir à une grande nation. Il n'a jamais pu s'habituer à voir une femme passer une revue, soit en jupon, soit en hussard, comme le faisaient Catherine et Marie-Thérèse.

Pendant que l'ancienne reine d'Espagne Marie-Christine est à Madrid auprès de sa fille, sur laquelle elle exerce sans doute autant d'influence qu'elle pouvait en exercer sur le roi Ferdinand, celui qui eut l'honneur d'aller la demander en mariage, accablé par la vieillesse et les infirmités, se trouve dans un pays étranger, sans qu'il lui soit permis d'aller dans son pays natal, même comme voyageur.

Si les hommes qui possèdent le pouvoir en Espagne ne se laissaient pas aveugler par l'esprit de parti ou dominer par des passions mesquines, il leur demanderait de quel droit on peut refuser l'entrée de l'Espagne à un homme qui non-seulement est Espagnol de naissance, mais qui est d'une famille espagnole depuis un temps immémorial, et aussi espagnole que les nobles montagnes de Castille, d'où elle descend. Parce que M. de Labrador ne veut pas prêter un serment qu'il croit contraire à sa conscience et à son honneur, est-ce une raison pour lui interdire le retour dans son pays? Même sans prêter serment, aussitôt qu'il serait rentré en Espagne, ne serait-il pas sujet du gouvernement établi, et soumis aux lois? D'après les anciennes lois d'Espagne, on n'exigeait de serment que de celui qui prenait possession d'une place pour l'exercice de laquelle il était d'usage de demander ce serment. Si M. de Labrador allait en Espagne, ce ne serait pas pour demander de l'argent, dont il n'a pas besoin; ni des places, car il en a occupé plus qu'il n'aurait voulu; ni la restitution de son collier de la Toison d'or, dont il a été privé par une simple signature d'un ministre, c'est-à-dire par un acte nul de plein droit. Il ne demanderait, pour le reste de ses jours, que l'air de sa patrie, et, après sa mort, que les six pieds de terre que l'on accorde au plus simple mortel. Ce ne serait pas une grande récompense pour les éminents services qu'il a rendus à son pays et pour ceux qu'il a tâché de rendre à l'Europe.

, M. de Labrador souhaite que l'Europe n'ait pas à éprouver de nouvelles convulsions ; mais tout annonce qu'après avoir semé des iniquités , on n'aura à recueillir que des douleurs (14).

Puisse la justice divine réparer, sans qu'il en coûte trop cher aux principales puissances de l'Europe , la persécution inouïe qu'on a exercée contre l'Espagne depuis le temps de Philippe II , en la privant de toutes ses possessions en Italie et en protégeant le soulèvement de ses possessions en Amérique , au profit, non pas du commerce de l'Europe , mais de la puissance des Provinces-Unies, qui joue en Amérique le même rôle que l'Angleterre en Europe !

NOTES.

Note (1), page 2.

Ce digne Espagnol vécut assez pour se mettre en rapport avec le duc de Wellington pendant que ce général occupait une partie du Portugal, et, lorsqu'il faisait le siége de Ciudad-Rodrigo, don Justo Garcia l'instruisait chaque jour des mouvements de l'armée française, en lui envoyant des hommes sûrs qui, sans être payés, le mettaient au courant des marches de l'ennemi, et l'informaient de la situation de cette partie de la Castille et des ressources que l'armée y trouverait. Ce fut alors que Wellington eut des relations avec les députés de la province de Salamanque, appelés en Espagne *sesmeros de la tierra*. Le duc de Wellington parlait de ces Espagnols en exprimant son admiration pour leur bon sens et leurs excellentes qualités. Ce sont les hommes les plus riches de la province, et ceux qui connaissent le mieux les ressources du pays. Ils ne sont nommés ni par le gouvernement ni par les municipalités; ils sont députés de la province, parce qu'ils sont nés tels et que leurs ancêtres l'ont été. Il y en a qui possèdent de grandes richesses en terres et en troupeaux; malgré leur fortune, ils s'habillent de drap brun comme les paysans de la contrée. Ils ne font de dépenses

extraordinaires que lorsqu'il est question du mariage de leurs
fils, et alors on voit de ces noces qui ont donné à Cervantes
l'idée des noces de Gamache. Ces braves gens n'ont jamais demandé ni pensions ni décorations, ce qui est très-extraordi-
naire en Espagne, où la manie des croix et des distinctions est
une vraie maladie endémique. Au commencement du siècle
dernier et jusqu'au temps du roi d'Espagne Charles III, il n'y
avait d'autres ordres de chevalerie que les quatre ordres militaires et celui de Malte. Charles III, qui avait fondé à Naples
l'ordre de Saint-Janvier, fonda en Espagne celui qui porte son
nom, et il y établit des grands cordons et de simples croix de
chevaliers, parmi lesquels un certain nombre jouissait d'une
pension de 1,000 francs. Cette croix se portait à la boutonnière
avec un ruban bleu et blanc. Du temps du feu roi Ferdinand VII,
un de ses favoris fit créer en faveur des chevaliers qui jouissaient
de la pension la distinction d'un crachat, d'abord fort modeste,
brodé en bleu et en fil d'argent. On y substitua ensuite une
plaque d'argent à pointes de diamant, qui devait d'abord être
plus petite que la plaque des grands cordons. Comme il était
impossible de faire observer ce qui avait été fixé relativement aux
dimensions de cette plaque, elle se confondit bientôt avec la
plaque du grand cordon, et, comme on l'accorde au premier
venu, le grand cordon lui-même a perdu presque toute sa valeur.
On a ajouté à cet ordre de Charles III l'ordre américain d'Isabelle
la Catholique, et plus tard celui de Saint-Ferdinand, imitation
de celui de Marie-Thérèse, mais imitation qui a dégénéré de
suite, parce qu'on a fait de cette décoration, non pas le prix des
services militaires, mais l'effet de la prodigalité des ministres.
On y a ajouté l'ordre de Saint-Herménégilde pour récompenser
les militaires qui ont le plus de service, ce qui l'a fait surnom-
mer l'ordre de la végétation. On doit ajouter à tout cela les croix
et les médailles pour des actions de guerre qui souvent ne mérite-

raient que l'oubli. Un seul exemple suffira pour faire connaître jusqu'à quel point on a poussé en Espagne la fureur de ces distinctions. En 1810, lorsque les Français se disposaient à entrer en Andalousie, il y avait un officier nommé Echevarri que l'on avait destiné à combattre les contrebandiers, mais qui n'avait aucune instruction. Plus tard on lui avait donné le commandement d'un bataillon que l'on avait formé en tirant des galères les condamnés les plus jeunes. Cet Echevarri était devenu maréchal de camp, et il forma le dessein de s'opposer au passage des Français. A cet effet, il réunit trois cents contrebandiers, partie à cheval, partie montés sur des mulets. Il mit en réquisition quelques centaines de paysans, et il alla occuper le pont d'Alcolea sur le Guadalquivir. Il était assez ignorant pour croire qu'avec sa faible troupe et une compagnie de milice qui se trouvait là, il pourrait entraver la marche de l'armée française. Les Français n'auraient eu besoin que de quelques détachements pour s'emparer du pont; mais ils ne voulurent pas sacrifier inutilement du monde et ils allèrent passer le Guadalquivir à quelques lieues de là. Il ne fut tiré que quelques coups de fusil, dont l'un blessa légèrement un jeune officier des milices, qui plus tard se trouva prisonnier à Dijon en même temps que l'auteur de cette brochure. Rien de plus amusant que d'entendre raconter par ce jeune officier les bravades du général Echevarri, et sa surprise lorsqu'il apprit que les Français avaient passé le Guadalquivir. Cependant ce brave général fit approuver par les cortès la création d'une médaille, sur laquelle on lisait cet exergue : « *Salut de l'Espagne.* »

A l'imitation de cette médaille du Salut de l'Espagne, il y a eu des milliers de croix et de médailles. Il n'y a point de militaire espagnol ayant servi quelque temps qui ne soit chargé de tant de décorations que, s'il ne portait pas son uniforme, on le prendrait pour un marchand ambulant étalant des échantillons de croix et de médailles. Depuis qu'on est devenu imitateur de tout ce qui se fait dans les pays étrangers, on aurait dû, en fait de décorations, imiter le gouvernement prussien. Le maréchal Blucher se trouvait avec un corps d'armée en Silésie, lorsqu'il reçut l'ordre de marcher sur Paris en même temps que les autres armées des alliés Dans cette grande marche, le maréchal Blucher eut à soutenir six batailles et vingt-trois combats. Bien qu'il ne fût pas toujours vainqueur, il ne laissait pas, dès le lendemain de l'action, de publier un ordre du jour qui contenait invariablement ces mots : *en avant* ; en sorte que, depuis cette époque, ses soldats le désignaient toujours sous le nom de général *En avant*. Il arriva donc à Paris en même temps que les autres armées ; et, pour récompenser une campagne aussi laborieuse et aussi importante, on décerna à tous ceux qui avaient fait partie de cette armée une croix en bronze faite des canons pris à l'ennemi, et cette croix fut commune au général et aux soldats. Ce serait un exemple à suivre pour mettre fin à cette parade de décorations et de distinctions. A la vérité, dans la guerre d'Espagne, il n'y a pas eu un seul général à qui on eût pu donner le nom de *En avant* ; mais les soldats, battus dix et douze jours de suite, revenaient à la charge aussitôt qu'un officier les menait au combat en disant : *ce n'est rien*. C'est à ces soldats que l'on doit donner le nom de *no importa*, que l'on disait être le plus grand des généraux.

Note (2), page 2.

A l'étude des éléments du droit de la nature et des gens, que l'on faisait alors, on ajoutait un examen approfondi des ouvrages de Grotius et de Puffendorf, aussi bien que des traités de paix et d'alliance conclus entre les différents gouvernements de l'Europe. Ces études sont devenues inutiles depuis la révo-

lution française. Le directoire exécutif et Bonaparte trouvèrent
un moyen plus simple pour déclarer la guerre ou pour faire
la paix. Ce moyen consiste à calculer le nombre de ses troupes
et celui de la puissance sur laquelle on veut faire des con-
quêtes. Malgré son grand génie militaire et son immense puissance, Bonaparte se trompa dans ses calculs lorsqu'il se décida a envahir l'Espagne. Il semblait qu'après qu'il fut tombé
à Waterloo, son système aurait dû périr avec lui, mais malheureusement le congrès même de Vienne l'a continué.

Note (3), page 8.

Il est possible que, dans un temps plus ou moins éloigné,
l'Espagne et le Portugal ne forment qu'un seul État. Il est possible
aussi que ces deux peuples continuent de former deux gouvernements différents. En ce cas, il faudrait qu'ils fussent étroitement
unis par une amitié solide et durable, fondée sur leur récipro-
que utilité, et qu'ils eussent le bon esprit de se soustraire à toute
influence étrangère ; car ce sont les influences étrangères qui
ont toujours été la ruine de la Péninsule hispanique. Formant
une seule monarchie ou deux États séparés, les Espagnols et
les Portugais doivent figurer en Europe, même après qu'on les
a privés de leurs colonies. Celles de l'Espagne occupaient la
sixième partie du globe, et les habitants de tant d'immenses
royaumes, sous le drapeau auguste de Castille, gagnaient tous
les jours en population et en prospérité. On a dit dans le temps
que le soleil ne se couchait jamais dans les possessions de la
monarchie espagnole. Cette phrase, qui pourrait paraître
une fiction poétique, était une pure vérité. Le Portugal, de
son côté, en outre de ses possessions en Afrique et en Asie,
était maître du Brésil, ce royaume si fertile et si vaste, qui,
peuplé par une race européenne, aurait été plus que suffi-
sant pour former deux ou trois puissants empires. Malgré

tant de catastrophes, l'Espagne et le Portugal, par l'abondance,
par la variété et par l'excellence des produits de leur sol, peuvent se passer de l'Europe entière, et les habitants de ces deux
pays conserveront leur dignité, parce qu'à la bravoure, à la
constance et aux plus nobles qualités de l'âme, ils joignent une
force de corps, capable de résister à toutes les fatigues. Ainsi,
l'Espagne et le Portugal, grâce à la libéralité de la nature, pourront regretter moins la perte de ces grandes régions soumises
naguère à leur autorité.

Note (4), page 16.

Le rapport que le comte de Toréno a fait sur le mouvement d'Aranjuez dans son *Histoire de la guerre et de la révolution d'Espagne* est très-exact. On prétend qu'une des filles de
don Francisco Saavedra, la seule qui est vivante, communiqua
à M. le comte de Toréno un journal que son père avait tenu
sur tout ce qui était arrivé en Espagne à cette époque. Le comte
de Toréno ne pouvait avoir un guide plus sûr, puisque M. de
Saavedra était un homme de beaucoup d'esprit, très-instruit,
parlant et écrivant l'espagnol avec une pureté remarquable, qui
le rapprochait de Jovellanos, dont il était l'intime ami. On
trouve en effet dans le rapport que le comte de Toréno fait de
cet événement, des réflexions qui appartiennent sans doute à
M. de Saavedra; mais le style appartient à M. Toréno, qui, ayant
lu plus de livres français que de livres espagnols, ne se contente
pas d'écrire l'histoire dans un style simple; mais, à l'exemple
de plusieurs écrivains français de l'école moderne, il cherche
à amuser plutôt qu'à instruire ses lecteurs. Il s'est donc servi
d'un style fleuri, qui ressemble fort à celui qu'on emploie dans
les romans. Ainsi, quand M. de Toréno parle de l'entrée des
soldats et des paysans dans les salons de l'hôtel du prince de
la Paix à Aranjuez, il dépeint les paysans sales et déguenillés,

pour faire contraste avec la magnificence, le luxe recherché et les ornements précieux de l'habitation de Godoy. Les paysans d'Aranjuez, pas plus que ceux des autres parties de l'Espagne, ne sont salés ni deguenillés, si ce n'est dans les récits des mauvais romanciers qui publient des voyages en Espagne. L'auteur de ces mémoires avait servi sous les ordres de don Manuel Godoy, et, dans ce même mois de mars où l'émeute eut lieu, il avait visité plusieurs fois l'hôtel de ce favori. L'ameublement en était convenable, mais il n'y avait rien de cette magnificence romanesque, ni de ces richesses, ni de ce luxe dont parle le comte de Toréno. Les salons de cet hôtel n'étaient pas réservés, comme il le dit, à ce qu'il y avait de plus brillant à la cour. Don Manuel Godoy donnait des audiences à tout le monde, et les paysans d'Aranjuez et les soldats espagnols ne sont pas des sauvages à rester stupéfaits à la vue d'un ameublement qui n'était ni plus riche ni plus recherché que celui de toutes les autres personnes de la classe élevée.

La part que les gardes du corps prirent au mouvement d'Aranjuez fut l'œuvre du baron Capelleti, chargé d'affaires d'Espagne à Bologne, qui était venu à la suite de la reine d'Étrurie et qui était extrêmement actif. Il se mit d'accord avec ses anciens camarades dans les gardes, et il fut convenu qu'un certain nombre d'entre eux se tiendraient à cheval dans leur caserne, prêts à se rendre, à un signal donné, aux environs de l'hôtel du Prince de la Paix pour empêcher son départ avec la cour.

Ce que le comte de Toréno dit sur le comte del Montijo, qui, sous le faux nom de *Tio Pedro*, était à la tête des paysans de la Manche qui s'étaient rendus à Aranjuez pour empêcher le départ de la cour, est exact. Le prétendu Tio Pedro se donnait le titre de greffier (escribano) d'un village de la Manche. Il avait mis sur un de ses yeux un morceau de taffetas noir pour faire croire qu'il avait une difformité à cacher ou quelque blessure

Si l'intendant de la maison du duc d'Olivarès était venu lui dire : « Monseigneur, je vous félicite de ce que désormais vous n'aurez plus à dépenser de l'argent pour la réparation de votre hôtel ni pour l'entretien de vos propriétés, parce que je viens de les céder à vos créanciers; » il est probable qu'il l'aurait fait jeter par la fenêtre.

Le comte duc d'Olivarès a été pourtant plus heureux que la plupart des hommes éminents de l'Espagne. Son portrait a été fait à pied et à cheval par Velazquez, et il y a encore à présent à Madrid une porte connue sous le nom de Portillo del conde duque de Olivarès.

A Philippe IV succéda son fils Charles II, prince d'une si faible santé que l'histoire lui a donné le surnom de *malade*. Il n'était pas plus fort d'esprit que de corps; tombé en enfance avant le temps, il se croyait ensorcelé et il ne prenait jamais son chocolat sans avoir plongé une croix dans la tasse pour se préserver de nouveaux sortiléges. Le malheur de l'Espagne voulut qu'on lui conservât le trône, ce qui donna lieu aux intrigues des puissances étrangères, et, après sa mort, à la guerre civile entre les Espagnols de la couronne de Castille et leurs frères de la couronne d'Aragon.

La branche allemande de la maison d'Autriche a été en général plus favorisée que la branche espagnole. Quant aux princes de la maison de Lorraine, qui ont succédé à l'impératrice Marie-Thérèse, ils ont été presque tous remarquables par la bonté de leur cœur, par la simplicité de leurs goûts et par une sorte de bonhomie. Ces qualités font aimer les princes, autant que le courage et un grand caractère les font admirer. Ceux qui ont été à Vienne en 1814 et en 1815 ont pu voir l'amour que la population entière de cette capitale avait pour l'empereur François. Ce souverain avait été malheureux dans la guerre; il n'avait pas choisi des ministres ni des géneraux capables de remplir les devoirs que leurs charges leur imposaient; malgré cela, S. M. I. était adorée de ses sujets, et l'on n'aurait jamais cru que, dans l'année 1848, une grande partie des sujets de son empire se seraient révoltés contre son autorité et qu'il aurait fallu demander à la Russie le secours d'une nombreuse armée pour conserver la couronne à son successeur.

L'empire d'Autriche compte une population de 46 millions d'habitants. L'empereur a une armée très-nombreuse, très-brave et très-fidèle, mais tous ces avantages ne l'auraient pas préservé d'une ruine totale sans l'appui de son puissant allié. Il a été même question d'avoir recours à la Prusse, à la Bavière et à d'autres puissances d'Allemagne.

L'empire d'Autriche était, avant cette funeste guerre civile, comme ces corps qui paraissent pleins de vigueur, mais qui ont un vice organique-qui, malgré toutes les apparences de la santé et de la force, les conduit au tombeau. Ce vice organique de l'empire d'Autriche est la réunion d'un très-grand nombre de nations d'origine différente, de goûts et d'intérêts contraires. L'empire d'Autriche compte parmi ses sujets les habitants de la Hongrie, qui composaient autrefois un royaume très-puissant par l'abondance et la richesse des produits de son territoire et par le courage de ses habitants. Quoique ceux-ci n'appartiennent pas à une seule race et qu'ils n'aient pas les mêmes croyances, ils se rappellent que le pays qu'ils habitent a été indépendant et ils voudront toujours le redevenir.

La Bohême a formé aussi jadis un puissant royaume, et ses habitants ont les mêmes motifs que les Hongrois pour se soustraire à une domination qui n'est pas celle de leurs anciens souverains. A cela il faut ajouter cette grande partie de la Pologne qui fait partie de l'empire d'Autriche. Les Polonais ne renonceront jamais à leur nationalité. Ils sont les Espagnols du

6

Nord, ils ont beaucoup de courage et une grande constance, qui sont les qualités les plus essentielles pour réussir.

L'empire d'Autriche possède aussi en Italie ce qui fut détaché de la domination d'Espagne par suite de la guerre de succession de cette couronne ; or il n'y a point en Europe de peuples qui se ressemblent moins que les Allemands et les Italiens, et, comme leurs intérêts sont opposés, l'Autriche aura toujours besoin d'avoir en Italie une armée d'occupation comme dans un pays nouvellement conquis.

Les autres sujets de l'empire d'Autriche sont les Tyroliens, les Croates et les habitants des provinces que l'Autriche a conquises sur les Turcs.

Le royaume de Prusse n'a que le tiers de la population de l'empire d'Autriche ; mais il a le même vice organique que son voisin. Il y a en Prusse des Allemands, descendants des sujets de ce grand maître de l'ordre teutonique qui embrassa la réforme de Luther et, de chef religieux et catholique qu'il était, devint prince séculier ; il y a des Silésiens, que la Prusse a conquis et détachés de la Silésie autrichienne ; il y a un grand nombre de catholiques, sujets autrefois des trois électeurs ecclésiastiques ; il y a des Polonais et des Saxons détachés de la Saxe par un des actes les plus blâmables du congrès de Vienne. Malgré tous ces éléments de faiblesse, la Prusse a été placée parmi les grandes puissances de l'Europe, parce qu'elle a trouvé le moyen d'avoir une armée très-nombreuse, très-disciplinée et très-brave, et qu'à force d'ordre et d'économie, elle a pu soutenir en Europe le rang auquel elle s'est élevée sous le grand Frédéric. L'auteur de ces mémoires n'aime pas les révolutions, mais il croit que l'Autriche et la Prusse pourront difficilement en éviter une nouvelle avant longtemps.

Si l'on compare l'état présent de l'Autriche et de la Prusse

avec celui de l'Espagne, qu'elles n'ont pas daigné compter parmi
les grandes puissances, on verra que l'Espagne, pour peu
qu'elle soit bien gouvernée, aura augmenté sa puissance quand
ces autres gouvernements auront perdu la leur. La grande
monarchie qui s'étend depuis les Pyrénées jusqu'à la Méditer-
ranée d'un côté et à l'Océan de l'autre, ne compte parmi ses
habitants qu'une seule race, ayant la même origine, les mêmes
croyances, les mêmes mœurs, les mêmes intérêts et les mêmes
préjugés, si l'on veut. Elle restera debout quand les plus
grands empires seront tombés.

Note (6), page 33.

Le ministre qui tenait ce langage avait rempli les mêmes
fonctions au temps de Charles III. Il avait joui pendant de
longues années du traitement de ministre et de riches comman-
deries ; il n'est donc pas extraordinaire qu'il voulût qu'on réta-
blît tout sur l'ancien pied. Pourtant le temps écoulé depuis la
mort de Charles III jusqu'en 1808, est une des époques les plus
désastreuses et les plus humiliantes pour l'Espagne. Charles IV
s'occupait exclusivement de sa passion pour la chasse et de
l'enfantillage appelé Maison de Ferme ou Casa del Labrador,
qu'il avait fait bâtir dans le jardin d'Aranjuez, et qui n'a jamais
servi ni pour donner un logement à la famille royale ni pour
une fête quelconque. C'était tout simplement un magasin de
pendules, de petits meubles et de curiosités, achetés la plupart
à Paris à des prix exorbitants Le rez-de-chaussée de cette petite maison étant au-dessous du niveau du Tage, devenait en
hiver un petit lac. Malgré cela, lorsque le marquis de Labrador arriva à Aranjuez en 1808, Charles IV, à qui la goutte ne
permettait plus l'amusement de la chasse, avait donné l'ordre
de réunir 2 millions de réaux (500,000 francs) pour augmenter
cette bicoque. Il faut savoir que, pendant ce temps, les domes-

tiques de la cour portaient des livrées râpées ou trouées. On
avait donné à l'auteur une voiture de la cour avec deux laquais,
et, ayant remarqué le mauvais état de leurs livrées, et soup-
çonnant qu'ils n'étaient pas payés de leurs gages, il leur donna
de sa bourse une somme chaque semaine, et l'inspecteur des
écuries du roi le remercia de cet acte de générosité. Ces détails
paraîtront incroyables, surtout si l'on considère qu'à cette
époque l'Espagne conservait encore ses immenses et riches colonies. Charles IV ne voulant pas être troublé dans ses goûts,
et la reine et le favori ne voulant pas l'être non plus dans les
leurs, on laissait insulter l'Espagne par les plus petites puissances.

NOTE (7), page 33.

Cette extraordinaire prétention de la France n'était pas la
première de la même nature qu'elle eût eue depuis la révolution. Lorsque Bonaparte, premier consul, signa les prélimi-
naires de la paix d'Amiens, sous prétexte d'urgence, sans attendre les plénipotentiaires espagnols, il céda à l'Angleterre
l'île de la Trinité, colonie espagnole.

Si ces faits avaient pu se répéter et cette doctrine prévaloir,
le premier consul de la république française et le ministre du
roi Louis XVIII auraient réalisé le rêve ambitieux de Louis XIV,
prétendant qu'il n'y avait plus de Pyrénées.

Les Français et les Espagnols sont des peuples très-braves,
mais chacun d'eux l'est à sa manière : le Français, plein de vanité, ne veut reconnaître la supériorité d'aucune autre nation,
et l'Espagnol, plein de fierté, ne peut souffrir d'égal ni en courage ni en loyauté; pour le reste, il ne s'inquiète de la supériorité d'aucune autre nation. On pourra peut-être avec le temps
aplanir les pics les plus élevés des Pyrénées, sillonner leurs
flancs par des chemins de fer, et les percer de tunnels; mais

dans la réalité les Pyrénées seront toujours des montagnes in-
surmontables, tant que les deux peuples conserveront leurs
caractères distinctifs.

NOTE (8), page 44.

Il est vrai que ces trente mille hommes étaient très-braves, et
commandés par un de ces hommes extraordinaires que l'on
voit paraître très-rarement dans le monde. Le duc de Wellington
vainquit en Portugal et en Espagne les plus renommés des maréchaux et des lieutenants de Bonaparte, et presque toujours
avec des forces inférieures, rarement avec des forces égales et jamais avec des forces supérieures. Pour compléter ces triomphes,
il battit Bonaparte lui-même à Waterloo, ce qui le plaça parmi
les plus grands génies militaires qui aient paru. Le duc de
Wellington a été encore favorisé par la Providence en ce qu'il
n'a jamais tiré l'épée que pour la défense de la justice et du
droit. Il n'a jamais terni sa gloire, ni par des actes de cruauté,
ni par ces basses perfidies qui ont déshonoré d'autres grands
hommes de guerre.

Le duc de Wellington se rendit à Cadix en 1813, pendant
que M. de Labrador était ministre des affaires étrangères.
M. de Labrador fit alors au duc de Wellington, par ordre de
la Régence, tous les honneurs que la situation des affaires permettait. Il fut ensuite son collègue au Congrès de Vienne.

A Paris, pendant l'ambassade du duc de Wellington, et
à Londres, lors d'un voyage qu'il y fit, il eut l'occasion d'admirer le duc de Wellington comme homme privé, ainsi qu'il l'a-
vait admiré comme homme public. Il remarqua surtout son
bon sens, qualité bien plus rare que la pénétration et l'esprit.
Les témoignages d'estime et d'amitié que le duc de Wellington
a donnés à M. de Labrador ont procuré à celui-ci une des
plus grandes satisfactions que son amour-propre ait éprouvées.

Note (9), page 54.

Aujourd'hui, le titre de duc est en faveur en Espagne, et cette faveur augmente tous les jours comme celle du coton. Je ne serais pas plus étonné si ma cuisinière me donnait un jour une soupe de coton, que si mon confiseur prenait le titre de duc de la Marmelade et de grand cordon de l'ordre du Caramel. Peut-être aussi un de ces jours, mon concierge va me remettre en rentrant chez moi une carte de visite de maître Crispin, cordonnier de son état et s'appelant duc de la Semelle et grand cordon du Cuir verni. Si tout cela vous paraît trop ridicule, j'ajouterai que je voudrais même que le titre de duc devînt plus commun, parce qu'alors on n'en voudrait plus, et tous les Espagnols deviendraient des archiducs. Peut-être trouverait-on un moyen de mettre fin à ces créations de ducs par douzaines (duques adocenados), ce serait de faire pour les ducs ce que l'on fait pour les canons, que l'on désigne toujours par leur calibre. On dirait par exemple le duc un tel, du calibre de 100,000 écus, et on descendrait jusqu'au duc de 3,000 francs. De cette manière, le titre de duc ne tromperait personne, comme il arrive à présent. Si vous trouvez cela trop amer, je vous dirai qu'avec des paroles douces on ne fera jamais marcher un Espagnol d'une certaine classe ; comme les muletiers ne feront jamais marcher leurs mulets et leurs ânes avec des paroles caressantes.

Note (10), page 58.

Ceux qui n'ont pas connu le roi Charles IV n'ont pas une idée exacte de lui. Il ne manquait pas d'esprit naturel et avait assez d'instruction; mais Charles III lui avait inspiré le goût de la chasse, et, lorsqu'il revenait fatigué, il ne voulait s'occuper de rien. Aussi reçut-il comme un bienfait de la part de la reine la présentation du jeune Godoy comme ministre, et il fut encore plus enchanté lorsque la reine demanda à être admise au con-

seil ; car alors Charles IV, calculant que son avis ne pouvait
prévaloir, parce qu'il avait contre lui l'opinion de la reine et
celle du favori, cédait à sa paresse naturelle et ne prenait aucune part aux délibérations. A Naples, il était plus à son aise
qu'au palais Borghèse de Rome, où il habitait avec la reine et
Godoy. Il disait un jour qu'il aimait beaucoup Naples à cause
de son climat ; mais qu'il préférait finir ses jours en Espagne,
où il n'aurait rien à craindre, n'ayant jamais fait de mal à personne. « Il n'en serait pas de même, ajoutait-il, pour Madame et
pour Godoy, qui ont été la cause de la ruine de l'Espagne. »

NOTE (11), page 63.

Ceux qui n'ont pas connu de près M. de Châteaubriand ne peuvent s'imaginer combien il était insignifiant dans les relations or-
dinaires de la vie et combien peu d'influence il avait sur ses compatriotes. Il prenait rarement part aux questions qui se traitaient
devant lui, et cela, non par orgueil, mais par timidité. On avait
déjà remarqué ce défaut lorsqu'il était ministre des affaires
étrangères, et il en donna des nouvelles preuves à Rome. Homme
d'un brillant génie, auteur de pages d'une admirable éloquence,
il n'avait aucune facilité pour l'improvisation, et, s'il répondait,
c'était dans des termes si généraux et si confus, qu'on aurait cru
qu'il voulait envelopper sa pensée dans une sorte d'obscurité
majestueuse. Il adressa aux cardinaux réunis en Conclave un
discours dans lequel on ne remarque pas un seul mot qui soit
digne de la circonstance. Ce discours est même inférieur à celui
de l'ambassadeur belge, où l'on ne trouve pourtant pas une
seule idée lumineuse.

NOTE (12), page 63.

Un ambassadeur qui, au commencement du siècle, eut la
commission de demander une princesse en mariage pour le prince
des Asturies, trouva le moyen d'enfler son compte au point de

se faire payer 300,000 francs, qu'il employa à l'acquisition d'un hôtel à Madrid.

Il existe au bureau des affaires étrangères d'Espagne, un compte pareil d'un grand seigneur qui, étant ambassadeur à Lisbonne, eut aussi l'occasion de faire un compte où, en outre de la vaisselle, on n'oublia pas même de porter les balais.

Lors du couronnement du grand duc Léopold comme empereur d'Allemagne, l'ambassadeur d'Espagne à Vienne dressa un compte d'une somme énorme, et l'ambassadrice, qui était très-bonne ménagère, y ajouta un si grand nombre de caisses de cire de Venise, que l'éclairage de l'ambassade à Vienne se faisait encore avec cette cire cinq ou six ans après. Ceux qui seront surpris de ces détails, ne le seraient pas s'ils savaient qu'en Espagne, tous ceux qui peuvent approcher du trésor royal se croient près d'une fontaine publique, où l'on peut étancher sa soif à plaisir.

Note (43), page 66.

M. de Labrador avait fait dans sa jeunesse une étude approfondie des anciens gouvernements, et il a été toujours grand admirateur de celui de la République romaine, le seul qui ait vraiment été un gouvernement d'hommes; car tous les autres n'étaient que des gouvernements de pygmées. Ce gouvernement, malgré les absurdités du polythéisme, malgré le scandale de ses divinités, avait su inspirer au sénat et aux tribunaux des principes de morale dignes d'admiration, vu surtout que le christianisme n'était pas encore apparu, et qu'il n'y avait d'autres lumières que celles de la philosophie, divisée en sectes ennemies. M. de Labrador a toujours admiré dans le gouvernement de la République romaine, une force d'organisation qui a survécu à tous les siècles; malgré les changements que l'usage des armes à feu a introduits dans l'art de la guerre, les fondements de la discipline militaire se trouvent toujours dans les armées romaines. Pour une compagnie de cent soldats, il y avait dix ou douze chefs, de façon que, sur huit ou dix hommes, il y en avait un qui se faisait obéir sous peine de mort, et cette tactique est suivie dans les Républiques modernes, où l'on commence par proclamer la liberté et l'égalité. C'est sans doute une plaisante égalité que celle où, pour huit hommes, il faut un chef. Il en est de même pour les places de l'administration. où dans les temps actuels, il y a, pour six travailleurs, au plus, un chef qui les commande.

Parmi les gouvernements modernes, M. de Labrador a toujours admiré celui de la Grande-Bretagne, qui, sous le nom de monarchie, avec toute la richesse, la pompe extérieure et les génuflexions du gouvernement royal, n'est qu'une république aristocratique, dont les chefs sont les plus anciens nobles et propriétaires de la Grande-Bretagne. Ce sénat de rois se recrute parmi tout ce que l'Angleterre produit de plus distingué dans les armées de terre et de mer, dans la diplomatie et la justice, et, pour être plus sûre d'être obéie, cette chambre des lords partage l'autorité avec la chambre des communes, qui réunit ce qu'il y a de plus remarquable par la richesse, l'industrie, le talent. Ceux qui n'admireraient pas le gouvernement de la Grande-Bretagne n'ont qu'à se faire représenter une mappemonde et ils verront qu'elle a trois cent millions de sujets dans les Indes, qu'elle a un pied dans la Chine, qu'elle peuple de nouveaux continents dans l'Australie et qu'il n'y a pas de port ni de rade où l'on ne trouve un bâtiment anglais prêt à protéger le commerce de son pays ou à faire reconnaître sa supériorité maritime ; et, pour bien comprendre tout ce qu'a d'étonnant ce giganteste édifice, il faut en considérer la base, laquelle n'est qu'un coin de terre, que le soleil éclaire à regret, comme le disait avec plus de vérité que de politesse le président du Directoire exécutif français.

M. de Labrador n'a jamais aimé les gouvernements despotiques, et il croit que, quand même le chef d'un pareil gouvernement serait le plus éclairé des hommes, s'il n'est absolument impossible, il risquera de communiquer à son gouvernement les enfantillages d'un gouvernement de femmes ou les violences de la tyrannie la plus sanglante. Il y a un gouvernement pire encore, c'est le gouvernement arbitraire dépendant de l'influence des personnes attachées au service du souverain. Malheureusement on ne manque pas, en Europe, d'exemples de ces deux espèces de gouvernement, également contraires à la raison.

Quintilien a défini l'orateur, *vir bonus dicendi peritus* « un honnête homme savant dans l'art de bien parler. » Le commencement de cette définition conviendrait à toutes les personnes vouées à des fonctions publiques. Un diplomate serait un honnête homme connaissant le droit de la nature et des gens, savant en politique, instruit dans les traités et les liens qui unissent les gouvernements entre eux. Un roi serait un honnête homme, capable de se mettre à la tête de son armée, ou au moins de se mettre dans ses rangs; assez instruit et assez laborieux pour présider les conseils de ses ministres et les séances de son conseil d'État. Il devrait être bon époux et bon père, mais assez sévère pour ne pas permettre que l'influence de sa famille s'étendît au delà de sa sphère naturelle, c'est-à-dire de l'alcove, du boudoir et du salon. Il devrait être assez jaloux de son autorité pour ne permettre à personne de s'occuper du gouvernement de son royaume, sans en avoir été officiellement chargé. Instruit de ce qui s'est passé dans les derniers temps dans le palais des rois d'Espagne, il devrait laisser les domestiques à leur place, sans réunir les fonctions de valet de chambre à l'uniforme de colonel ou de général, ainsi qu'il a été fait sous le dernier roi. Les anciens rois de Castille, dans le diplôme qu'ils faisaient expédier à un valet de chambre, disaient qu'ils le nommaient parce qu'il était honnête homme et qu'il ne savait ni lire ni écrire. Cette dernière clause paraîtra par trop primitive à notre époque, mais les anciens rois ne voulaient pas que leurs valets de chambre se mêlassent des affaires.

Le rôle d'un roi d'Espagne, pour ce qui est de ses rapports avec les gouvernements étrangers, devrait revenir à son ancienne dignité et à la glorieuse indépendance de sa couronne. Cette indépendance fut perdue lors que Charles III conclut avec le roi de France le traité connu sous le nom de pacte de famille. Depuis le moment funeste où il fut mis à exécution, l'Espagne, qui avait été, pendant des siècles, rivale et souvent rivale heureuse de la France, devint l'humble vassale de sa voisine; elle s'éclipsa, et, au lieu d'être un astre brillant, elle devint un triste satellite, tournant autour d'une grande planète.

Le premier effet de ce déplorable traité fut la détermination de Charles III de s'unir à la France pour protéger l'insurrection des colonies anglaises. L'Espagne possédait alors deux mille lieues de territoire, depuis le Nouveau-Mexique jusqu'au détroit de Magellan; en s'unissant à la France pour protéger l'insurrection des colonies anglaises, elle commença à donner aux habitants de ses propres possessions en Amérique, les idées qui ont amené la perte de ces contrées. Pourtant Charles III fut un des meilleurs rois d'Espagne des temps modernes; mais les Anglais l'avaient humilié pendant qu'il était roi de Naples, et il voulut se venger; seulement il choisit très-mal le moyen de le faire.

Le comte d'Aranda, qui signa le traité dont on vient de faire mention, était un homme de beaucoup de mérite, très-actif et très-laborieux. Il servit toujours son roi et son pays de sa personne et de son argent, n'ayant jamais voulu recevoir ni solde, ni appointements, ni aucune indemnité pour subvenir aux dépenses des grandes places qu'il occupa (*), entre autres, de celle de capitaine général de l'armée espagnole et de commandant en chef dans la guerre de l'Espagne contre les Portugais et les Anglais, qui se termina par la paix de 1764. Il fut président du conseil de Castille et ambassadeur à Paris ; mais, pendant son séjour à la cour de France, la famille royale le traitait plutôt en ami qu'en ambassadeur étranger, et ce fut probablement cette amitié qui lui fit oublier les intérêts de son pays pour plaire à la cour de France. L'Espagne doit vivre en paix avec la France ; mais elle ne doit jamais lui donner que la main gauche, tenant la droite prête à tirer l'épée, pour peu que la France exige que l'amitié de l'Espagne pour elle se change en dépendance.

Vivent les Pyrénées ! et puissent leurs bases s'élargir et leurs cimes s'élever pour rendre plus difficiles les passages qui conduisent de France en Espagne ! Mais ne suffit-il pas qu'elles restent telles qu'elles sont ? L'Espagne n'aura jamais rien à craindre de la France, pourvu que les Espagnols n'oublient pas qu'ils sont Espagnols. Il y en a eu qui, invités aux Tuileries, ravis de se voir préférés à leurs compatriotes et devenus courtisans de Louis–Philippe, lui demandèrent auquel de ses enfants il destinait la couronne d'Espagne. On a loué, et avec rai-

---

(*) Son exemple a été suivi dans un autre temps par le duc de l'Infantado, qui ne voulut jamais non plus accepter ni solde, ni appointements, ni indemnité pendant qu'il fut capitaine général de l'armée espagnole, ambassadeur à Londres, général en chef de l'armée de Catalogne pendant la guerre de l'invasion de Bonaparte, membre de la régence de Cadix, et plus tard président du conseil de Castille. Tous ceux qui l'ont connu savent qu'il était très-poli et très-obligeant pour tout le monde, et M. de Labrador, lié avec lui de la plus étroite amitié, sait par sa propre expérience combien il était un ami sûr et constant. Sans doute ces illustres exemples seront suivis par d'autres nobles espagnols, que leur fortune mettra à même de pouvoir les imiter.

son, l'adresse, la souplesse et la sagacité de Louis-Philippe; mais il ne faut pas qu'il soit fier d'avoir converti des Espagnols en Français, bien qu'il y eût parmi ces Messieurs, et des pères conscrits de la constitution de 1812, et des apôtres de l'égalité. Leur conversion n'a pas été un grand miracle : le plus noir des rois d'Angora ou de Guinée aurait opéré la même transformation, pourvu qu'il eût flatté leur vanité. Tous les hommes ont un péché originel, qui nous fut transmis par Adam; en Espagne, il y en a un second, la vanité, fondée sur la supériorité réelle ou imaginaire que chaque Espagnol croit avoir sur ses compatriotes. La fable du Renard et du Corbeau paraît avoir été inventée pour les Espagnols, et je parierais qu'un corbeau espagnol était venu d'Espagne en France se percher sur un arbre du jardin de Lafontaine. Rien de plus espagnol que l'action du corbeau qui, pour convaincre le renard de ce que son ramage répond à son plumage, laisse échapper sa proie. Choisissez le plus basané et le plus disgracieux des enfants de l'Ebre ou du Tage; si vous voulez vous en rendre maître, vous n'avez qu'à lui dire qu'il est le plus beau des Espagnols, et que toutes les jolies femmes sont folles de lui; il laissera tomber à vos pieds le cigare de la Havane, que nul, parmi ses compatriotes, ne sait fumer avec autant de grâce.

M. de Labrador s'est toujours fait une gloire d'être Espagnol; mais il ne dissimule pas les défauts de sa nation. Le plus grand est l'envie que tout Espagnol porte en général à ceux de ses compatriotes qui se distinguent. On pourra parcourir l'Espagne d'un bout à l'autre, et l'on ne trouvera aucun monument érigé en l'honneur d'un grand homme, si ce n'est une statue de Cervantes érigée par le commissaire de la Croisade, M. Varéla. On dirait, en parcourant l'Espagne, que ce n'est pas pour elle que Colomb fit la découverte de l'Amérique; on dirait que le Grand Capitaine n'était pas Espagnol; que don Juan d'Autriche était étranger à l'Espagne ; que Cortès, Pizarre et tant d'autres grands conquérants lui étaient étrangers, puisqu'il n'y a pas un seul monument élevé à leur mémoire. Il n'y en a pas non plus en l'honneur du duc d'Albe, qui eut *le tort* de vaincre tous les ennemis de l'Espagne et de conquérir le Portugal dans le court espace d'un mois, et que les étrangers n'ont cessé de calomnier, n'ayant jamais pu le vaincre.

Un roi d'Espagne doit rendre à l'armée espagnole la dignité qui lui convient, et qu'elle a perdue par le nombre incroyable de ses généraux et de ses officiers supérieurs. Dans les armées de toutes les nations d'Europe, il n'y a que les généraux dont on peut avoir besoin pendant la guerre où pendant la paix, et ce nombre est toujours en proportion avec l'armée. En Espagne, on a introduit l'usage de donner des grades sans tenir aucun compte de la force de l'armée ; d'après l'état militaire d'Espagne, publié au commencement de cette année 1849, le cadre des généraux est ainsi composé : neuf capitaines généraux, soixante et onze lieutenants généraux, deux cent-vingt-deux maréchaux de camp et trois cent-soixante brigadiers généraux; ce qui fait un total de six cent soixante-deux généraux, nombre monstrueux quand même il s'agirait d'une armée vingt fois plus nombreuse que l'armée espagnole. Tout ce désordre vient de l'usage d'ajouter aux places effectives un nombre indéfini de grades purement nominaux. Cette innovation fut l'œuvre du comte d'O'Reilly, pendant qu'il était inspecteur général de l'infanterie espagnole. Ainsi cet oubli de toutes les règles de l'organisation militaire fut introduit en Espagne par un étranger, comme bien d'autres abus qui ont fait dégénérer un grand nombre d'institutions espagnoles. A cet abus des grades militaires on doit ajouter le scandale de donner à un enfant qui vient de naître le grade, la solde et l'ancienneté de capitaine. On a été jusqu'à fixer à des officiers de cette espèce, la solde que l'on donne

dans l'Amérique espagnole, parce qu'elle est plus forte que
celle que l'on donne en Espagne. Par ce moyen, un enfant qui
vivra jusqu'à cinquante ou soixante ans, sera nécessairement
général et peut-être le doyen des généraux, ou pour mieux
dire, il sera le plus ancien de tous ceux qui auront vécu aux
dépens de ce peuple espagnol, que les étrangers calomnient en
l'appelant fainéant, tandis qu'il travaille pour se nourrir et
nourrir ses enfants, pour payer d'énormes contributions, et pour
solder une armée innombrable d'employés et d'enfants d'employés; car, en Espagne, l'employé le moins rétribué ne don-
nera jamais à ses enfants un état, ni ne leur fera apprendre un
métier comme on le fait dans les autres pays. En Espagne, les
enfants des employés ne doivent être que des employés.

NOTE (14), page 69.

Lorsque éclata en France le fléau politique appelé révolution,
les apôtres de la nouvelle doctrine se contentèrent de parler
de liberté, d'égalité et de fraternité. Nous sommes en temps
de progrès. Il y a maintenant une autre secte plus audacieuse,
qui publie que la propriété c'est le vol, ce qui veut dire qu'il
ne doit plus y avoir de société; car, sans propriété, il ne peut y
avoir d'agriculture, et, sans agriculture, il n'y aurait que des
sauvages, vivant de la pêche et de la chasse. Ils ajoutent que les
femmes doivent être communes, ce qui veut dire qu'il n'y aura
plus de famille. Ils prétendent aussi qu'il ne doit pas y avoir des
gouvernements différents, ni de nations distinctes, et qu'il doit
s'établir une fraternité générale entre tous les peuples. Le christianisme avait établi comme dogme que nous descendons tous
d'Adam et d'Ève, et que nous sommes parents. Il avait établi
que tout homme doit regarder un autre homme comme son
prochain. Ces doctrines ont civilisé le monde, et, si elles
étaient observées, on n'aurait pas besoin de tribunaux ni de

punitions. Mais le dogme moderne de la fraternité de tous les peuples est encore une plus grande chimère que celui de la paix universelle de l'abbé de Saint-Pierre. Il faudrait savoir comment on s'y prendrait pour qu'un enfant du Gange, qui pleure si en marchant il a écrasé sans le vouloir une fourmi ou une puce, devînt le frère d'un Caraïbe, qui tout joyeux tourne devant le feu sa broche chargée de chair humaine.

> El Indio llora de amargura lleno
> Si una hormiga pisó mientras paséa,
> Y el Caribe vorax frio y sereno
> Humana carne en asador voltéa.

> Naturam expellas furca tamen ipsa redibit.

En français, on donne à cette maxime une tournure plus gaie : « Et l'on revient toujours à ses premières amours. » Les quatre vers que je viens de citer faisaient partie d'un petit poëme que j'ai composé il y a plus de cinquante ans, et, pour être si vieux, ils ne me paraissent pas plus mauvais que des vers qui ont valu des places d'ambassadeur, de ministre des affaires étrangères, et, ce qui vaut mieux, des écus. Ils étaient bien niais les poëtes du bon vieux temps, qui se contentaient d'une couronne de laurier, dont ils ne pouvaient tirer d'autre parti que celui d'en mettre les feuilles dans leurs sauces ; il était très-bon aussi cet Horace, qui trouvait insupportables les poëtes médiocres. Nous autres Espagnols nous sommes de meilleure composition, et nous préférons les couplets du poëte Calaïnos et ceux de Mingo Revulgo aux services les plus honorables et les plus utiles qu'on ait rendus en diplomatie ou en finances, voire même à la guerre.

PARIS. — IMPRIMÉ PAR E. THUNOT ET Cᵉ, RUE RACINE, 26.

CPSIA information can be obtained at www.ICGtesting.com
Printed in the USA
BVOW01s1105090115

382676BV00021B/216/P

HMS
BELFAST
POCKET MANUAL

Compiled and introduced by
Lt Cdr John Blake FRIN RN

OSPREY PUBLISHING
Bloomsbury Publishing Plc
PO Box 883, Oxford, OX1 9PL, UK
1385 Broadway, 5th Floor, New York, NY 10018, USA
E-mail: info@ospreypublishing.com
www.ospreypublishing.com

OSPREY is a trademark of Osprey Publishing Ltd

First published in Great Britain in 2018

A catalogue record for this book is available from the British Library.

ISBN: HB 9781472827821; eBook 9781472827845;
ePDF 9781472827838; XML 9781472827852

18 19 20 21 22 10 9 8 7 6 5 4 3 2 1

Index by Kate Inskip

Front endpaper: Image courtesy of Mrs Greenup/R. Cosby's (www.maritimeoriginals.com)

Typeset by Deanta Global Publishing Services, Chennai, India
Printed and bound in Great Britain by CPI (Group), UK Ltd, Croydon CR0 4YY

Osprey Publishing supports the Woodland Trust, the UK's leading woodland
conservation charity. Between 2014 and 2018 our donations are being
spent on their Centenary Woods project in the UK.

To find out more about our authors and books visit www.ospreypublishing.com.
Here you will find extracts, author interviews, details of forthcoming events
and the option to sign up for our newsletter.

CONTENTS

Her Majesty's Ship *Belfast*
Pennant Number C35

INTRODUCTION

Today, HMS *Belfast* is an important example of our nation's cultural heritage. She is moored in the heart, in the Pool, of London, positioned close by those other hallmarks of British history, the Tower of London and Tower Bridge – a fact that reflects her significance. Visited by more than 250,000 people every year, she represents for the Imperial War Museum the role of the Royal Navy in our history. Here, we explore the fascinating story of both her commissioned life and her preservation.

The many people who have been associated with the ship in their very different ways, and who have contributed to this pocket manual, reflected that she was a 'happy ship' – an accolade not bestowed on every vessel. In accordance with this, rather than being a dry work of reference the book seeks to describe both the important strategic environment in which HMS *Belfast* was procured and operated and the spirit of the ship, which led to her being preserved as a representative of the Royal Navy. Compiled from original material and documents of the time, the pocket manual catalogues the ship from her launch in 1938 at Harland and Wolff (the same shipyard as the RMS *Titanic)* and her equipment and operation through to her role in a variety of naval operations during her eventful 25-year career and, latterly, her current role as a museum ship.

I, too, during my time in the Royal Navy, came to regard the ship in which I served with affection. Although perhaps prima facie this regard may seem unexpected to civilians, the sentiment is something, possibly created by the atmosphere that a ship emanates once commissioned, that most sailors experience. With this in mind, it is unsurprising that ships are called 'she', and have been for centuries, and HMS *Belfast* is no exception to this tradition.

Historically, the term *cruiser* (sic) traces back to the 18th century and referred to an 18-gun ship of the brig-sloop class of the Royal Navy. This was the same as a ship-sloop except for the rigging, with only a foremast and mainmast, while a ship-sloop was rigged with three masts. More cruizers were built by the British during the Napoleonic Wars, with 110 vessels constructed to this design, making the cruizer (or cruiser as it came to be known, although the innovating and energetic reformer of the Royal Navy, AF Jacky Fisher, spelt it cruizer as late as 1900) the second-most numerous class of sailing warship built to a single design for any navy at any time.

The function of the early cruizers for the fleet was not dissimilar to that of the cruiser of the 1930s. The cruiser class of the first half of the 20th century denoted a ship capable of independent employment on a foreign station. This required its crew to have the ability to make running repairs and have a large radius of action. Looking within this overarching role of the cruiser there was a multifunctional aspect: to be a scout for a fleet of battleships (and later aircraft carriers); to be on hand to provide firepower to deter colonial trouble in the British Empire as well as to protect trade interests; to be available to protect principally Britain's merchant shipping fleet worldwide; and, during peacetime, to maintain and extend Britain's influence around the world by 'showing the flag'.

Described by AF Jacky Fisher as 'eggshells armed with sledgehammers', before the advent of radio large numbers of cruisers were needed for trade protection, for convoys or at merchant shipping focal points around the world. However, the arrival of radio, and later radar – which was introduced into HMS *Belfast* just before World War II – profoundly changed the way cruisers were able to operate and the number of cruisers needed by the Royal Navy was considerably reduced thereby.

The difficulty for Britain in the late 19th century was that, while potential enemies (viz, Russia, Germany and France) could build relatively small numbers of cruisers to provide a threat and to attack trade shipping, Britain needed huge numbers to beat off potential attackers and had to position them wherever an attack might be possible. What's more, the financial burden on the Empire could be the winning factor for her enemies: what the French at the time called *la guerre industrielle* – an economic war – which, it was thought, would make Britain bankrupt. Radio changed all that and allowed for a smaller number of cruisers to be vectored to points at which there might be trouble.

The cruiser role of protecting the Empire was entwined with the dominance of Britain as the financial centre of the world. Not only did the overseas colonies and dominions need trade protection for what has been called the 'formal Empire', but the 'informal Empire' did too. This latter category was made up of many countries worldwide that favoured trade with Britain because of the implicit acceptance that Britain would protect their free trade. This created a self-serving situation that benefitted both Britain and her trading partners. Trade followed the flag. China was an important example and this explains why the Royal Navy kept a large and expensive fleet throughout the inter-war years – one that was far larger than that of any other country with Asian interests. The cruiser, with powerful guns, a strong detachment of marines and good command and control facilities on board, answered the needs of colonial and informal Empire protection. Kuwait, for example, was saved from Saudi attack in 1921 and Iraqi attack in 1961 (albeit with a carrier force).

After World War I various treaties were signed by the dominant powers: Great Britain, the USA, Germany, Italy and Japan. The Washington Naval Treaty, concluded on 26 February 1922 by the victorious powers of World War I, limited cruisers to 10,000 tons' displacement with maximum 8in. guns, but without restriction on numbers. Japan and the USA built to this limit, but the Royal Navy cruisers of the Kent, Norfolk and London classes were relatively too expensive and too big for the task and the York class of 8,000 tons was built. The London Naval Treaty of 1930 superceded the earlier Washington Naval Treaty and was itself superceded by a further London Naval Treaty in 1936, which tried again to limit the naval arms race while allowing the USA and Britain naval parity. The Town class was the outcome, with a size limitation of 10,000 tons and bearing 6in. guns – a class that featured HMS *Southampton*, which was laid down in November 1934.

At that time, British warship designers consistently sought to minimise weight, which was associated with cost, deciding on length and space requirements later in the design. These changed with the advent of World War II and the rapid advance in radar and wireless equipment, since there was now a need for anti-aircraft guns and internal space for increased electric power, which added significantly to top weight. However, it was known that the Japanese were not adhering to any size limitations in their naval construction programme and were building much heavier ships.

HMS *Belfast*'s capture in 1939 of the German merchant ship *Cap Norte* (*Belfast*'s crew included the future AF Lord Terence Lewin, then a midshipman in charge of the boat that carried the capturing boarding party); her enduring performance guarding and supporting merchant ships of the Arctic Convoys to Russia; her role in the sinking in 1943 of the German pocket battleship *Scharnhorst*; her leading role in the D-Day landings as a command and control ship, with accurate army support bombardment; her involvement in the Korean War; and subsequent flag-showing during the 1950s and 1960s, with inspirational captains such as R Adm Sir Morgan Morgan-Giles, all gave her a pedigree history that has deservedly been recognised through her preservation as a tribute to those involved with her. Her battle honours, proudly displayed today on her quarterdeck, visually and succinctly summarise this extraordinary career.

It was Sir Morgan Morgan-Giles, captain from January 1961 to July 1962 who, as MP for Winchester, so determinedly led the move to preserve HMS *Belfast* for the nation. That the Russians should pay more than £1 million for the replacement of her masts with Russian steel, completed in October 2010, is testament to the wider affection in which she is held.

The ship is open to visitors and this, along with the highly active volunteers of the HMS Belfast Association who work with the Imperial War Museum, keeps her alive. These volunteers hold meetings, commemorative services, VIP visits and, through their association magazine *The Seahorse*, keep veterans and members in touch and help to relive her past achievements through the exhibits and parts of the ship fitted out with contemporary functions on board.

She serves to remind us all of the debt we owe to the Royal Navy in protecting this island nation and that we depend on trade and food from throughout the world (with some 95 per cent coming by sea) for our survival. The Kaiser and the Nazis nearly starved Great Britain during two world wars with their U-boat campaigns and we should never let ourselves be hostage to such a situation again. As a collective tribute to the Royal Navy and the Merchant Navies she is representative of all classes of ship. Go and visit HMS *Belfast!* You will not regret it.

John Blake FRIN 2018

CHAPTER 1

 HMS _Belfast_: From conception to launch

BATTLE HONOURS FOR HMS _BELFAST_

Ben Warlow states in the preface to Battle Honours of the Royal Navy –
the publication officially authorised to list the honours:

'The award of Battle Honours to Her/His Majesty's ships is intended
to foster esprit de corps among their officers and ships' companies
who are thereby encouraged to take a personal interest in the wartime exploits not only of their present ship, but also of ships of the
same name which have distinguished themselves in the past.

The Battle Honours Committee ... makes recommendations for awards to the Navy Board, which will authorise any official Honours considered appropriate... If awards are made too freely, they lose much of their value... Battle Honours have generally been awarded for successful war service rather than as a record of service.'

HMS *BELFAST*'S MOTTO

'*Pro tanto quid retribuamus*'

Formal translation from the Latin: 'For so much, how shall we repay?'

The sailors' translation: 'We give as good as we get.'

The motto is taken from the Latin Vulgate Bible, Psalm 116, Verse 12. There have been many varying translations.

HMS *BELFAST*'S ENSIGN

HMS *Belfast* is especially permitted to fly the White Ensign, normally flown by Royal Navy ships in active commission.

HMS *BELFAST*'S BADGE

Field – Blue

Badge – Upon waves in base white and blue, a sea horse gorged with a mural crown proper.

The badge of BELFAST – the blazon, or technical description, is occasionally provided by the College of Arms with the Sealed Pattern, but not always; and of course, blazons can vary. It should be an accurate technical description, from which a heraldic artist could draw a similarly accurate and acceptable version of the badge.

The *Belfast* badge is in the card index of the SNBC records, and is therefore the version dating from the creation of the badge in 1937. The sea horse and mural crown proper may not be immediately obvious in terms of colours, but the proper colour of a crown of any variety is normally gold, and that is how the mural crown is depicted in the arms of BELFAST and on the Sealed Pattern. The proper colour of a mythological creature is distinctly more awkward, but for the sea horse generally seems to have been primarily a fishy silver, which often tends to a greenish colour – a herald would not usually put green on blue, since it does not show up well.

HMS *BELFAST*'S CREST

Cdr Ferguson (RN, FI, Mech E) recounts how the original design was conceived:

'I recall that the ship was without a crest before the launch, being the first *Belfast* ever (Job No 1000) and that, having the skeleton of a seahorse I picked up on the shores of Lake Avernus (shades of Agrippa), this idea of a crest was born; particularly as the seahorse appears also in the crest of the City of Belfast. My drawing was passed from the Admiralty to the College of Heralds who arranged the red gorged crown for the seahorse and presumably had it redrawn; I had a letter back from the Admiralty informing me that the design was accepted with this minor modification. On Trafalgar Day, 1971, I had the seahorse with me and gave it to the admiral.'

HMS *BELFAST'S* BELL

The following letter from the First Lord of the Admiralty gives details of the specification of *Belfast*'s bell.

The First Lord of the Admiralty
Whitehall Gardens
London
17 January 1938

Town Clerk
Belfast

Sir,
With reference to your letter of the 3rd December 1937 concerning the presentation of a silver bell and flags to H.M.S. BELFAST by the city of Belfast, I am commanded by My Lords Commissioners of the Admiralty to inform you that the presentation bell would be for use as well as ornament and would take the place of the ship's bell which would ordinarily be provided.

2. The specification for H.M.S. BELFAST provides for a "watch bell of Service Pattern and size with the ship's name legibly engraved or cast thereon" and is to be of the following dimensions:-

Inside diameter . . . . . 19"
Inside height . . . . 16"
Weight . . . . 148 lbs. (excluding weight of clapper which should be 1/17th of the weight of the bell).

A drawing of the bell is enclosed.

3. My Lords would be glad if they could be consulted concerning the design of any devices which the City Council may desire to have engraved on the bell.

HMS *BELFAST*'S IDENTIFICATION

VISUAL AND RADIO CALL SIGNS

International call signs and visual signal letters for all Royal Navy ships were noted in the Signal Department, Admiralty reference O.U. 5516/40. *Belfast*'s visual signal letter group is GGCN and her sister ship HMS *Edinburgh* was GGCP. (Information kindly supplied by the Curator, HMS *Collingwood* Heritage Collection (CHC).)

Today the book used is *ACP 113 (Allied Communications Publications) Call Sign Book for Ships*. The Sponsoring Authority for all ACPs is the Combined Communications-Electronics Board (CCEB), which is comprised of the five member nations: Australia, Canada, New Zealand, the UK and the USA.

A ship's international call sign and radio call sign are the same, e.g. for *Belfast* GGCN.

However, the visual call sign of a ship is her pennant number. Currently *Belfast* has a pennant number of C35, which was issued post 1948 when the Admiralty rationalised pennant numbers by allocating a Flag Superior letter to denote the type of ship, e.g. C = Cruiser. Prior to 1948 Flag Superiors weren't used and records held at the HMS *Collingwood* Heritage Collection show her pennant number as C35 and her sister ship *Edinburgh*'s as C16.

CONCEPT AND RAISON D'ÊTRE FOR A CRUISER IN THE ROYAL NAVY IN THE 1930S

The need for a cruiser was outlined in various Admiralty papers and the abstracts below give the arguments that were put at the time. That thinking matured into the cruiser designs that eventually became HMS *Belfast* as laid down in 1938. The keynote factors were versatility to act as an independent warship; being strong and speedy enough to protect merchant shipping and trade routes; to be protected by armour plating against a battleship's shells but speedy enough to outrun a battleship to fight another day; impressive enough to 'show the flag' when Britain's Empire and dependant countries would experience some of the personality of the mother country and help foster trading relations with other countries. Their design, however, had to be frameworked within the Treaties of Washington in 1922 and London in 1930.

Captain Arthur W. Wheeler RN wrote a five-page article in the Number One issue of the 1986 Imperial War Museum Review *on the raison d'être for cruisers in the Royal Navy, titled 'The Provenance of a Warship', of which the following is an extract.*

"War in the Far East is the basis on which our preparations are to be made."

Cabinet decision quoted in a Naval Staff paper dated 28 October 1926.

The surrender of the German High Seas Fleet in 1918 and the restrictions later imposed on Germany by the Treaty of Versailles, effectively removed what, until then, had been the principal threat to British maritime supremacy. On this premise alone, *substantial cuts* could safely be made in the strength of the Navy. The Government of the time, faced with an exhausted economy, sought to take advantage of this, but the Empire remained as great a strategic burden as ever and its existence depended on an immense volume of seaborne trade. New concerns for the defence of that trade soon began to emerge.

In naval terms, Anglo-American relations were uneasy. During the War the subordination of American warships to British overall command had only been accomplished with difficulty. After the Armistice, there was much disagreement about the disposal of the

German Fleet, which only ended when the interned crews solved the problem by scuttling their ships. More generally, there was an undercurrent of resentment in the USA against the very existence of the British Empire and against the naval supremacy which Britain had hitherto maintained to defend it. A powerful lobby in the USA advocated building a navy which was "second to none", in other words at least equal to the British.

Britain had been brought close to defeat not through battle fleet encounters but by massive destruction of her merchant shipping by submarine and surface attack. [Ships to counter this] needed to be able to steam long distances without refuelling. They needed a powerful gun armament, good sea-keeping qualities to provide a stable gun platform, some armoured protection and a high maximum speed. The class of ship which most clearly approached this most exacting combination was the cruiser. More traditionally designed to act in support of the main fleet, it came increasingly to be seen through British eyes as the principal means of trade protection, and successive British cruiser designs were to reflect this trend.

On the poacher/gamekeeping principle, the cruiser was also regarded as the type of warship best suited to commerce raiding, so British cruiser designers had also to take account of the equivalent designs of potential enemies and ensure that, if possible, British ships would at least equal their likely adversaries.

The central aim of naval policy is to prepare for war. In the 1920s the primary objective of British foreign policy was disarmament and the abolition of war. To this extent the two were in opposition and because naval policy was necessarily subordinate to foreign policy, the Naval Staff were sometimes obliged to settle for new warship designs which diverged appreciably from those dictated by purely naval considerations.

This led to the development of the 10,000 ton, 8" gun county class cruisers, 13 of which were to join the Fleet between 1928 and 1931. At the 1920 Washington Conference it was agreed that the relative numbers of British, American and Japanese capital ships were to be in the ratio 5:5:3. To many Japanese, the acceptance of the lower ratio represented a slight to their national prestige and this grievance grew in the years following the Conference.

The London Naval Treaty was due to expire in 1936 and in 1935 the second London Naval Conference met to decide what should succeed it. The Japanese, having already publicly denounced the Washington Treaty, proposed a "common upper limit". The Japanese proposal won no support and their delegation withdrew from the Conference. The class of Japanese cruisers described in the Admiralty letter was named Mogami after the first ship to be built. Compared with these fifteen gunships, the British Leanders mounted only eight guns, and the Arethusas only six. The guns in these British ships were mounted in twin gun turrets, but by the early 1930s a new mounting carrying three guns had been developed.

Anxious to order the ships in the 1936 programme the Admiralty decided to abandon the quadruple mounting and fit the standard triple turrets instead. The weight thus saved was used to increase the armour protection. So the final design was settled with a main armament similar to *Southampton*, but with more anti-aircraft guns and a larger fuel capacity.

After an eventful wartime career in Atlantic, Arctic and home waters, she sailed to join the British Pacific Fleet for what promised to be a long campaign against Japan.

That campaign never took place. The atomic bombs were dropped, Japan surrendered, and *Belfast* was never to encounter the adversary which had so concerned her designers.

HMS *Belfast* was an improved version, along with HMS *Edinburgh*, of ten light cruisers of the 'Town' class and was ordered from Harland and Wolff shipyard in Belfast with the Yard number 1000 on 21 September 1936, and laid down on 10 December 1936.

They had four improved triple gun turrets with 6in. guns and armour plate fitted to the sides and deck. Four Admiralty pattern three-drum boilers set in separate boiler rooms, two side by side forward and one astern the other in the after space, produced steam that drove high- and low-pressure Parsons turbine engines, along with a cruising turbine in each system, driven respectively by high- and low-pressure steam. These turned the ship's four propellers. Commanding officers were to find her delightfully responsive to manoeuvre.

The fitting out for her first commission included water pumps, air compressors, water-distilling machinery, electric generators, refrigeration, ventilation, capstans for the anchors and crane engines, galley ranges, even cabin radiators – the whole panoply required for a crew of some 800 to operate and live within this warship.

Ships in the Royal Navy at that time, including HMS *Belfast*, were designed by the Department of Naval Constructors, headed by the Director of Naval Construction (DNC), while machinery was the responsibility of the Engineer-in-Chief (E-in-C) and ordnance the Director of Naval Ordnance (DNO), and a separate Department of Electrical Engineering was created in the inter-war period. An anti-submarine Directorate, concerned with Asdic (now Sonar) and torpedoes, and a Naval Air department were created. All these departments produced specifications that were then included in the final construction plans.

Constructors' notebooks are now kept in the National Maritime Museum's Brass Foundry, and Ships Covers in The National Archives, which make it possible to reconstruct all British cruiser designs prepared between 1920 and up to the last missile cruiser in 1956. This of Sir Charles S. Lillicrap, head of cruiser design in the late 1930s and later DNC: 'The key design tool was the summary weight breakdown typically included in the Legend, the summary of ship characteristics presented to decision-makers'. Typically, the designer began with a target weight and with demands for particular armament, protection and speed. Displacement, based on the weight of these factors suggested overall dimensions of the ship based also on previous experience. The constructor added these factors and calculated them from the overall allowable (by treaty) weight to decide how much protection weight to give, which was built to cover the hull belt and deck over the machinery, along with boxes for the magazines' shell rooms. In practice, this method of ship design worked because DNC split his organisation into sections, which included one for cruisers, rather than the US method of one department designing one aspect for all classes of ship.

Policy, including ship requirements, was decided by the Board of Admiralty, which included the First Sea Lord, operational chief of the Royal Navy and Naval Staff, and who was involved in decisions concerning material; his deputy, the Second Sea Lord (with additional responsibility for personnel); the Third Sea Lord (Controller); Fourth Sea Lord for logistics; and Fifth Sea Lord for fleet aircraft.

Elsewhere, storm clouds were gathering in Europe with the Italian invasion of Abyssinia in 1935 and the Spanish Civil War of 1936–39.

Against this political and geographical background the purpose of HMS *Belfast*'s genesis and design was decided, and her construction could begin. The decision to choose her name, however, was more than mere whimsy – naming the Town class after (anomalously) cities revealed ulterior motives that could provide a spawning ground for recruitment, elicit ship loyalty and achieve adoption by the city. This was a clever ploy that worked well for both the *Edinburgh* and the *Belfast*.

The Treaty of Versailles of 1919 stated in its Article 181 that the German naval forces in commission could not exceed six battleships, six light cruisers, 12 destroyers and 12 torpedo boats, while Article 190 limited the displacement of capital ships to 10,000 tons. On 6 February 1922, the USA, the British Empire, France, Italy and Japan signed the Washington Naval Treaty. Under the terms of this treaty, the five major naval powers agreed to limit the standard displacement of their capital ships to 35,000 tons (35,560 metric tons), and the calibre of their heavy guns to 16in.. The total capital ship standard tonnage was distributed as follows:

- USA 525,000 tons (533,400 metric tons)
- British Empire 525,000 tons (533,400 metric tons)
- France 175,000 tons (177,800 metric tons)
- Italy 175,000 tons (177,800 metric tons)
- Japan 315,000 tons (320,040 metric tons)

The London Naval Conference of January–April 1930 was intended to review the Washington Naval Treaty, but France and Italy refused to ratify it because of the low battleship tonnage ratios they were assigned.

In the early 1930s, German naval shipbuilding was still restricted by the Treaty of Versailles, and it was not until 18 June 1935, when Britain's Foreign Minister Sir Samuel Hoare and the German Ambassador Joachim von Ribbentrop signed the Anglo-German Naval Agreement in London, that its restrictions were finally lifted. Germany was then allowed to build a surface fleet numbering up to 35 per cent of that of Britain, and up to 45 per cent in the case of submarines. This meant that Germany could now build 184,000 tons of battleships – in other words, five 35,000-ton battleships. Between December 1935 and March 1936 the five major powers met again in London. Japan withdrew from the conference since her demands for parity with the USA and the British Empire in capital ship tonnage were not met. So, an escalator clause was added, and allowed countries to build battleships of up to 45,000 tons in case a non-signatory power were suspected of building ships outside the treaty limits. Since Italy and Japan did not sign the treaty, the standard displacement of 45,000 tons was understood to be acceptable by the other powers, including Germany.

Table showing comparisons of Battleship and Cruiser construction of principal maritime nations in 1930s

Great Britain.			
King George V . .	Laid down, 1.1.37.	35,000 tons,	14-in. guns.
Prince of Wales . .	Laid down, 1.1.37.	35,000 tons,	14-in. guns.
3 ships . . .	To be laid down, 1937.	35,000 tons,	—
United States.			
2 ships . . .	Ordered, 1.1.37.	35,000 tons,	16-in. guns.

Japan.				
4 ships	. .	Projected, one or two to be laid down, 1937.	35,000 tons,	(Probably 16-in.)
France.				
Dunkerque	. .	Laid down, 1932.		
		Launched, 1935.		
		Completed, 1936.	26,500 tons,	13-in. guns.
Strasbourg	. .	Laid down, 1934.		
		Launched, 1936.		
Richelieu	. . .	Laid down, 1935.	35,000 tons,	15-in. guns.
Jean Bart	. . .	Laid down, 1937.		
Germany.				
Scharnhorst	. .	Laid down, 1934.	26,000 tons,	11-in. guns.
Gneisenau	. .	Launched, 1936.		
1 ship "F"	. . .	Laid down, 1936.	35,000 tons,	14-in. guns.
1 ship	. . .	To be laid down, 1937.		
Italy.				
Vittorio Veneto	.	Laid down, 1934.	35,000 tons,	15-in. guns.
Littorio	. .			

The following table summarises the cruiser activity of the six principal Powers during 1936: —

Cruisers Completed During 1936.

Great Britain.	United States.	Japan.	France.	Italy.	Germany.
Amphion	Quincy	Suzuya	Jean de Vienne	E. di Savoia	—
Apollo					
Penelope					
3	1	1	1	1	—

Cruisers Launched During 1936.

Great Britain.	United States.	Japan.	France.	Italy.	Germany.
Aurora	Vincennes	Kumano	Georges Leygues	G. Garibaldi.	—
Southampton	Brooklyn			D. d. Abruzzi.	
Newcastle	Philadelphia				
Glasgow	Savannah				
Birmingham	Nashville				
Sheffield					
6	5	1	1	2	—

Cruisers Continued (but not Launched) during 1936.

Wichita	Tone	Gloire	"G"
Phoenix	Tikuma	Marseillaise	"H"
Boise		Montcalm	
Honolulu			
4	2	3	2

Cruisers Laid Down During 1936.

Helena	"J"
St. Louis	
2	1

Liverpool
Manchester
Gloucester
Belfast
Edinburgh
5

8-in. Gun Ships.

HMS *Belfast*'s specifications 1939

Length overall:	613ft 6in
Beam:	63ft 4in
Displacement (during trials):	10,420 tons
Draught:	17ft 3in
Shaft horse power:	80,000 (300rpm)
Speed:	32.5kts
Oil fuel capacity:	2400 tons
Armament:	12–6in in triple turrets
	12–4in HA/LA in twin mountings
	16–2pdr AA in 8-barrelled mountings
	8–0.5in AA in quadruple mountings
	6–21in torpedo tubes in triple mounting
	15 Mk VII depth charges
Aircraft:	2 or 3 Supermarine Walrus amphibians
Armour:	
Main belt:	4½in NC
Bulkheads:	2½in NC
Decks:	3in NC (over magazines). 2in NC (over machinery)
Weights:	
General equipment:	560 tons
Armament:	1265 tons
Armour:	1790 tons
Hull:	4725 tons
Machinery:	1435 tons
Aircraft equipment:	120 tons
Refrigerating machinery and lubricating oil:	105 tons
Total:	10,000 tons

Captains of HMS *Belfast* – 1939 to 1963

5.8.39–4.1.40	Captain G.A. Scott, D.S.O., R.N.
3.11.42–28.7.44	Captain F.R. Parham, D.S.O., R.N.
29.7.44–8.7.46	Captain R.M. Dick, C.B.E., D.S.C., R.N.
9.7.46–20.11.47	Captain H.B. Ellison, D.S.O., R.N.
22.9.48–7.4.50	Captain E.K. Le Mesurier, M.V.O., R.N.
8.4.50–22.11.51	Captain Sir Aubrey St. Clair-Ford, Bt., D.S.O., R.N.
23.11.51–26.11.52	Captain A.C. Duckworth, D.S.C., G.M., R.N.
12.5.59–30.1.61	Captain J.V. Wilkinson, D.S.C., G.M., R.N.
31.1.61–1.7.62	Captain M.C. Morgan-Giles, D.S.O., O.B.E., G.M., R.N.
2.7.62–15.8.62	Captain M.G.R. Lumby, D.S.O., D.S.C., R.N.
16.8.62–7.2.63	Captain W.R.D. Gerard-Pearse, M.V.O., R.N.
16.7.63–24.8.63	Captain H.C.J. Shand, D.S.C., R.N.

Flag officers who flew their flag in HMS *Belfast* – 1939 to 1963

1943	Vice Admiral Sir Robert Burnett K.B.E., C.B., D.S.O.
1944	Vice Admiral F.H.G. Dalrymple-Hamilton C.B.
1945–1946	Rear Admiral R.M. Servaes C.B.E.
1946–1947	Vice Admiral Sir Denis Boyd K.C.B., C.B.E., D.S.C.
1948–1949	Vice Admiral A.C.G. Madden C.B., C.B.E.
	Admiral Sir Patrick Brind K.C.B., C.B.E.
1950–1951	Rear Admiral W.G. Andrewes C.B., C.B.E., D.S.O.
1951–1952	Rear Admiral A.K. Scott-Moncrieff C.B., C.B.E., D.S.O.*
1959–1960	Vice Admiral V.C. Begg C.B., D.S.O., D.S.C.
1961–1962	Rear Admiral M. Le Fanu C.B., D.S.C.
	Rear Admiral J.B. Frewen C.B.
1962	Vice Admiral J.G. Hamilton C.B. D.S.C.
1963	Rear Admiral F.R. Twiss C.B.,C.B.E.
	Rear Admiral H.C. Martell C.B., C.B.E.

HMS *BELFAST*'S LAUNCH

HMS *Belfast* was ordered from Harland and Wolff shipyard in Belfast, Number 1000, on 21 September 1936 and her keel laid down on 10 December 1936. Her prestigious launch by the wife of the then Prime Mister Neville Chamberlain on 17 March 1938 (appropriately, St Patrick's Day) provided an impetus and focus of local interest and adoption, exemplified in the presentation by the Belfast City Council dignitaries of a magnificent silver ship's bell. Her subsequent career as a major member of the Royal Navy, however, proved the worth of her loyalty by the city and her succeeding crews. After fitting out and builders' trials she was commissioned into the Royal Navy on 5th August 1939 under the command of Capt G. A. Scott DSO RN. Of her budgeted cost of £2,141,514 the improved triple-turret guns cost £75,000 and the two Supermarine Walrus aircraft cost £66,500.

Mrs Neville Chamberlain launched HMS Belfast *on St Patrick's Day, 17 March 1938, breaking the traditional bottle of champagne across the bows with the words 'God bless her and all who sail in her'.*

EQUIPMENT

Summary of machinery

Boilers
Four Admiralty 3-drum with superheaters and air preheaters.

Main engines
Four Parson's-type geared turbines made by Harland and Wolff, designed to produce 80,000shp.

Gear ratios:	High pressure	11·2 to 1
	Low pressure	8·03 to 1
Cruisers to high pressure		2·77 to 1

Evaporators
Two twin-shell evaporators by G. & J. Weir (6 tons/hour). One auxiliary single shell.

Auxiliary machinery
Three turbo generators by W. H. Allen (350kW).
Two diesel generators by Paxman (230kW).
Four high-pressure air compressors.
Two low-pressure air compressors.
One Vao air-conditioning plant.
One diesel generator by G. C. E. (400kW).

Fuel expenditure and range – six months out of dock, temperate waters; four boilers, four shafts

Speed	Revs	Fuel expended tons/hour	Miles Range
10	88	4·1	5,380
11	96	4·5	5,390
12	104	4·9	5,400

Speed	Revs	Fuel expended tons/hour	Miles Range
13	112	5·3	5,420
14	120	5·6	5,500
15	128	6·1	5,400
16	138	6·6	5,333
17	146	7·1	5,270
18	154	7·6	5,202
19	164	8·7	4,807
20	174	9·6	4,583
21	184	10·7	4,325
22	194	12·0	4,040
23	204	13·2	3,840
24	214	14·8	3,570
25	224	16·4	3,355
26	236	18·6	3,080

Figures above dotted line are for cruising turbines.

Steaming arrangements

The following arrangements of engines and shafts were available:

Turbines	Boilers	Shafts	Controlling Engineroom	Use
Main	Four	Four	Forward E.R.—outer shafts	Manoeuvring and pilotage
			After E.R.—inner shafts	
Main	Two	Two	Either Forward E.R.—outers or after E.R.—inners	Passage speeds 15 to 22 kts. required

Turbines	Boilers	Shafts	Controlling Engineroom	Use
Cruising	Two	Two	Either Forward E.R.—outers or after E.R.—inners	Economical steaming
Cruising	Two	Four	Forward E.R.—outer shafts	Passage speeds up to 20 kts
			After E.R.—inner shafts	

SUMMARY OF ARMAMENT

Main armament
12 x 6in. 50-calibre breech-loading Mk XXIII guns in four triple Mk XXIII mountings. Total weight, 615 tons, plus 28 tons for the hoist. It was the main battery gun used in Royal Navy cruisers from 1930 and throughout World War II.

Secondary armament
12 x 4in. Mk XVI* quick-firing guns on six HA twin Mk XIX mountings; two after mountings removed April 1945, remainder modified to RP 50 (remote power control, again modified to RP 51 in May 1959).

QF 2-pounder Mark VIII (multi pom-pom)
The Royal Navy had identified the need for a rapid-firing, multi-barrelled close-range anti-aircraft weapon at an early stage and one that would utilise the enormous stocks of 2-pounder ammunition left over from World War I. In 1930 the **QF 2-pounder Mark VIII**, usually known as the *multiple pom-pom* and nicknamed the 'Chicago Piano' entered service for ships of cruiser and aircraft carrier size.

Saluting guns
4–3pdr Mk I (removed 1942).

Torpedoes
6–21in. Mk IV on two triple 21in. torpedo tube mountings.

AA Armament

Particulars of 1939 Primary & Secondary Armament (Gunhouses, Turrets, Fire Control Systems, Ship's Complement etc):

	2pdr	2pdr	2pdr	40mm	40mm	40mm	40mm	40mm	20mm	20mm	20mm	20mm	0.5in
Gun Mk	VIII	VIII	VIII		NI	NI/I	NI/I	NI/I	IV	IV	IV	IV	III
Mounting Mk	VIA	VII	XVI	V	III	VII	Boffin	VII	V	III	VII	V	III
Type of mounting	8-barrel	quad	single	twin	single	single	single	single	twin	single	single	single	quad
1939	2	–	–	–	–	–	–	–	–	–	–	–	2
1942	2	–	–	–	–	–	–	–	5	4	–	–	–
1945 (May)	2	4	4	–	–	–	–	–	4	2	4	–	–
1945 (August)	2	4	4	–	3	–	2	–	–	–	2	–	–
1948	2	4	2	–	3	2	2	–	–	–	–	–	–
1959	–	–	–	6	–	–	–	–	–	–	–	–	–

Gunhouse armament

The gunhouses were armoured as follows:

Gunhouse floor:	D quality plate
Shield, side, rear and roof:	2 in. in NC plate
Shield, front:	4 in. NC plate

Turret capabilities

Turret Capabilities: Triple Mark 23 Turrets

Elevation:	45°, elevating power or hand.
Extreme range:	at 44°—24,800 yd. with 112lb. shell
Training arcs:	120° on either side of the fore and aft line.
Rate of training:	5°/second (both training engines)
	7°/second (one training engine only). Hand training available.
Rate of fire:	8 rounds per gun per minute.
Rate of supply:	10 rounds of shell and 10 of cordite charges per minute.
Ramming:	by hand.
Breech mechanism	hand-worked.

weight of projectile:	112 lb.
weight of charge:	30 lb.
elevation:	45°
loading angle:	between 5° depression and elevation.

HA armament 1939

Twelve x 4in. quick-firing Mark XVI* guns on HA Twin Mark XIX mountings.

The close-range weapons 1939

1. Two ·5in. quadruple mountings, one on each side of the hangar top.
2. Two 8-barrelled 2-pdf quick-firing Mark VIII pom-poms on Mark VIA mountings, with cosine sights, sited at superstructure level abreast the mainmast. These mountings had originally been designed to be sited further aft but, by the Board's decision of MFO 192/36, in order to clear the blast from the 6in., the pom-poms were removed to this new position, which would inevitably be exposed to blast from the 4in. HA at high elevations.
3. Two Vickers GO (gas-operated) machine guns.

For landing parties: ten ·303 Lewis for seamen, six ·303 Bren for Royal Marines.

MAIN ARMAMENT FIRE CONTROL

The Director Control Towers (DCTs)

The 6in. triple turrets were controlled from the two armoured Director Control Towers, one above the upper bridge, the other on the after superstructure.

The following personnel manned the front compartment:

Director Layer; Director Trainer; Cross Levelling Operator; Auxiliary Trainer.

The rear compartment was manned by:

Control Officer (a lieutenant-commander); Rate Officer; Spotting Officer; Inclinometer operator.

The Transmitting Station (TS)

The Main Armament Transmitting Station was sited immediately above the 4in. HA magazine and was therefore protected by the main armoured belt and by the armoured deck. In this compartment was the calculating machine – The Admiralty Fire Control Table – which converted the range and bearing received from the Director Control Towers into gun elevation and gun training. These two components were then transmitted electrically directly to the guns and turrets. At Action Stations, the TS was manned by the Royal Marines.

The Admiralty Fire Control Table (**AFCT**)

Centrally in the TS stood the Admiralty Fire Control Table Mark VI, No. 18, a mechanical calculating machine. Fed with data from the Fore DCT and the After DCT, the main function of the table was to produce continuous gun elevation and gun training and to transmit these readings to the turrets.

The High Angle Control System (**HACS**)

The 4in. HA armament was controlled by the High Angle Control System, Mark IV. The HACS Comprised:

- Two sided-HA Director Towers (HADT) on the lower bridge, forward.
- One centreline HA Director Tower on the after superstructure.
- One HA Calculating Position (HACP) forward, next to and for'd of the TS, and protected by the armoured belt.
- One HA Calculating Position, port side aft, abaft the after Engine Room and protected by the armoured belt.

Starshell and bombardment The 4in. armament was used to fire starshell in order to illuminate a surface target for the main armament.

Pom-Pom fire control The pom-pom directors were sited on each side of the after superstructure, forward of the after HACT and on shielded platforms at a level above the 44in. searchlight projectors.

Ammunition supply: main armament

6in. shell per gun:

HE, AP or SAP	200
Practice, low angle	34
high angle	2·5
Stowage: shell	turret shell rooms
cordite (flashless)	turret magazines
Supply: mechanical hoists in turret trunks	

Ammunition supply: secondary armament

4in. HA shell per gun

Fused shell	250
Practice HA	65
Practice LA	4
Target smoke	4

Note: 200 4in. starshell (flashless cordite) *per ship* was the total illumination outfit, i.e. 12·5 rounds per gun.

CLOSE-RANGE WEAPONS (AA)

Pom-poms: 2,500 rounds per barrel – 40,000 rounds total.
Stowed:

(i) in pom-pom and ·5in. magazine, sited beneath the main central store, below the armoured deck and next to 'B' 6in. magazine.

(ii) belted ammunition in ready-use lockers between the mainmast tripod legs on the pom-pom gun deck.

5in. machine-guns: 2,500 rounds per barrel – 20,000 rounds total.

Vickers Gas Operated (GO) ·303in.: 5,000 rounds in pans and in small arms magazine below armoured deck and forward of the bomb room, which was adjacent to the 4in. magazine.

Lewis and Brens: variable amount of ·303in. in portable boxes in small arms magazine.

Saluting guns: landed on outbreak of hostilities

Sub-Calibre: 140 rounds per parent gun, plus 1,680 fused for practice.

Summary of fire control gear fitted throughout *Belfast*'s commissions

Main armament

1942	6in Mk XXIII DCT
	Fore director fitted with 22ft rangefinder and Type 284 surface warning radar
	15ft rangefinder fitted to aft DCT, 4 Type 283 blind barrage directors fitted, 1 port and starboard lower bridge, 2 on 01 deck after superstructure
1945	Both 6in directors fitted with Type 274 gunnery radar
1950	22ft rangefinder removed from fore DCT
1939	Two (1 fore, 1 aft) 6in triple Mk XXIII armoured DCTs, both fitted with 15ft rangefinders. Fore director fitted with dial sight
1942	Forward director re-equipped with 22ft rangefinder and Type 284 fire control radar; 4 Mk II blind barrage directors with Type 283 radar added, 2 port and starboard lower bridge 2 on 01 deck aft superstructure
1945	Both 6in directors fitted with Type 274 fire control radar. Blind barrage directors altered to Mk III
1950	All rangefinders removed from directors
1959	Both directors up-graded and fitted with RP 40; 274 radar retained. All barrage directors removed

Secondary armament

1939	3 HACTs with 15ft height-finders
1942	All directors fitted with Type 285 radar
1950	All height-finders removed from directors

AA Armament

1939	2 Mk II pom-pom directors located on the after superstructure deck forward of HACT

1942	2 pom-pom directors Mk II replaced by Mk IV fitted with Type 282 radar
1945	4 additional Mk IV pom-pom directors were fitted on sponsons: 2 forward of after funnel and 2 midway between both funnels
1950	All replaced by tachymetric directors
1959	All HACTs and pom-pom directors removed and replaced by 8 close-range blind-fire directors fitted with Type 262 radar

Additional fire control gear

1939	Upper bridge fitted with 6 air lookout sights, 4 searchlight sights, 2 starshell sights and 2 captain's sights
1940	2 12ft rangefinders removed from lower bridge
1959	4 Type 274A lookout sights and 4 Type 275 gunnery control sights added

DEPARTMENTS ABOARD

Torpedo department
Torpedoes: Six 21in. Mark IV torpedoes were carried in the triple TR 21in. Mark IV* torpedo tubes mounted on the upper deck in the waist on each side. No spare torpedoes were carried.

Torpedo Warhead Room: Starboard side, platform deck, abreast 'X' barbette. Torpedo control sights were mounted, one on each side of upper bridge.

Searchlights 44in.: Four stabilised Mark VII searchlights, two on after control deck, two in wings of hangar top, controlled from stabilised sights at the four searchlight control positions on the upper bridge. Six air look-out sights, three each side, were abreast the S/L control positions.

Searchlights 20in.: Signalling projectors – four, two on top of for'd 40in. S/Ls, two on lower bridge.

Paravanes: Four paravanes 'S', Mark I, were used for severing the mine mooring wire.

Depth Charges: 6in. rails; spares on port quarter of quarterdeck.

THE ASDIC COMPARTMENT: 1939

A Type 132 set was installed.

NAVIGATIONAL DEPARTMENT: 1939

Equipment: Pitometer log Walker log for emergency use.

Type 758N Echo-sounder – Chart House D/F Set (FCI) in D/F Office. 60Khz–20Mhz.

Compasses: Two Pattern 1015 Admiralty Gyro Compasses. One Brown B Gyro Compass, in Wheel-house as stand-by steering compass.

Action Plot: ARL table in Bridge Plotting Office on lower bridge.

Propellers: Outboard turning when proceeding ahead. 11ft 3in. dia., pitch 13ft 9in. Made by J. Stone & Co. Ltd Weight: 6·82 tons.

HMS *BELFAST*'S COMPLEMENT

The ship's complement: 1939 and beyond

The ship was designed as a flagship and, on commissioning, the authorised war complement was as follows:

	Flagship	Supernumerary Accommodation available	Private ship
Wardroom	37	13	24
Gunroom	7	–	7
Warrant Officers	13	3	10
Messmen	2	2	–
CPOs and Men in enclosed messes	188	–	160

	Flagship	Supernumerary Accommodation available	Private ship
Ratings in broadside messes	634	–	580
Total	881	18	781
1953	974		930
1961	886		862
1962			
Peace complement	582		542

RAS (REPLENISHMENT AT SEA)

Using a jackstay – a strong wire connecting an RFA tanker or replenishment vessel to a warship while they steamed parallel courses 100ft (30.5m) apart, allowed refuelling and the taking on of ammunition, stores and victuals; and the transfer of the sick and mail at sea, thus precluding any necessity to do so in harbour, giving much more flexibility to commanders-in-chief and longer 'time on task'. The supporting role of the Royal Fleet Auxiliary ships that normally provide these essentials (fuel, stores) is of huge importance. Key to a successful transfer was knowing the heights and positions for transfer connections, and distances.

HMS *BELFAST'S* BOATS

The ship's boat complement changed throughout her life, as did her Carley float outfit, which, combined with the boats, were capable of accommodating her war complement, when she carried 30 floats.

Ships' boats not only gave practice for young officers and ratings in seamanship, but were essential as liberty boats when, for example, *Belfast* was moored to a buoy or at anchor; for inter-ship communications; to tie up to a buoy; for inter-fleet pulling and sailing regattas; and for boarding suspect vessels.

Replenishment at sea positions with particulars of rigging

RIGGING	DIMENSIONS			ALL DISTANCES ABOVE AWL			
Masts:	1939	1948	1959	Masts:	1939	1948	1959
Foremast:				**Foremast:**			
Lower mast	102ft. 0in.	86ft. 6in		Highest fixed part	125ft. 0in.	111ft. 0in.	
" " struts ea (2)	49ft. 6in.	47ft. 6in		Highest part including Lightning conductor	127ft. 0in.	125ft. 0in.	
Signal yard	40ft. 0in.	40ft. 0in		Highest part of D/F pole above AWL (including D/F frame coil)	144ft. 9in.	–	
Upper yard (W/T)	24ft. 2½ in	24ft. 3in.		Overall to AWL	–	–	123ft. 1⅜ in
Housing of D/F pole	6ft. 6in.						
Mainmast				**Mainmast**			
Lower mast	96ft. 3in.	79ft. 7in.		HF Part	108ft. 0in.	95ft. 0in	
" " struts ea (2)	54ft. 0in.	53ft. 0in.		Highest part of Topmast (including Lightning conductor)	119ft. 1in.		

RIGGING	DIMENSIONS			ALL DISTANCES ABOVE AWL			
Masts:	1939	1948	1959	Masts:	1939	1948	1959
Topmast	16ft. 0in.	–		Highest part of W/T pole	–	108ft. 0in.	
W/T yard	24ft. 2½ in.	18ft. 4in.		Overall to AWL	–	–	111ft 8⅛in.
Housing of topmast	6ft. 7in.	6ft. 7in. (radar mast)					
Radar mast		19ft. 5in.					
Booms							
Lower booms 2ea	40ft. 0in.	40ft. 1in.					
Quarter booms 2ea	10ft. 6in.	10f 3in.					
Sounding booms	33ft. 6in.	33ft. 6in I2)					
D/F pole	17ft. 8⅜ in.						

CAMOUFLAGE

HMS *Belfast*'s camouflage applied during her 1945 refit followed the scheme applied by Devonport Dockyard; the 'standard light tone scheme'.

The Camouflage Directorate of the Ministry of Home Security employed artists to work out camouflage patterns to help break up the outline of a warship, although the marine artist Norman Wilkinson was credited with creating dazzle ship camouflage

Motor Boats

Type	Construction	Beam (excl rubbers)	Speed	Bhp	Weight with 2 men	Lifesaving capacity	Remarks
35ft fast motor boat (FMB)	Carvel-built hard chine	8ft 6in	17-22kts	65/100 (twin) *Vosper*	90cwt	46	3 carried; reduced to 2 in 1945 – admiral's barge
36ft motor and pulling pinnace	Clinker-built round bilge	9ft 9in	7½kts	20 *Vosper*	130cwt	76	Used for liberty men and laying stream anchor
35ft medium speed boat	Carvel-built round bilge	9ft 2in	12-13kts	72/144 (twin)	127cwt	30	Replaced 35ft FMB in 1959; 3 carried, one as admiral's barge
25ft fast motor boat	Sheer strake clinker-built; hard chine carvel-built	6ft 9in	17-23kts	65/100	45cwt	30	1 carried port side of after funnel until 1952

25ft motor cutter	Clinker round bilge	7ft 8in	6½-7½kts	11½	50cwt	26	1 carried from 1959
27ft motor whaler	Double skin carvel round bilge	7ft	6½kts	11½	50cwt	23	2 carried as seaboats from 1959
16ft fast motor dinghy	Sheer strake clinker; hard chine carvel (skimming dish)	5ft 6in	14-24kts	24/28	18cwt	12	1 carried stowed starboard side of after funnel; 1942 stowed on top of 36ft motor pinnace; 1945 stowed on boat deck behind bridge superstructure
35ft landing craft personnel (large)	Hard chine	11ft 8in	18kts	225	125cwt	30	1 carried from 1948 until 1952. Handed over to HMS *Newcastle*

Sailing Boats

Type	Construction	Beam (excl rubbers)	Rig	Oars	Weight	Lifesaving capacity	Remarks
32ft cutter	Clinker (drop keel)	8ft 6½in	Single mast dehorsey or lug sloop	8 × 15ft 4 × 14ft	52cwt	59	2 carried until 1945
27ft whaler	Clinker (drop keel)	6ft	Two mast montagu	4 × 17ft 1 × 16ft	26cwt	27	2 carried underneath catapult deck on gantries until 1940; re-embarked on quadrantal davits in 1945 until 1956, then stowed on boat deck
14ft dinghy	Clinker (drop keel) – RNSA dinghy	5ft 4¾in	Single mast gunter	4 × 8ft	10cwt	6	2 normally carried for recreation purposes

Anchors and cables

Anchor	Type	Weight	Cable	Remarks
Bowers	Byers stockless	110cwt	15 lengths 12½ fathoms 2⅛in diam forged steel, 4 lengths 6¼ fathoms 2⅛in diam forged steel	2 carried port and starboard, used for anchoring and mooring
Sheet	Byers stockless	110cwt	1 length 2 fathoms 2⅛in diam forged steel, 150 fathoms 6½in steel wire hawser	1 carried starboard side until June 1943
Stream	Admiralty pattern with stock	14cwt	150 fathoms 2½in	1 carried for keeping ship's stern stationary in tidal stream
Kedge	Admiralty pattern with stock	10cwt	150 fathoms 2½in	Used for moving the ship by winding in on hawser

during World War I, whereby a ship should be painted 'not for low visibility, but in such a way as to break up her form and thus confuse a submarine officer as to the course on which she was heading.' Schemes devised for capital ships emphasised identity confusion rather than concealment. Through 1941 it became evident the polygons were too small to be differentiated at effective camouflage ranges. Simplified Admiralty light and dark disruptive schemes were promulgated in 1942 to use larger and simpler polygons with no more than four colours. Light disruptive schemes were intended for use in the higher latitudes where skies were often overcast. Dark disruptive schemes used darker colours, providing more effective disruption where bright sunlight could be expected. *Belfast* was painted in two tones of grey, light and dark, to the instructions given here, with the reasoning that one of the colours chosen would be tricky to see under differing light circumstances.

Today, *Belfast* is painted with a World War II Admiralty disruptive camouflage scheme that employed polygons of varying shades of grey, blue and green so at least two of the colours would blend with background sea or sky under different light conditions.

CONFIDENTIAL
INSTRUCTIONS FOR PAINTING CAMOUFLAGE DESIGN
(TYPE A.D.)

1. The pattern of the camouflage when applied to the ship need not follow the drawing accurately within 3 feet.
2. Decks are to be painted 507.A. omitting Semtex or other composition if laid.
3. Non slip deck paint may be used on decks where a non slip foothold is necessary. If used this should be of grey not lighter than 507.A.
4. "507.A." refers to Admiralty Pattern 507.A. Dark Grey Home Fleet Shade.
    "507.C." refers to Admiralty Pattern 507.C. Light Grey for use on foreign stations.
5. Masts and Crow's nest should be painted white.
6. All athwartship vertical surfaces not shown on the diagrams to be painted 507.C.
7. The underside of all horizontal surfaces overhanging decks, bridge decks etc., to be painted white. This includes the underneath horizontal surfaces of Director Towers, undersides of Turrets etc.
8. That part of the deck itself that is overshadowed by the turret should in each case be painted white.
9. Boats should be painted white below the waterline. This may be impracticable, but if possible, it will proof [sic] a great help

in counteracting the large mass of contained shadow in the area of the boat's stowage.

10. Boat's chocks should be painted white.
11. Cranes to be painted 507.c.
12. Decks under torpedo tubes should be painted white.
13. Roofs of turrets should be painted 507.A.

BELFAST'S COMMUNICATION SYSTEMS

The below Information is provided by HMS *Collingwood* Heritage Collection and covers the different kinds of radio used on the ship.

P38/2 FIGHTER DIRECTION SYSTEM RECEIVER PART

FM12 MF DF OUTFIT

This was medium frequency, and used for direction finding.

KCH/KCR/KFA/KFD/KGA CONTROL OUTFITS

Control Units KC & KF (K = Control. 'C' could not be used because it was already assigned for other communication purposes. F = Flying)

KG CONTROL UNITS

This series (now in addition to CCS and CWS) was fitted in the late-war years to enable British and American transmitters and receivers to be used remotely.

87M

This is a VHF Tx/RX used for fighter aircraft communication.

TYPE 405

Designed in 1936, Type 405 is a warning telephone outfit, better known as a ship's tannoy system, and was a Type of intercom with buzzers and alarms between various positions throughout the ship. Over the tannoy came spoken orders, pipes, bugle calls, action station clangers/siren and warnings.

73X

This is a UHF set working on about 600Mhz. It used supersonic CW and was being developed by Marconi. Development was stopped by the war. In 1939, Type 73 was listed as being CONFIDENTIAL. There were several variants of the set in addition to the Type 73 (basic model), viz, 73X (first experimental model), 73C (CCS), 73D (CWS).

FC 1

This was a D/F (direction finding) outfit used for simultaneous reception on M/F (medium-frequency 60–600kc/s) and H/F (667–20,000kc/s) with arrangements for tasking D/F bearings on M/F or H/F alternatively. It needed two operators with separate open aerials and receiving outfits.

AIRBORNE AND SURFACE EARLY DETECTION: RADAR

Typically, in 1939 cruisers were fitted with:
WA Type 281
Interrogator Type 243
WS Type 273Q
GS Type 284
GA Type 243

By 1945 *Belfast*'s radar types had mushroomed to include:

Type 242	IFF
Type 243	IFF
Type 253	IFF
Type 277	AA height finding and surface warning
Type 281	Air warning
Type 282 & 283	Pom-Pom directions and blind barrage
Type 274	6in. armament
Type 285	HA
Type 293Q	Close-range height finding and surface warning

This photograph of HMS Belfast's Walrus aircraft taken by then Mid Terence Lewin, later Admiral of the Fleet Lord Lewin, is by kind permission of Lewin of Greenwich. The Walrus was used principally for reconnaissance, on anti-submarine patrol, recording gunnery fall of shot and enemy early warning. The Belfast had two. However, the introduction of radar in the fleet made an aircraft on board a cruiser redundant; the aircraft left on 6 June 1943 and the hangars were converted – one to a messdeck and the other to a church and cinema, while the catapult area housed more boats.

The Walrus

Information on the Walrus supplied by The Fleet Air Arm Museum, Yeovilton

Aircraft type:	Supermarine Walrus (Seagull V)
Mark:	V
Primary Role:	Reconnaissance and Air/Sea rescue, amphibious
First Flight:	21.6.1933
Date operating with FAA squadrons:	1935–1945

Manufacturer:	Saunders-Roe (SARO)
Engine:	One 775 HP Bristol Pegasus VI radial engine
Wing Span:	45.8 ft (13.97 m)
Length:	37.2 ft (11.35 m)
Height:	15.3 ft (4.65 m)
Wing Area:	610 sq ft (56.67 sq m)
Empty Weight:	4,900 lb (2,223 kg)
Max. Weight:	7,200 lb (3,266 kg)
Speed:	135 mph (217 km/h)
Ceiling:	17,090 ft (2,210 m)
Range:	600 mi (966 km)
Armament:	Two Vickers 'K' guns – in nose and dorsal positions; 760lb of Bombs and Depth charges under wing
Crew:	3–4
Squadrons:	700, 701, 702, 710, 711, 712, 714, 715, 716, 718, 720, 722, 728, 730, 733, 737, 740, 742, 743, 747, 749, 751, 754, 757, 763, 764, 765, 771, 772, 773, 777, 778, 781, 782, 783, 787, 788, 789, 796, 836, 1700
Battle Honours:	Atlantic, Arctic, West Africa, Eastern Mediterranean, Singapore

The Walrus Mk 2 had a wooden hull. They were built by Saunders-Roe of Cowes, Isle of Wight. After a number were built (*British Flying-Boats & Amphibians 1909–1952* G.R. Duval (PUTNAM) indicate 6), the production reverted to the original Alclad (corrosion-resistant aluminium) hull, due to the extra weight of the wood plus water absorbed.

The aircraft endeared itself to all who became involved and was affectionately called various names, some unprintable. Shagbat, Flying Pig, Dick and Steam Pigeon were a few of the better known. It was recognised as a solid beast and would take a lot of punishment. It was known to have been spun, looped, rolled and stall turned: the stall was viceless. It was said, before the war, that it was the only aircraft strong enough to do a bunt. Some of these aerobatics would, no doubt, make life a little uncomfortable for the crew. The floor boards, bilge water, oil from the hydraulic reservoir and loose objects would have caused some consternation. It was also known for one of the propeller blades to be fitted back to front, in which case the aircraft refused to fly!

(Further information can be found at www.fleetairarmarchive.net/Aircraft/Walrus.htm)

SHIP-HANDLING CHARACTERISTICS

1. The ship handles very well, but she is a heavy ship and takes some stopping.
2. When steadying on a new course, "Midships" 10° before, and opposite wheel 3°-5° before, for slow swing, and 5°-7° before, for a fast swing.
3. She has a fairly quick roll and is rather wet.
4. The following reductions in speed have been used:

(a) Anchoring	10 cables	8 knots
	3 cables	Stop
	1 cable	Slow astern; increasing to half astern as necessary
(b) Mooring	10 cables	8 knots
	2 cables	Stop
	Let go (first anchor)	Slow astern
(c) Coming to a buoy	10 cables	8 knots
	3 cables	Stop
	1½ cables	Slow astern
(d) Going alongside	8 cables	Slow ahead
	2 cables	Stop
	1 cable	Slow astern; increasing to half astern as necessary

These distances have been used when steaming on 4 shafts with 4 boilers connected. Should only two boilers be connected it is necessary to start going astern about a quarter of a cable earlier.

5. There is quite a noticeable difference in the acceleration when four boilers are connected and when two are connected. Gain and loss of speed allowances under normal circumstances and in speeds range 8-20 knots have been:

(a) With normal rate of increase/decrease 55 yards per knot

(b) With E.R. using timed increase/decrease 80 yards per knot

In practice, if the E.R. are given warning the 55 yard per knot figure is fairly good, but a good deal depends on the personalities in the engineroom.

When accelerating with four boilers connected use 55 yards per knot figure, and when accelerating with two boilers connected rather more should be allowed and 60 yards/knots is a fair estimate for an increase in speed.

6. If only two shafts are connected turning at rest becomes a very tedious affair, and should only be attempted if there is no leeway problem.

Otherwise for turning at rest 80 revs ahead and 90 revs astern with 20° wheel has been found satisfactory. The ship is slow to turn, though, when dead stopped and due allowance should be made when leaving harbour in formation, as *BELFAST* always seems to take longer than anyone else to get pointed.

7. Sternboards.

This has been tried with success in Grand Harbour, Malta. The ship turned in the entrance with a little headway on between St. Elmo breakwater and Ricasole point. Having pointed the stern down harbour, 120 revs astern were rung on and the ship having gathered sternway steered quite well. When 720 feet from the required stopped position engines were rung on to half ahead 150 revs, and the ship stopped in the required position.

This method of approaching the buoy was quicker than approaching the buoys direct and turning in the berth.

8.   Weighing.

Caution is needed when weighing to avoid the cable getting jammed on the P.V. ram on the forefoot. Should the cable be growing around the bow it is advisable to point the ship to open the hawse or give the ship a kick astern to achieve the same effect. This should be particularly guarded against when weighing in company.

9.   Suez Canal.

The ship was a little sluggish at 7½ knots (canal speed) but stable. At 106 revs (12 knots) in the southern part of the canal steering became a little erratic (tide was against). The most comfortable speed seemed to be between 86 and 96 revs on four shafts. Some opposite wheel was needed occasionally on the turns but the ship did not take a sheer. 19 knots were rung on through the Bitter Lakes with no adverse effect.

10. Approaching a buoy with two shafts only.

The following plan was used with success in calm conditions, with two boilers connected.

10 cables	8 knots
8 cables	Slow
3 cables	Stop
1½ cables	Slow astern
1¼ cables	Half astern (80 revs)

Cut off distances
From G.D.P looking directly ahead   32 yards from bow
From G.D.P looking directly astern   35 yards from stern
From Compass platform looking ahead   58 yards from bow
From Compass platform looking astern   61 yards from stern

Chapter 2

HMS *Belfast*'s role in World War II

TIMELINE OF KEY EVENTS

1939	Capture of *Cap Norte*
	Damaged by a magnetic mine
1939–42	Repairs in Devonport
1942–43	Arctic convoys
26 Dec 1943	Sinking *Scharnhorst* (Battle of North Cape)
1944	D-Day landings

CAPTURE OF *CAP NORTE*

AN ACCOUNT BY REAR ADMIRAL GEORGE THRING CB, DSO*

When R Adm George Thring CB, DSO joined HMS Belfast in August
1939 as a lieutenant-commander, the ship was being taken in hand from her
builders, Harland and Wolff, in Belfast. He saw active service throughout
World War II, mainly on convoy duties (including an Arctic convoy), and
later in Korea. After a number of senior appointments he retired in 1958.*

*This account of his time in the ship, taken from his personal
recollections, by kind permission of his son, Cdr Edward Thring RN,
describes his impressions on joining; how she was employed as part of the
Home Fleet 18th Cruiser Squadron based at Scapa Flow; and the capture
of the German merchant vessel Cap Norte (13,165 tons) of the Hamburg
Sud-America line while carrying wheat imports and German reservists.*

I am sure the majority of us thought that war would come, probably
before the end of the year; therefore "Britain's latest Cruiser" was to
us a matter of life and death.

The ship did not yet belong to us, and we were still spectators. Early
on in the proceedings, when steaming at comparatively high speed,
everything stopped. The ship slowed down, out of control, all lights
went out and nothing worked. It gave us an uncomfortable feeling for

a short time; was this the sort of thing that might happen in action? However the fault was soon discovered; some inexperienced man had connected the boilers to an oil tank which was nearly empty.

We were still very new, and very green. However we were undoubtedly a very happy ship. The organisation ran smoothly, and people smiled. We still had experts from Vickers on board performing feats with gun mountings; and we had another civilian for wireless or gyro compasses; they remained until the job was finished, without complaint.

Then came Sunday, 3rd September 1939 and with it war, submarine scares, aircraft alarms and so on. Surprisingly nothing happened; the Hun apparently was doing one thing at a time.

Trials were marvellous, everyone returned to Belfast with the feeling that she was a fine ship, and all that was now required was from our side, the Naval side, to make her efficient by organisation and training.

We were literally "pitchforked" straight into a large scale naval exercise. Someone had to be "the enemy", we became the "Hipper". Her duty was to start from the Horn's Reef (of Jutland fame) and try to break through the Northern patrol, extending as in the last war from Scotland to Iceland. On the way to Horn's Reef we learnt how to darken ship, a certain amount of simple gun drill and how to master the new control system. Damage and breakdowns were also practised in a small way. Off the Horn's Reef we sighted a large liner, one of the "Strength through Joy" cruises of Hitler Youth, returning to the Fatherland.

We were also visited by a German Seaplane, who flew close round the ship, inspecting, and probably photographing "Britain's latest Cruiser" from every angle. He gave us a friendly wave before leaving us alone. I wonder where that young chap is now!

Our "Hipper", taking a most audacious route, much too much so for the careful planning Hun, got through to "raid" the Atlantic, with nearly all her oil fuel in hand. As soon as the exercise was over the Home Fleet assembled at Invergordon.

The first shoots were quite satisfactory. Never had a ship had a battery of six four inch high angle guns on each side before, and each side was out to rival the other. Shells went in all directions, control was very limited. The aircraft, towing the sleeve target stood up to it for a time; the aircraft went home, and reported us as a public menace! Which we undoubtedly were; but we had learnt how to let the guns off – control would come with practice.

At about this time our "Walrus" arrived; we should have had three but there were not three to be had. Catapult trials were carried out. We also exercised hoisting it in by crane, a far more tricky business than shooting it off. Incidentally, that is the last we saw of our aircraft, which went to shore base for anti-submarine patrol round the Orkneys. For North Atlantic in Winter aircraft were not required.

We joined a power force for a high speed sweep to the North. It was an inspiring sight to see the HOOD and RENOWN again; both old friends of Home Fleet peace time cruises and exercises.

Our job was to prevent others escaping to join her on the trade routes. The SCHARNHORST and GNEISNAU were a formidable pair and would undoubtedly try to slip through; more pocket Battleships similar to the GRAF SPEE were also available, not to mention modern eight inch cruisers. It is a significant fact, showing the Germans' complete failure to appreciate Naval Warfare (other than U-boats), that they did not sally forth at once into the Atlantic before our aircraft were more available to shadow them, and when our shipping was still moving from peace time to war time routes, and almost completely uncovered. Indeed when they did slip through, they made singularly little use of their opportunities.

This time we were to take our place in the famous Northern Patrol. This meant intercepting and boarding every ship met, leaving armed guards on board, and sending them in for examination. We found our boat work exercises had been well spent. It is necessary for a cruiser to keep moving during boarding operations, due to the U-boat menace, and to the possibility of the ship being a disguised raider, armed with unseen torpedo tubes and guns. We boarded many ships, two of which were of more than normal interest. The first was a Norwegian Whale factory.

The second event was of far greater interest. One morning we sighted a fairly large liner eastward bound. We increased speed to intercept, and saw she was flying Swedish colours; later we could read her name, that of a Swedish ship not known to be in the area, according to Lloyds, and not quite the same size to look at. We unfortunately had no picture for comparison. Weather again was rough. We got very close to the "Neutral", getting more suspicious every minute. We could see a dark patch on her bow where something had been painted over, and all doubt was removed when we could read through the paint, due to the embossed lettering of her old paint, and read her original name "Cap Norte". The boat returned and an extra party was sent on board, all possible precautions were taken by the boarding party to prevent scuttling; but in those days the technique had not been acquired by the Hun and possibly the Fuhrer's orders on the subject had not been received. Thus the first large prize fell to HMS BELFAST. It gave us a big thrill, and a feeling of accomplishment. I believe she still is the largest ship captured from the Germans, and she had a small but exceedingly valuable cargo.

The boarding party had no trouble. There were women and children on board returning to the Fatherland; for that reason, the Captain said he had not scuttled his ship, assuming that we would not board in the prevailing weather; but that we would just escort her in. He could then scuttle unhampered by a boarding party, on reaching calmer waters. The boarding parties' relations with their captives were not strained, courtesy prevailed; and one could not help feeling very sorry for that Captain, who had lost his ship, having left South America "under his lawful occasion" before war started. I saw that ship again some time later with her third and British name ["Empire Trooper"] lying alongside at Gibraltar.

We passed the Faroes and sighted Iceland on several occasions and judged the distance to be steamed from the Northern end of the patrol in order to fuel in the Shetlands, at Sollum Voe, our nearest British fuelling post. Sollum Voe is a bleak spot and gives little opportunity for recreation; we went in behind the hastily improvised defences, fuelled, possibly had a night's rest, and then to sea again.

News programmes came through regularly on the B.B.C. and the absence of real news was the most remarkable thing. But one could not help feeling that the Navy was the only part of the Nation actually doing anything.

At Scapa we were always having some sort of air raid warning. Soon the Armed Merchant Cruisers, taken up and hastily converted, started to arrive at Scapa. Old friends, they were to take over the contraband control patrol, and their other duty of reporting a breakthrough of a raider. Their arrival made us free for our proper function, that of a Fleet Cruiser.

In the early hours of the morning a Signalman came into my cabin, and showed me a signal to the effect that the ROYAL OAK had been sunk, and that the Fleet was to go to sea at once.

It has since been disclosed that the ROYAL OAK was torpedoed by Prion, that fine submarine "ace", who subsequently showed Huns how new techniques could enable U-boats to attack convoys. His exploit was daring, his navigation of a very tricky channel superb, one cannot help taking one's hat off to a fine Seaman and brilliant Submariner, who has since paid the penalty. He was sunk by Walruses 6 March 1941.

The account by R Adm George Thring continues with his description of HMS Belfast's *crippling from a German magnetic mine, which saw her put out of action and taken to Devonport for a two-year rebuild.*

Then came orders to proceed to the Clyde. The passage through the Minches was trying. It was our first experience of high speed steaming in close formation at night and zig-zagging. A critical moment arrived when the "snotty"(*Midshipman*), who was watching the time, announced that the watch had stopped, and that he did not know when the next zig should be. At the same time a blinding storm blotted out the next ahead. One could not help wondering if all this risk was worth it, in view of the small number of U-boats out. It was very good practice all the same.

At this time we had heard of the first of the magnetic mines. It caused a certain amount of disquiet. We gathered there were two sorts, big ones for attacking the fleet, and little ones for merchant ships.

We were not left in doubt very long. Our flagship and ourselves proceeded into the Firth of Forth for exercises; AA armament was as usual partially manned in case of enemy interference. We had decided it would be a good thing to wire up a microphone from the air defence position to the ship's loud speaker system, partly as a means of getting guns onto a target quickly, and partly to keep the remainder of the ship's company "in the picture", who could not see what was going on, due to their work being between decks. Some sort of running commentary was indicated, such as "Goering has just come on to bowl at the Forth Bridge end". "The first over was mainly wides; but one ball narrowly missed so and so". However this innovation was only at present a make-shift arrangement. The Chief PO Telegraphist was first explaining to me what switches to make. He told me, with a note of anxiety, that it was his only spare "mike", and that it was very delicate, due to not being in a proper holder. He had just given it to me, with a final word imploring me not to drop it, when the earthquake occurred, and crash went the mike onto the steel deck!

As far as I remember I held on tight to the rail round the control platform; and then, as the heaving underfoot ceased, had a look round. The Chief PO Tel and I were "garlanded" with wireless aerials. The first thing that caught my eye was the top mast at a drunken angle of about thirty degrees to the rest of the mast. The next thing I noticed was my Brother-in-law's motor boat completely wrecked on the catapult deck!

The ship behaved exactly as during that first break down on trials. All machinery ceased to function; all electric power broke down. It should have been perfectly obvious that the ship had either been torpedoed or mined.

All communication had failed with my guns and most of them could not be trained. I therefore decided to leave the control position, and see what I could do to help the Commander. I found out that he, armed with every torch he could find, was busy shoring up hatches and generally controlling damage, ably assisted by the engineers. There was no sense of giving orders quickly, since the loudspeaker system had been cut off. However, we had organised "boatswains mates" and messengers just for this eventuality, who were most useful.

On deck we prepared the ship for towing. There was a most convenient tug, who had been sent out to tow the target for our shoot. The tug took us in tow and pointed us slowly towards home.

The apparent damage, as viewed from the upper deck, was not great. It was also reported that the ship was not making water seriously. The most evident phenomena was the presence of oil fuel almost everywhere between decks, and the complete wreckage of mess decks.

We had actually touched off a large magnetic mine right under the foremast. One result of this was that a column of water, stated by the flagship to have risen as high as the mainmast, deposited itself on the after part of the ship, largely on the Gunnery Officer and his Gunner, who were damp, but unhurt.

Casualties occurred mainly in the two ends of the ship which "whipped" furiously as the "earthquake" took place. The medical team did marvellous work.

After a time electric supply came to life. By a great effort the Engineers managed to get the partially damaged diesel generator going. This gave us light, wireless, internal communications by loud speaker and telephone, and one of the two electric cranes. By means of the latter we were able to hoist on board a salvage pump which had been sent out together with two tugs. The three tugs between them towed us at 5 or 6 knots towards home, which fortunately was not far off.

Then we were safely taken in tow. The galleys had been wrecked forward; however the Paymaster Commander and the canteen staff between them organised sandwiches. The spirit room was found to be intact, and a rum ration was issued; a little later tea started to appear, after which comforts everyone seemed to buck up again.

Once in the Rosyth dockyard, as the water was pumped out, the ship started to rest on the chocks. This caused her to creak and groan like an animal in pain. Rivets were sheared, and the deck itself began to crack. Pumping was therefore stopped, and the ship left floating, just clear of the chocks.

It was quite clear that the keel had been bent upwards, the two ends of the ship having sat on the chocks before the midship section. Only one man died. Patients were allowed to have their relations up to see them.

Christmas on board was rather cold and grim. Early in the New Year we paid off. Special trains came into the dockyard to embark men bound for Portsmouth barracks, whence they would be scattered to the four corners of the earth. Behind us in the dock was the wreck of one of the finest ships ever built. Our hearts were very heavy.

The Naval Constructors made a magnificent temporary repair, binding the ship in a cradle, of sufficient strength to enable her to steam on two shafts, from Rosyth to Devonport. Her reconstruction took a long time. I am sure it gave us all, of the original commission, a great thrill, when we later heard the BELFAST had played a leading and most successful part in the sinking of the SCHARNHORST.

Mid Lewin (later AF Lord Lewin) was the coxswain of the ship's cutter (boat) that took the boarding party to the blockade runner merchantman Cap Norte – *disguising herself as a Swedish neutral: the SS* Ancona – *and took the surrender of the merchantman.*

SHIP'S LOG DURING THE *CAP NORTE* INCIDENT

HMS *Belfast*—October 9, 1939—at sea

0800	Latitude 63° 51'N Longitude 07° 35'W
	Wind: ESE Force 4
	Weather and visibility: blue skies, seven miles
0800	a/c to MLA (Mean Line of Advance) 263° St'd 4 in. Defence Watch closed up
0854	Sighted steamship bearing 278° Co SE
0900	Courses and speeds as requisite for closing ship
0915	Ordered SS *Tai Yin* to stop
0946	Armed guard boarded
1102	SS *Tai Yin* ordered to Kirkwall
1104	Sighted liner bearing 300°. Closed as requisite. Ordered SS *Ancona* (Swedish) to stop. Ship was found to be SS *Cap Norte* (German)
1210	Strong armed guard boards
1313	2nd armed guard left ship and boarded
1347	*Cap Norte* proceeded
1354	Proceeded. Course 105° 15 knots.

HMS *BELFAST* STRUCK BY MINE

HMS *Belfast* ship's log records in a matter-of-fact manner, giving drama to the event, the occasion when she struck a German mine.

Damage to the hull of HMS Belfast *taken in Devonport Dockyard 1940.*
(Getty Images)

Tuesday, November 21, 1939: At Rosyth (see Glossary for abbreviation explanations)

	(Leave granted to ship's company: Nil)
0800	*Wind: SW Force 3*
	Weather and visibility: blue skies, seven miles
	Sea and swell: 7
	Barometer: 1032.2 (rising)
0917	Weighed and proceeded. Course and speed as requisite for leaving harbour and carrying out firings in company with *Southampton*
0947	Passed through A/S boom. 1005 out paravanes
1030	a/c to 025° 1037 295° 1042 115° 1049 060°
1058	Violent explosion felt in *Belfast*. Extensive damage
1140	Taken in tow by tug *Krooman*
1314	Prepared to abandon ship

From: *D4*
To: *Belfast*

Please keep me informed of your condition so that I can inform C in C Rosyth	1112
Light PL TOD 1117	21/11/39

To: *D4*
From: *Belfast*

Keep Destroyers on the move screening me	1115
Light PL TOD 1116	21/11/39

To: *Belfast*
From: *D4*

Do you require towing?		1114
REPLY: Yes certainly		1115
Light PL TOD 1115	TOD 1116	21/11/39

To: C in C Rosyth (R) C S 2
From: *Belfast*

"A" Boiler and Engine Room out of action. Improbable that steam can be raised. Explosion was abreast "A" Boiler Room	1116
Light PL TOD 1119	21/11/39

To: *Belfast*
From: *Euryalus*

Can we be of any assistance? Divers are dressed and all ready	
Light PL TOR 1120	21/11/39

To: *Euryalus*
From: *Belfast*

Return to harbour and be ready to help when we return to harbour	1125
Light PL TOD1127	21/11/39

To: *Belfast*
From: *Whitley*

Shall I come alongside your starboard side forward to facilitate passing tow	
Light PL TOR 1130	21/11/39

To: *D4, Whitley*
From: *Belfast*

Tug *Krooman* is endeavouring to tow me if he is able to do so, keep *Whitley* screening	1130
Light PL TOD 1133	21/11/39

To: *Whitley*
From: *Belfast*

Keep on the move	1131
Light PL TOD 1132	21/11/39

To: *Krooman*
From: *Belfast*

Come alongside starboard bow, slip your targets	1133
Light PL TOD 1155	21/11/39

To: *Belfast*
From: *Euryalus*

Shall I take the target from Tug?	
REPLY: Yes tug has slipped target endeavour to get them in tow	1137
Light PL TOR 1126 TOD 1138	21/11/39

To: *D4*
From: *Belfast*

Report to Rosyth that Tug *Krooman* is towing, but further assistance is urgently required. Ship will not be able to steam and probably not steer. Approximate casualties Dead NIL Injured 16	1148
Light PL TOD 1152	21/11/39

To: *Belfast*
From: *D4*

Is it certain that it was a torpedo please?	1211
REPLY: No I cannot tell as nothing was seen	1216
Light PL TOR 1214 TOD 1216	21/11/39

To: *Belfast* for C D
From A S

Outer caisson of lock is open. Ship can enter lock whenever there is sufficient depth of water to navigate main channel	1249
Light PL TOR 1333 TOD 1549	21/11/39

To: C-in-C Rosyth, CS2, CD
From: *Belfast*

Explosion at about 80 and possibly two other right aft. Ship flooded to waterline from 66 to 93.4 in. HA magazine flooded. Making water in forward Engine Room and possibly "A" Boiler Room. Steam cannot be raised except for one dynamo as all Turbo oil fuel pumps out of action. Steering gear in use. Draught increased to two feet forward four inches aft. Oil fuel cannot be pumped out forward. Casualties Dead NIL, 21 injured, some seriously. Hope to arrive for immediate docking 1500, essential to dry dock immediately.	1259
Light PL TOD 1300	21/11/39

To: A S
From: C D

Propose to berth *Belfast* in "Y" berth. Will you please clear berth, rough time of arrival 1630 today Tuesday.	1303
Light PL TOD 1325	21/11/39

To: *D4*
From: *Belfast*

Destroyers are to continue screening up to the Gate so far as navigationally possible and to remain in close company till ship enters basin.	1318
Light PL TOD 1332	21/11/39

To: *Belfast*
From: *D4*

C in C and R A D think I am hunting. May I take *Gurkha* and *Isis* and search when you have reached Inchkeith.	1349
Light PL TOD 1349	21/11/39

To: *D4*
From: *Belfast*

Yes I had no idea that you were supposed to be hunting. Many thanks for your screening.	1351
Light PL TOD 1355	21/11/39

To: C D
From: *Belfast*

At 1315 draught was as follows:	23 feet 9 forward	
	22 feet aft	
Light PL TOD 1400		21/11/39

Summary of Mine Damage Report 21-11-39 by D.N.C. Dept Admiralty Bath (DNC 4B/R1) - Restricted

The effect of the mining on this ship was most severe, causing 100% disablement.

Although the direct impingement of the explosive forces caused negligible hull damage, the secondary effect was that the vessel broke her back in the region of the break of the forecastle. In this neighbourhood this class of ship undergoes a quick change of inertia of cross section, due to such causes as the stopping of the Upper Armour Deck, Side Armour and Inner Bottom. Just forward of this quick change of inertia is a relatively heavy concentration of load, caused by 'A' and 'B' turrets and the bridge structure. The structure was evidently unable to withstand the very rapid and large amplitude motions induced by an underwater explosion of the type encountered.

The main machinery was also fully disabled, firstly due to fractures of oil fuel pump discharges entirely robbing the burners of fuel, and secondly, had steam been available, it is doubtful if the main engines could have been run for very long without defects developing sufficiently seriously to cause them to be shut down.

The main armament and a large portion of the secondary armament would probably have failed to function if attempts had been made to fire it.

REPAIRS AT DEVONPORT

When HMS *Belfast* had completed her 26-month refit in Devonport she was updated to become the Royal Navy's strongest cruiser, able to take on an 8in.-gun enemy ship or any other cruiser worldwide. In summary this table shows her modernisation. Of particular note is that she was fitted with the latest radar, which concentrated on U-boat hunting, whereas German radar focussed on gunnery. *Belfast*'s radar was later to play a key role in finding the *Scharnhorst*.

HMS *Belfast*'s modernisation

Armament:	November 1942
Main:	as at 1939
Ammunition:	as at 1939
Radar:	1 × Type 284 on for'd DCT—main armament surface

1 × Type 273 General warning, surface; in lantern aft of for'd DCT

4 × Type 283 blind barrage directors for 6 in. armament

1 × Type 252 IFF (Identification Friend or Foe) to combine with 273

1 × Type 251 IFF

High Angle:	**November 1942**
Guns and Mountings:	as at 1939
Ammunition:	as at 1939
Fire Control:	The three HA Directors were modified to Mark IVs to take Type 285 radar for radar controlled fire
Radar:	3 × Type 285
	1 × Type 281 *Air Warning*, Transmitter aerial on foremast; receiver aerial on mainmast
	1 × Type 242 *Air Warning IFF* aerials on top of 281 receiver
Close range:	**November 1942**
2-pdr. Pom-poms:	The two Mark II mountings were replaced by two Mark VIII RPC (Remote Power Control)
Ammunition:	1800 rounds per barrel
	14 rounds per belt; 10 belts per tray
Fire Control:	The Mark II Directors were replaced by two Mark IV pom-pom directors and repositioned near the mountings
	2 × Type 282 radar being fitted to the directors. The guns and directors were RPC. The weight of a director was 36 cwt
Operation:	Power or hand: maximum elevating and training speed, 16 degrees/second loading was carried out by using the energy of the recoiling barrel

Sights:	Cosine

20 mm. Oerlikons

Twins:	Ten ·20 mm. Oerlikon guns in five Mark V twin mountings equipped with tachymetric sights were fitted in exposed positions about the ship. The mountings were shielded, power controlled and later tied to radar sights; 1 on roof of "B" turret, 1 on each wing of the lower bridge, for'd; 2 right aft on the quarterdeck and protected by concave and roofed shelters
Control:	RPC through HA barrage directors
Singles:	Eight single Oerlikons, Mark IV on Mark IIIA fixed pedestal mountings were fitted, four each side on the catapult deck
Ammunition:	2400 rounds per gun in Ready Use lockers and stowage in pom-pom magazine
	Though hand operated and sighted by eye-shooting using a 300 kwt. sighting ring, these single Oerlikons were comforting weapons. With an effective range of 1000-1200 yd., the gun was very versatile being manufactured in America as well as Britain and all parts being interchangeable.

Details:	Calibre:	20 mm.
	MV:	2725 ft./sec.
	Rate of fire:	465/480 r.p.m.
	Length:	8 ft.
	Weight of gun:	173 lb.
	Weight of pedestal:	140 lb.
	Elevation:	75°
	Training:	360°

·5 in. Machineguns:	Removed—replaced by twin Oerlikons

TORPEDO DEPARTMENT

Six-21 in. Mark IV torpedoes were replaced by six-21 in. Mark VIII**

Depth-charge Outfit was enlarged:

15 Mark VIIs—ship

12 Mark VIII—aircraft

Rangefinder unit (22 ft. Duplex and PIL FM7 rangefinder on an MR II anti-vibration mounting) with air-disturbing, desiccating and window-cleaning units.

The after DCT was fitted with 15 ft. FX2 rangefinder on an MR13 anti-vibration mounting.

The two lower Bridge rangefinders were removed.

A loud-hailer system was fitted to incorporate all close range weapons.

A Type 760 Echo Sounder was fitted.

Two extra paravanes were carried, totalling six Mark VII and Mark VII* which replaced the original outfit.

THE AIRCRAFT

Fearnought fire covers were fitted to the hangars.

Two Walrus amphibians were carried until June 6, 1943 when they were landed and the catapult removed.

A collection of papers was found among the documents of Capt P. H. E. Welby-Everard, DSC, OBE, DL, RN. He served in HMS Belfast as her commander from 1942 until 1944. This is the first of four articles and describes a little-recorded dockyard problem. They are reproduced with the kind permission of his son, Roger Welby-Everard.

HMS *BELFAST* – RATS

After being mined in 1939 the ship was over two years in Devonport dockyard undergoing a major reconstruction below the waterline during which period she became overrun with rats. When the interior of the ship was made habitable again towards the end of this long refit, and once the ventilation was restarted and the ship's company began living aboard, the rats got disturbed from their comfortable quarters between decks and many of them moved out to the huge pile of old and other rubbish that had accumulated ashore. During the last week or two before commissioning the Dockyard Rat-catcher was reported to have killed 250 rats alongside the ship.

Rats were, however, still plentiful on board and we would have liked to have had the ship fumigated before commissioning but the 48-hour delay this would have entailed was not acceptable in wartime so we had to take the rats to sea with us. On the upper deck was a large vegetable locker made of wire mesh, the inboard side being panelled with wood to protect it from the heat of the boiler uptakes. After a month or two it was apparent that numbers of rats had made their home in this panelling and on the next occasion that the locker was nearly empty of vegetables the Commander shut the entire Shipwrights staff into the locker with instructions to strip this panelling completely; an exciting rat hunt took place inside the locker, watched with interest by those outside, and when the Shipwrights were released they brought with them 67 dead rats.

1942–43 ARCTIC CONVOYS AND NORTHERN WATERS OPERATIONS

In the History of the Second World War the term Arctic Convoy conjures up an image of endurance against great odds, of battles fought in the Arctic night in which ice, snow and high winds added to the horrors of war. It was indeed conditions in the Arctic which set the convoys to Northern Russia apart from other theatres of war. In winter seamen fought a continual battle against gales and ice in almost perpetual darkness; in summer the sun rarely set and there was no respite from the threat or reality of attack. In fact the Arctic convoys were amazingly successful. Of a total of forty outward convoys comprising of 811 ships only 68 were sunk. Those that got through delivered great quantities of tanks, aircraft, ammunition, and other essential war materials which made a significant contribution to Russia's role in the war.

Terence Lewin; Admiral of the Fleet KG, GCB, LVO, DSC

12 convoys, *Belfast* veteran, First patron of the Russian Convoy Club

The log of *Belfast*'s activities from December 1942 to August 1945 gives but a mild view of the intensity of operations as the crew

endured extreme cold and nerve-wracking worry of a German attack
by U-boat, aircraft or surface units of the German Navy.

1942	
December 10	Left Plymouth for Scapa
December 25	Scapa, *10th Cruiser Squadron (Home Fleet)*
1943	
February 17	Arrived Seidisfjord, Iceland

Russian Convoys

1943	
February 19	Off Seidisfjord in company with *Cumberland, Sheffield, Bluebell, Camellia* and destroyers
February 21	Left Seidisfjord with *Cumberland* and *Norfolk* to cover Russian Convoy JW53
March 1	Murmansk
March 2	Left Kola Inlet with *Cumberland* and *Norfolk* to cover Russian Convoy RA53

Northern Blockade Patrol: 1943

March 29	Left Hvalfjord
	Ordered to reinforce Patrol "White" with *Intrepid*—Search for Blockade Runner
March 30	Patrol "White" with *Glasgow, Intrepid* and *Echo*
April 2	Sailed to relieve *Cumberland* on Patrol "White"
April 7	On west coast of Iceland to Patrol "White"
April 13	Arrived at Hvalfjord having been relieved on patrol by *Cumberland (10th Cruiser Squadron) (Home Fleet)*
May 27	Arrived Scapa from covering mine-laying operations, SN111B

June 18	Arrived Rosyth to give leave and for quick docking. Ship to sail for Scapa so as to arrive July 1
July 1	Arrived Scapa
July 7	Sailed from Scapa to the north-eastward in company with *London*, *Kent* and one destroyer
	OPERATION "CAMERA", a diversionary sweep off Norway to exploit, during the Sicilian Landings, Hitler's continued fear of an Allied counter invasion of that country. Operation was successful because the cruisers were mistaken for a transport convoy
July 9	Arrived Scapa in company with *London* and *Kent*
July 27	Left Scapa
July 29	Arrived Scapa

Russian Convoys: 1943

August 15	After HM the King's visit to the Home Fleet, CS10 in *Belfast*, screened by *Onslow* and *Orwell*, left Scapa to create a diversion off the South Norwegian coast—OPERATION FN, a covering sweep for the JW/RA Russian Convoys
August 17	Returned to Skaale Fjord with *Onslow* and *Orwell*
August 22	Left Scapa
August 28	Sailed from Hvalfjord with *Norfolk* and *Impulsive* to cover destroyers in OPERATION "LORRY": stores and mail to Russia
September 3	Returned to Hvalfjord with *Norfolk* and *Impulsive*: OPERATION "LORRY" Left Hvalfjord with CS10 for reconnaissance and search in the Spitzbergen area: the enemy had landed a meteorological party on this desolate island, an action the Allies were to imitate. CS10 was ordered to investigate an intelligence report of a German raid on the island

September 10   Arrived Hvalfjord

September 25   In vicinity *of* Reykjanes searching to south-east
                 OPERATION SF; suspected enemy break-out of
                 blockade runner

September 27   Arrived Scapa

Home Fleet Offensive Sweep: October 5/6,1943

                 10th Cruiser Squadron (Home Fleet) Sailed from
                 Scapa in company with *Duke of York, Anson*, U.S.
                 Aircraft Carrier *Ranger* and U.S. Heavy Cruiser
                 Tuscaloosa to attack shipping targets in the Bodo
                 area with the air striking group from *Ranger*

                 OPERATION "LEADER": diversionary, as well as
                 offensive, to ease pressure on the Russian convoys,
                 was successful

October 6   Scapa: self-refit, boiler-clean and leave period

October 29   Left Scapa

---

*This second extract from the papers of Capt P. H. E. Welby-Everard tells
of an unusual way the crew enjoyed a varied diet.*

HMS *BELFAST* – FISH FOR ALL

When the ship joined the home fleet at the end of 1942, after the
long reconstruction at Devonport, she carried an aircraft which could
be catapulted off at sea and could carry antisubmarine depth charges.
The pilot was an RNVR (Lieutenant Commander Sergeant) who was
extremely keen but our service did not have much use for his aircraft.
The aircraft was later landed.

On one occasion we anchored in Quel fjord in Iceland for a short
period between patrols in the Denmark Strait, and the pilot, obtaining
the Captain's permission to carry out a depth charge practice, was
hoisted out and took off for his exercise. Some considerable time
later the aircraft was seen to be entering the fjord on the surface
and appeared to be having some difficulty in taxi-ing back to the

ship; fortunately it was calm weather. As the aircraft approached the ship it was seen to be very low in the water but eventually arrived alongside and was hoisted on board. It was then discovered that it was loaded to the gunwales with cod as the pilot had seen a shoal of cod out to sea and had dropped his depth charge in the middle of the shoal. He then landed on the surface and taxied around picking up stunned fish until the flying boat could take no more with safety; with the weight of fish on board he was unable to take to the air and had to taxi in slowly many miles back to the ship. Everyone in *Belfast* had a welcome meal of fresh fish as a result of this depth charge practice.

This third extract from the papers of Capt P. H. E. Welby-Everard recounts how an unexpected VIP's visit necessitated painting the ship, even though Belfast *would be in rough seas on operations in a couple of days.*

HMS *BELFAST* – THE "TIDDLEY B"

In 1943 *Belfast*, under the Command of Captain F. R. Parham (Executive Officer Commander P. H. E. Welby-Everard) and flying the flag of Rear Admiral R. L. Burnett commanding the 10th cruiser Squadron, was serving in the Home Fleet and at one period in the first half of that year found herself in harbour at Scapa Flow together with a high proportion of the fleet. One morning, after the Admiral had been to see the Commander-in-Chief in HMS *Duke of York*, the Captain sent for his Commander and informed him, in confidence, that H. M. The King was to inspect the Fleet in three days time and that the Admiral had suggested it might be an appropriate occasion to paint ship.

For wartime conditions the ship was not looking too bad and the Commander would not normally have considered painting the ship at this time but the Admiral's hint was as good as an order particularly, as appeared to be the case, if the Admiral was giving *Belfast* an opportunity to steal a march on the rest of the fleet. The Commander sent to the ship's Painter and ordered him immediately to prepare the paint pots and brushes as it was intended to paint the whole superstructure the next day. The time available did not permit the painting of the ship's side as well as the superstructure; the latter was clearly the more important under the circumstances.

The news soon got round the ship and there was doubtless a great deal of "tooth-sucking" amongst the seamen who thought that the Commander must have taken leave of his senses to have such an idea when we all knew that in a few days time we could expect to go to sea on operations. However, the ship's company will always rise to the occasion and *Belfast* was a very happy ship, and all the next day all hands turned to with a will and a coat of paint was applied to the whole of the upper deck. When on the next day the hands were normally employed cleaning up after painting, scrubbing decks and polishing brightwork it is certain that everyone realised that something special was in the wind but it was not until that evening that they could be told that the King was visiting his fleet on the morrow and would come on board *Belfast* and inspect the Ship's Company.

And so it happened – H. M. King George VI came to Scapa and went on board many of his ships including *Belfast* when he walked round the upper deck inspecting the Ship's Company and later had

King George VI visited HMS Belfast at Scapa several times. On 13 May 1944, he was on the bridge with Rear Admiral FHG Dalrymple-Hamilton, who was to command the squadron looking on, as she sailed around the assembled ships at Scapa prior to D-Day (pages 77–81). Photograph courtesy of Simon Tosswill from the private collection of his father Captain Richard Tosswill RN, Executive Officer HMS Belfast 1944.

tea in the Admiral's cabin. When the King left the ship the Ship's Company manned the upperworks and gave Three Cheers for His Majesty the King. The following day the fleet went to sea, and in line ahead, manned ship and cheered the King as the Destroyer taking him back to Scapa Flow steamed down the line; a memorable occasion for everyone in the fleet in wartime.

It was readily apparent to all that Admiral Burnett had indeed enabled his flagship to steal a march on the rest of the fleet because *Belfast* was the only ship with a fresh coat of paint, really looking her best on this occasion; and His Majesty commented on her appearance accordingly. As a result of this achievement *Belfast* got the nickname in the fleet of "The Tiddley B".

SINKING THE *SCHARNHORST* (THE BATTLE OF NORTH CAPE)

ACTION OF 26 DECEMBER 1943 – SINKING OF THE SCHARNHORST

This extract is from the account of the Scharnhorst action written shortly afterwards by HMS Belfast's *commander (second-in-command) from 1942 until 1944, Capt Philip Welby-Everard DSC, OBE, DL RN. While written mainly for his wife and family, his account is reproduced here with the kind permission of his son, Roger Welby-Everard.*

AN INTRODUCTION

As far as the action itself was concerned I, as Commander, had virtually nothing to do; my action station is on top of the after superstructure at what is called the Emergency Conning Position, a rather draughty and exposed place, but from which I have all the necessary communications to take over control of the ship in the event of damage to the bridge. I'm also responsible for what is called Damage Control if the ship is hit and files have to be dealt with etc. Fortunately I was not called upon to do any of these things as the ship was never hit and therefore my duties were limited to the promulgating of information on the progress of the action to the majority of the ship's company who are between decks and see nothing, and, as it was a long action, organising supply of food to the men at their action stations when opportunity offered.

Although I was therefore little more than an onlooker of the action itself, it was a special interest for two reasons. Firstly, it was the first action of its kind, being fought continuously in either complete darkness or in the dim light that is all you get for a few hours in these latitudes at that time of year, in which full use was made of the modern fire control developments for which I was responsible during my two years at the Admiralty. Secondly, the ship and her company were in action for the first time and in the last 18 months all my energies had been directed towards producing an efficient unit from the half repaired hulk that I joined in June 1942, and the 900-odd inexperienced men that commissioned her the following November.

So, with only slight exaggeration, I can say I was watching the men I had trained, in my ship, use the instruments I had produced two and three years before.

PHASE I

Belfast was doing what had almost become a routine operation, mainly covering a North Russian convoy; in company with us was *Norfolk* and *Sheffield*, and of course the close escort of Corvettes and Destroyers with the convoy itself. We had already been at sea some days, all the time in the Second Degree of Readiness, which meant that everyone lives and sleeps at their action stations (or very close), except when a portion at a time go away for meals.

On the morning of Sunday the 26th of December, the weather was inclined to be rough but not cold for the area as the temperature was above freezing point. At 1040 (ship's time), we detected the presence of an unknown vessel in the vicinity, and shortly afterwards, *Norfolk* sighted her vaguely (it was still fairly dark) and opened fire. I'm fairly certain that *Norfolk* got a hit with her third salvo as I saw a flash as I watched her salvo fall. Being fitted with tracers, you can watch the shells all the way in the dark.

The enemy opened fire at *Norfolk*, and also hit her, though we did not hear this until later. The damage was not so serious and she had a few casualties. *Sheffield*, who was next in line to *Norfolk* fired one or two salvos. But during this phase, we saw nothing and did not fire. The enemy turned away and ran for it at 30 knots and the action did not last long as we turned back to position near the convoy, our object being its protection. We lost contact with the enemy shortly after 12 o'clock.

Belfast had as yet played no part, but we were all keyed up as at last it seemed that it was the *Scharnhorst* and our as yet un-encountered enemy of the last twelve months. I was able to broadcast that we thought it was the *Scharnhorst* this time though were not yet sure. The position was a little obscure, for a straggler from the convoy, that had failed to make a diversionary alteration ordered shortly before, was also detected and all was not quite clear at that time.

What did we think? Would *Scharnhorst* return? Would she fight it out with us? How should we get on? Knowing as we did that none of the 6 inch or 8 inch shells of us three cruisers could penetrate her armour whereas her 11 inch could knock us to pieces. The *Duke of York* was still a long way away, could we hold her until the *Duke's* 14 inch could be brought to bear? Those were the thoughts running through my mind.

However, for the moment *Scharnhorst* had legged it at 30 knots and in view of the time and the possibility of action shortly, the moment seemed right to arrange some food. So I put our action messing organisation into force and we all got a meal at our action stations – hot soup, meat pies and a jam tart.

PHASE II

I was back on the bridge, where I stay until action starts so as to keep in touch with the situation, when just after two o'clock we detected her again coming in to find the convoy. This time all three ships were in a position to open fire and no time was wasted in doing so, and *Scharnhorst* soon replied. Conditions were difficult, the best of the daylight was over and one never caught more than a fleeting glimpse of her or only saw the flash of her guns. All ships claim to have got a hit, but her salvos, though falling close did not touch us. Once again *Scharnhorst* wouldn't take it and turned away, this time to the southward towards her base, and as we knew, the *Duke of York*. This time, we all three closed to keep in touch and to ensure that the Commander-in-Chief in the *D of Y* should catch her. After a time both sides stopped firing as the range had opened and it was then a waste of ammunition to go on. The firing period lasted about 20 minutes.

Could we drive her into the arms of the *Duke of York* or would she turn round and rend us and escape that way? For four hours this chase continued, *Sheffield* dropped back due to a temporary engine defect, and *Norfolk* dropped back. *Belfast* put on her best speed, developing more horsepower than ever before, but we slowly lost ground though still keeping touch and continuing to report her every move to the C-in-C.

As the time approached for the *Duke of York* to get in touch it got very exciting but I was able to get a cup of tea and biscuits round to all quarters during this period.

Then at last, the *D of Y* got in touch and we watched and waited for the first salvos which we saw about 10 minutes to seven o'clock, the *Scharnhorst* then being about 11 miles ahead of us.

During this agonising period, everyone below was wondering what was going on. All I could tell them was that the *Duke* was in the right place and would cut her off if she went on. I didn't tell them that, during the last hour or so, we were by ourselves and had she turned round it would have been a hot corner for us!

Phase III

"The *Duke of York* has opened fire" – that sent a thrill through the ship when I was able to broadcast it at last.

Scharnhorst immediately turned to the eastward and went off at her best speed. That enabled us to close the range again as we watched the flashes and salvos of the two big ships, and those of *Jamaica* the cruiser with the *Duke*.

At about seven o'clock *Scharnhorst* opened fire again at us and we turned to a parallel course firing ourselves when good opportunities offered.

It was now of course quite dark and although our latest gadgets enable us to fire 'blind' this is with only limited accuracy and a short range and the *Duke* never got closer than 5 or 6 miles. Would she get a hit that would reduce *Scharnhorst*'s speed? That was the question.

Over an hour this action went on, both ships firing quite slowly owing to the difficult conditions – whether the *Scharnhorst* was hit during this period I don't know – the *Duke* wasn't except for a chip off one mast. Slowly the *Scharnhorst* increased the range with her superior speed and our hearts fell as it seemed that she might get away.

The German battleship Scharnhorst. (Getty Images)

At about 8.20 both ships ceased fire and the day seemed lost, but the Commander-in-Chief had sent in his destroyers to attack and had only stopped firing as they closed. At 8.30 *Scharnhorst* opened fire again with every weapon she had, in every direction, and another thrilling moment when I was able to broadcast – "The Destroyers are now attacking".

PHASE IV

The *Scorpion*, *Savage*, *Saumarez* and *Stordt* (Norwegian) were the four destroyers with the C-in-C, and they made a gallant attack in face of very heavy fire and got at least three torpedo hits which slowed the *Scharnhorst* and allowed the *Duke* to close the range. It was not long then before I was able to announce "The *Scharnhorst* is on fire" as the *Duke*'s 14 inch guns soon turned her into a blazing wreck once the range was short enough for her to see the enemy.

Scharnhorst put up a gallant fight – firing airguns to the end – *Jamaica* was then ordered to sink her with torpedoes, and at about 9.30 we fired three torpedoes, one of which we claim to have hit, and this was the last hit as she turned over and sank.

So went down the last of the German's fast armoured ships that was in a fit state to go to sea. The Destroyers closed and rescued survivors, I don't know how many but from those we saw on rafts etc in the water I should say that it was less than 100.

It was about 11 o'clock before we finally left the scene. So for some 12 hours we had been keyed up to the top pitch by a sequence of thrilling events. We still had to keep alert that night as *Scharnhorst* may have had Destroyers in the area or an air attack might arrive as we were only some 50 miles from the enemy occupied Norwegian bases. However, we got some food about midnight and the sailors their tot of rum and so ended an eventful day.

THE ADVERSARIES
German

Scharnhorst (Kapitän zur See Hintze), flagship of Rear-Admiral Bey.
Battle cruiser, 26,000 tons, 9 × 11 in., 12 × 5·9 in.

6 *Narvik Destroyers: Fleet Destroyers, 4 × 5·9 in., 8 × 21 in. torpedoes, 38 knots.*

Z–29 (Kapitän zur See Johanneson) 4th Destroyer Flottilla Leader Z–30, Z–33, Z–34 and Z–38

British
Force Two (Admiral Bruce Fraser)
   Duke of York (Captain The Hon. Guy Russell RN)
   Battleship, 35,000 tons, 10 × 14 in., 16 × 5·25 in.
   Jamaica Cruiser, 9 × 6 in., 8 × 4 in., 6 × 21 in. torpedoes
Destroyer Screen
1st. Sub-Division
   Savage (Commander Meyrick) Divisional Leader. 4 × 4·7 in., 8 × 21 in. torpedoes, 32 knots
   Saumarez
   Scorpion
2nd. Sub-Division
   Stord (Norwegian)
Force One (CS 10. Vice-Admiral Burnett in Belfast)
   Belfast *(Captain F. R. Parham) 12 × 6 in., 12 × 4 in., 6 × 21 in. torpedoes*

Norfolk 8 × 8 in., 8 × 4 in., 3 × 21 in. torpedoes
Sheffield 12 × 6 in., 8 × 4 in., 6 × 21 in. torpedoes
Destroyer Screen (36th Division)
71st. Sub-Division
   Matchless 6 × 4·7 in. (twins) 33 knots
   Musketeer (Commander Fisher) Divisional Leader 6 × 4·7 in.
   (twins) 33 knots
72nd. Sub-Division
   Opportune 4 × 4·7 in. All 8 × 21 in. torpedoes, 32 knots
Convoy Escort JWB5B
   Onslow (Captain McCoy) D 17 with 9 assorted destroyers,
   1 minesweeper, 2 corvettes
Convoy Escort RA55A
   Milne (Captain Campbell) with 6 assorted destroyers,
   1 minesweeper, 3 corvettes (1 Norwegian)

SINKING THE *TIRPITZ* – OPERATION *TUNGSTEN*

The *Belfast* was part of the fleet that put the *Tirpitz* out of action in Altenfjord, Norway, when on 3 April 1944, 42 Barracudas from the carriers 140 miles (225km) away with attendant fighter protection attacked and rendered her inoperable. After a number of follow-up attacks, the final attack by RAF Lancasters on 12 November 1944 damaged her to such an extent that she capsized and was never a threat again.

1944 – D-DAY LANDINGS

Belfast, flying the flag of R Adm Frederick Dalrymple-Hamilton, was the headquarters ship of Force E, part of the invasion force of France spearheaded by the Normandy D-Day coastal assaults. Her task was to bombard the resisting enemy forces and support the British and Canadian landings on Gold and Juno beaches. *Belfast* sailed from the River Clyde, arriving off the Normandy coast early on 6 June – without the Prime Minister, Winston Churchill, who only abandoned the idea of sailing in *Belfast* after the personal intervention of King George VI. Bad weather delayed the start until 6 June when at 5.30am *Belfast* opened fire on a German artillery battery at Ver-sur-Mer (poignantly ten miles from Bayeux, of tapestry fame), suppressing the guns until they were captured by the Green Howards, the 7th battalion of British infantry. On 12 June *Belfast* supported Canadian troops moving inland from Juno Beach and returned to Portsmouth on 16 June to replenish her ammunition. She returned two days later for further bombardment. However, during the night of 6 July German E-Boats tried to attack and *Belfast* weighed anchor and hid behind a smoke screen. With the fighting front now beyond *Belfast*'s gun range she sailed for Scapa on 10 July. Her 6in. guns had fired 1,996 rounds.

Adm Ramsey was the commander-in-chief of the Allied Naval Expeditionary Force that took the Normandy beaches during D-Day. This was his message to the sailors involved.

SPECIAL ORDER OF THE DAY ISSUED TO EACH OFFICER AND MAN OF THE ALLIED NAVAL EXPEDITIONARY FORCE

It is to be our privilege to take part in the greatest amphibious operation in history – a necessary preliminary to the opening of the western front in Europe which in conjunction with the great Russian advance, will crush the fighting power of Germany. This is the opportunity which we have long awaited and which must be seized and pursued with relentless determination: the hopes and prayers of the free world and of the enslaved people of Europe will be with us and we cannot fail them. Our task, in conjunction with merchant navies of the united nations, and supported by the allied forces, is to carry the allied expeditionary force to the continent, to establish it there in a secure bridgehead and to build it up and maintain it at a rate which will outmatch that of the enemy.

Let no one underestimate the magnitude of the task. The Germans are desperate and will resist fiercely until we out-manoeuvre and out-fight them, which we can and will do. To every one of you will be given the opportunity to show by his determination and resource that dauntless spirit of resolution which individually strengthens and inspires and which, collectively, is irresistible.

I count on every man to do his utmost to ensure the success of this great enterprise which is the climax of the European war.

Good luck to you all and god speed.

(Signed) B. H. Ramsey ADMIRAL
ALLIED NAVAL COMMANDER-IN-CHIEF EXPEDITIONARY
FORCE

*Winston Churchill reluctantly agreed that he would not go on board
HMS* Belfast *for the D-Day landings after King George VI had written
the letter shown here to him personally, but that HMS* Belfast *should be
given the privilege of opening the bombardment. There is, however, some
controversy over this as it is believed that another ship opened fire just
before, by mistake.*

Buckingham Palace
June 2nd 1944

My Dear Winston,

I want to make one more appeal to you not to go to sea on D-Day.
Please consider my own position. I am a younger man than you, I
am a sailor, and as King I am the Head of all three Services. There
is nothing I would like better than to go to sea, but I have agreed to
stay at home; is it fair that you should then do exactly what I should
have liked to do myself?

You said yesterday afternoon that it would be a fine thing for
the King to lead his troops into battle, as in the old days; if the King
cannot do this, it does not seem to be right that his Prime Minister
should take his place. Then there is your own position. You will see
very little, you will run a considerable risk, you will be inaccessible
at a critical time, when vital decisions might have to be taken, and
however unobtrusive you may be, your presence on board is bound
to be a very heavy additional responsibility to the Admiral and
Captain.

As I said in my previous letter, your being there would add
immeasurably to my anxieties, and your being there without
consulting your colleagues in the Cabinet would put them in a very
difficult position, which they would justifiably resent.

I ask you most earnestly to consider the whole question again, and not let your personal wishes, which I very well understand, lead you to depart from your own high standard of duty to the state.

Believe me,

Your very sincere Friend
George R.I.

This 'Report on the Meteorological Implications in the selection of the day for the Allied Invasion of France June 1944' shows the dilemma facing the supreme allied commander, Gen Dwight Eisenhower, and his staff over when to give the order for the D-Day landings. HMS Belfast, *as the directing ship for the landings on Juno and Gold beaches, was directly affected by this decision.*

Declassified 1976
POA D.S. STNUSCOU.
U.S.O. HMIG
REPORT
ON THE METEOROLOGICAL IMPLICATIONS IN THE SELECTION OF THE DAY FOR THE ALLIED INVASION OF FRANCE JUNE 1944.
(iii) <u>Decision to proceed on 6th June</u>.

As regards the decision to proceed with the plan after 24 hours' postponement on the basis of a meteorological forecast presented on Sunday evening, 4th June, Section VII (a), shows that the actual conditions in the hours immediately preceding and following the time of landings, though not the ideal or even the complete minimum requirements, were decidedly better than those on the preceding and succeeding nights.

The surface wind, and therefore the sea roughness, had moderated during Monday evening; and the amount of the cloud and the height of its base at various times of the night and early morning were such as to allow all phases of the assault to be carried out according to plan.

In particular, the conditions for airborne landings were somewhat better than forecast in that the cloud ceiling was at the unusual height of 4000–5000 feet; and by the time the heavy bombers were due to operate, the cloud was sufficiently broken to allow use of visual technique. The medium and fighter bombers were not hampered, nor were the spotting aircraft. The wind conditions on the beaches were within the limits set, though the sea and surf still suffered from the stronger winds of Sunday and Monday.

That the weather deteriorated again during Tuesday and continued poor into Wednesday could not have surprised the Supreme Commander and his Staff; considerable emphasis was put on this deterioration at the meetings leading to the final decision (Section V).

Belfast's War Diary: D-Day June/July 1944

June 6-9	Bombardment—assault support
June 12	Area JUNO, bombarding with *Diadem*, p.m. Withdrew to sail for Portsmouth
June 16	Ammunitioning at Portsmouth
June 18	Sails from Portsmouth for JUNO area
	Bombarding
June 19	The Great Gale
June 22	Overlord threatened—Mulberry harbour justifies itself
June 23	Bombarding
June 30	Bombarding with *Rodney* and *Argonaut*
July 6	Bombarding in JUNO area with *Emerald*, *Roberts* (monitor) and *Danae*
	Danger from human torpedoes and explosive motor boats, and oyster mines
July 8	Montgomery begins offensive and breaks out from Caen. *Belfast*, *Roberts*, *Rodney* bombarding in support
July 10	At sea
July 12	Arrives Scapa Flow

WARTIME MEMORIES OF HMS *BELFAST*

Canada arranged to take over the Cruiser "HMS Uganda" after repairs, and provided a trained crew to man it. I was part of a draft of "all ranks" sent to the Royal Navy for training on cruisers. I joined HMS *Belfast*, my first ship in November 1943, and became a crane driver. My Action Station was in "B" Shell Room.

The ship had two cranes in 1943, originally fitted to recover the Walrus aircraft after landing alongside.

The cranes were fitted just forward of the 4" guns. The operating platforms were about eight feet above the deck. In December, on our way to Murmansk, we anchored in Seydisfjord, Iceland, and I spent a forenoon watch on the crane. It was very cold with a strong wind and a six-foot swell. A boat came alongside, with an injured man in a basket stretcher who needed medical treatment. The crane had a heavy hook, and with the boat bouncing about, I was concerned that the hook might drop onto the stretcher, but the boat's crew managed to get the stretcher's sling onto the hook and I got the casualty onboard safely. I was chilled to the bone, and when relieved, I was late getting below for lunch. A 3-badge AB asked me where I had been, and when I told him, he handed me his rum issue and said, "Here, you need this more than I do". That was my first taste of rum and it lit a fire in my belly, which warmed me up. I do not remember the AB's name, but I've never forgotten his kindness.

In the Kola Inlet, Murmansk, I went ashore with some lads and we went up into the hills where we met two Russian soldiers on skis. A shipmate said as I was a Canadian I must know how to ski, and they wanted a demonstration. For the price of a few cigarettes, one soldier gave me his skis. The harness was quite primitive, with a strap over the toe and one around the heel. They were suitable only for cross-country skiing but the lads insisted that I go down the hill. At the bottom was a group of Petty Officers. I had a good fast run downhill, but at the bottom I tripped on sticky snow and collided with the group. They cursed me "for being a daft Colonial" but I think my shipmates thought it was hilarious and the Russians had a big grin when I returned the skis.

Russia was paying the Allies for raw materials in gold bullion. Before we left Russia, a barge came alongside and I picked up many boxes of gold bars. I remember these made a large pile on deck. When I visited the ship recently, I learned that the shipment amounted to 17 tons. At today's price, $1420 per ounce, the value would have been $772,480.000.00

During the Battle of the North Cape with SCHARNHORST, action in the shell rooms was hectic keeping the shell rings full while the guns were firing, but slack when the guns were still. An Officer on the bridge kept the crew informed about the battle. He told us the ship was making a torpedo attack. We would hear the Torpedo Officer giving the order to fire, and if we counted to 18, we would hear the result. I was sitting on the deck, leaning against the bulkhead, while counting. I heard two very distinct "bumps", which I'm sure were two hits. The ship reversed course to bring our other tubes to bear, but the SCHARNHORST was gone.

On D-Day, the Allies made their landings in Normandy and BELFAST was there to fire on the coastal defences. As the troops moved inland, the ship sent a signalman to work with the Army as a spotter, and to report the coordinates of targets, i.e. tanks, trucks, troop concentrations, for BELFAST to engage with broadsides. After several weeks, the beach was covered in debris. Shore parties from ships were sent to the Mulberry Harbour and on to the beach by "ducks". The "duck" I was in, pulled up on the sand to disconnect the propeller and engage the gears. I stood up on the back of it to get a view when the "duck" jerked forward and I "landed in France on the seat of my pants". I got back on the vehicle and we were taken to an area of the beach needing a cleanup.

The Germans had a mobile gun at the northern end of the beachhead, which harassed the activity on the beach and on the anchored ships. One of its shells landed in shallow water about 50 yards from us. As it exploded, we prostrated ourselves and the shrapnel rattled off the side of the beached landing craft behind us.

Later when our section of the beach was clean, I walked up to the village and looked into one of the houses. There was an open window facing the beach, and on the windowsill lay five rounds of rifle ammunition. The bullets were made of wood and dyed in different colours. I had no idea what they were used for, and I've never seen any reference to this type of ammunition.

When our guns were no longer required to support the troops, BELFAST returned to England. I returned to Canada for leave and then joined UGANDA on commissioning as a Canadian ship. We sailed to join the Pacific Fleet waging war against Japan.

Contributed by HMS *Belfast* Association Veteran number 661, Able Seaman R. W. Brown, Royal Canadian Navy (from *Seahorse Magazine*, summer 2011).

CHAPTER 3

 HMS *Belfast*'s time in the tropics

HMS *BELFAST*'S REFIT: SUNDERLAND JULY 1944 TO 18 APRIL 1945

On Belfast's arrival in the Tyne, Capt Parham, after nearly two strenuous years in command, handed over on 29 July to Capt R. M. Dick, CBE, DSC, RN, who was to command her over the next two years.

In addition to improving her accommodation for the tropics, the object of the refit carried out by the Middle Dock and High Shields Engineering Company was to modernise her with the latest weapons and fire control, in particular for defence against the Japanese 'suicide-planes', the kamikazes, although in the event Japan finally surrendered on 15 August after Hitler had shot himself in his Berlin bunker and the dropping of two atomic bombs.

In April 1945 Belfast carried out sea trials after completion of her nine-month refit.

MAY 1945: RECORD OF ALTERATIONS AND ADDITIONS
4 in. HA Armament
S3 and P3 mountings removed. Remaining Mountings S1, S2, P1, P2, modified to Remote Power Control (RPC). Auto-Selector-Alignment was fitted to the HACS Mark IV Tables.

Pom-Poms
2 x eight-barrelled Mark VIII guns on Mark VI mountings. RP10 (Remote Power Controlled). One each side of mainmast on Pom-pom deck controlled by: 2 Pom-pom Directors, Mark IV with Gyro Rate Units Mark 1 + Type 282 radar, mounted on sponsons high up on the forward edge of the after funnel.

4 x four-barrelled Mark VIII guns on Mark VII mountings, RP50, sited each side:

1 forward edge of Pom-pom deck, just abaft for'd funnel.

1 abreast after HADT on after superstructure controlled by:

4 Pom-pom Directors Mark IV with Gyro Rate Units Mark I and Type 282 radar, sited each side: 1 on sponsons, just aft of the for'd Pom-pom mounting on Pom-pom deck, 1 on after superstructure in sponsons forward of the after HADT.

20 mm. Oerlikons

Twelve twin mountings fitted and re-sited as follows:

6 x Twin Mark V 20 mm. powered-mountings with tachymetric sights
6 newly designed hand-worked mountings with tachymetric sights
These six twin mountings were sited as follows:

1 lower bridge wings.

1 lower bridge, after corners, to replace 44 in. searchlights which were landed with the after pair.

1 B gun deck, 1 abreast forward funnel, 1 abreast after funnel, 1 on quarterdeck (2 mountings abreast of each other).

In addition, two single Mark VII mountings were sited one each side of the after superstructure, in protected sponsons.

Magazine stowage was enlarged.

Radar

In May 1945 she carried:

Type	242—IFF	
„	243—IFF	
„	253	IFF
„	277	AA Height-finding and surface warning
„	281	Air warning
„	282	Pom-pom Directors and blind barrage
„	283	
„	274	6 in. Armament
„	285	HA
„	293Q	Close range height-finding and surface warning.

44 in. Searchlights: all landed
Aircraft: Hangar converted into recreation and accommodation spaces
Catapult: removed
DCT Rangefinder: for bombardment use only
Damage Control Headquarters: A secondary HQ was built on the port side, below the armoured deck, on the after side of 158 bulkhead, abreast "B" boiler room
Echo Sounder: was re-sited in the bridge plotting room
Depth Charges: 6 (15 spares)
Accommodation: The "internals" of the ship were greatly modified to make the heat of the tropics more tolerable

An interesting alteration was: "To improve laundry facilities by installing a shirt press and single sleeve form."

An elementary Action Information Organisation (AIO), was introduced into the Operations Room to sift and display all visual, radar and signal information for the Command to assess the threat and act upon, previously assimilated by the Action Plot.

Oil Fuel Replenishment and Transfer at Sea
The vast sea distances at sea in the Pacific had produced the Fleet Train of the huge American Task Force. It was vital therefore that *Belfast* should be modernised to the latest developments and standards of oiling at sea and she was brought up to date during this refit.

Replenishment speed was about nine knots.

Paravanes:

6 Mark VII Bodies with:	6–31 knot planes
	2–22 knot planes
	4–16 knot planes

The Starboard paravane towed from the for'd chain.
The Port paravane towed from the after chain.

PEACETIME DUTIES

At the war's end *Belfast* still managed to do sterling work in helping to evacuate the unfortunate emaciated survivors of the Japanese prisoner of war and civilian internment camps in Shanghai. In September 1945 the officers and men organised a party for the children in the

Children of British internee survivors in Shanghai enjoying a party on board thrown by the officers and sailors of the Belfast *on 28 September 1945. This drawing shows a bosun's chair rigged as a children's slide.*

(*Image courtesy of James Morris, Getty Images*)

camps. The most popular item on the menu was chocolate, which most of the children had never tasted before; the men even searched their lockers and every last piece of chocolate was consumed. *Belfast* continued on peacekeeping duties until the autumn of 1947, when she returned home for a well-earned rest and refit.

THE KOREAN WAR

The Korean War (25 June 1950 to 27 July 1953) was fought between North Korea, with the support of China and the Soviet Union, and South Korea with the support of 21 member countries of the United Nations (UN), principally the USA but including the UK, Royal Canadian, Royal Australian and Royal New Zealand forces. Two days after North Korea invaded South Korea on 25 June 1950 the UN sent a combined NATO (North Atlantic Treaty Organization) fleet and troops in their support, while China assisted North Korea with Soviet Union help.

Korea had been ruled by Imperial Japan from 1910 until, in August 1945, the Soviet Union declared war on it. As a result it was agreed that the Soviet Union would liberate Korea north of the 38th parallel while US forces subsequently would move into the south. By 1948, as a product of the Cold War between the Soviet Union and the USA, Korea was divided into two regions with separate governments. Both claimed to be the legitimate government of all of Korea, and neither accepted the border as permanent. On 27 June, the United Nations Security Council authorised UN forces to repel a North Korean invasion.

SHIPS THAT SERVED WITH HMS *BELFAST* IN KOREAN WATERS

HMS *Belfast* was part of Britain's naval contribution to implement the UN's decision to stop the invasion of South Korea by North Korea. The size and international nature of the intervention is shown by this list in the ship's commission record of US, Dutch, New Zealand, Australian, Canadian and British warships and Republic of Korea patrol craft that operated at the same time as HMS *Belfast* in Korean waters; as did the aircraft carriers HMS *Theseus*, *Glory*, *Ocean* and HMAS *Sydney*.

USS	*Missouri*	HMNZS	*Taupo*
USS	*New Jersey*	HMNZS	*Rotoiti*
USS	*Wisconsin*	HMNZS	*Hawea*
USS	*Iowa*	HMAS	*Warramunga*
USS	*Bataan*	HMAS	*Bataan*
USS	*Rendova*	HMAS	*Sydney*
USS	*Badoeing Strait*	HMAS	*Murchison*
USS	*Bairoko*	HMAS	*Condamine*
USS	*St. Paul*	HMAS	*Tobruk*
USS	*Toledo*	HMAS	*Anzac*
USS	*Rochester*	HMCS	*Athabaskan*
USS	*Manchester*	HMCS	*Cayuga*
USS	*Ozborn*	HMCS	*Nootka*
USS	*Lind*	HMCS	*Sioux*
USS	*Hank*	HMS	*Ceylon*
USS	*Fletcher*	HMS	*Cossack*
USS	*Apache*	HMS	*Constance*
USS	*J. A. Bole*	HMS	*Concord*
USS	*Lowry*	HMS	*Charity*
USS	*Chevalier*	HMS	*Consort*
USS	*Gurke*	HMS	*Comus*
USS	*Shelton*	HMS	*Cockade*
USS	*Porterfield*	HMS	*Kenya*
USS	*Eversole*	HMS	*Theseus*
USS	*Hanna*	HMS	*Glory*
USS	*Collett*	HMS	*Ocean*
USS	*Colohan*	HMS	*Cardigan Bay*
USS	*Hanson*	HMS	*Whitesand Bay*

USS	McDermott	HMS	St. Bride's Bay
USS	Wantuek	HMS	Morecambe Bay
USS	Sicily	HMS	Mount's Bay
USS	H. W. Tucker	HMS	Amethyst
USS	Brush	HMS	Alacrity
USS	Current	HMS	Crane
USS	Swallow	HMS	Unicorn
USS	Hart.	RFA	Wave Sovereign
USS	Kimberley	RFA	Wave Baron
HMNS	Evertsen	RFA	Wave Chief
HMNS	Van Galen	RFA	Wave Premier
HMNS	Piet Hein	RFA	Green Ranger
HMNZS	Tutira	RFA	Brown Ranger

Various LSTs, LSMRs etc. and Patrol Craft of the ROK Navy.

BREAKING NEWS
Conrad Jenkin, who was to become a rear admiral, but at the time was the sub-lieutenant in charge of the gunroom as well as foc'sle divisional officer and 6" gun control officer of HMS Belfast *in the 1950–52 commission, recounts the moment* Belfast *heard they were at war with Korea.*

In late June 1950, HMS *Belfast* was anchored in Hakodate in northern Japan, nearing the end of a cruise round that country. As the Sub of the Gunroom, responsible for the dozen or so Midshipmen on board, I had been invited one evening to dine with the Admiral, Rear Admiral Andrewes, Flag Officer Second in Command Far East Fleet (who retired in 1957 as Admiral Sir William 'Bill' Andrewes KBE CB DSO). He was flying his flag on board and was dining with the Commanding Officer, the Captain, Sir Aubrey St Clair Ford Bt DSO RN. There we all were, dressed in our formal evening uniform 'bum-freezers', seated round the great polished table covered with silver and all the bits and pieces of a smart naval dinner and with stewards hovering in the background, when there was a knock on the door and a signalman walked in, clutching a bit of paper in his hand. Looking slightly flustered, he walked to the end of the table where the Admiral was sitting and handed him the bit of paper; the Admiral read it – and read it again – and then looked up at the rest of us and said "Gentlemen, we are at war with North Korea".

We sailed the following day, preparing for war; all the guns were readied, the big 6" and the smaller 4", ammunition was fuzed and off we went south, awaiting our orders. Only days later we found ourselves off the east coast of North Korea bombarding their trains as they emerged from tunnels, hoping to hit them before they disappeared into the next tunnel. As the 6" Control Officer high above the Bridge, I remember feeling it all quite exciting though for the life of me, I don't remember ever hitting one.

Personal experiences

These extracts are taken from Rear Admiral J.L. Blackham, C.B., D.L. Memoirs Of A Naval Life and recall his experiences as the then commander (second-in-command) of HMS Belfast between his joining in June 1951 and leaving on 26 November 1952 during the Korean War. This was the same period as that covered by Alasdair Paton, whose extracts from his midshipman's journal are printed later on, after both transited in the troopship Dilwara. His memoirs were left by him to the Royal Naval Museum in Portsmouth, and these extracts are recounted with the kind permission of his son, V Adm Sir Jeremy Blackham KCB.

I finally left England in May 1951 in Her Majesty's Transport "Dilwara", a British-India passenger liner commandeered for war service, where I found myself designated Officer Commanding Naval Draft, and so entitled to a cabin to myself which was quite a luxury for a relatively junior officer in a trooper. It was not an arduous task, keeping an eye on a body of about 120 sailors and a dozen officers, and accompanying the ship's Captain on his daily rounds of the ship every forenoon. We had no trouble from our charges and arrived without event in Singapore, where I joined "Belfast", which had just completed a docking and short refit period.

Our Captain was Sir Aubrey St Clair-Ford (Bart), (8 April 1950 – 22 November 1951) a round and jolly man with a high colour in his face, so that he was widely known by a nickname, "Aubrey Strawberry"!

I relieved the Commander, W.W. Fitzroy, who left the day I arrived, and I found myself very much alone in my first seagoing job as a Commander. I well remember my first day, when I "cleared lower deck" to show myself to the ship's company and give them a short speech on my philosophy for conduct and discipline. Most of them had already done a period in Korea, so I could not tell them what they were in for, however it seemed to go down alright, and I set about the task of getting to know my way around the ship and, equally important, getting to know as many of the ship's company as I could by name.

We had a couple of days in Hong Kong for fuel and food, and I was happy to find my old friend "Jenny" and employ her again, with her girls as our "side party", with a promise that she would do so whenever we came back to Hong Kong, for "R and R", *(rest and recreation)*, and then we went on to Sasebo in Japan.

We had three cruisers, also two light fleet aircraft carriers, and a number of destroyers, frigates and minesweepers, some of them from Canada, Australia and New Zealand, as part of the United Nations Force under whose authority we were to operate. On arrival in Sasebo we embarked Rear Admiral A.K. Scott-Moncrieff, the Flag Officer 2nd-in-command, Far East Station, and became his flagship for the duration of our time out there.

The general plan was that the U.S. Navy operated on the East coast of Korea, while the Royal Navy operated on the West coast. At that time, the war between North and South Korea had settled down to something of a stalemate along the 38th parallel line. On the West side of the mainland there was a considerable British Army force sited on the 38th parallel between the rival warring armies, and we used to have some contact with them when we visited Inchon. For example we used to invite some officers and soldiers to fly down to spend a few days on board and enjoy the luxury of baths and good food, both of which were lacking where they were stationed.

The broad picture was that South Korea had been invaded by Communist North Korea, and the United Nations had intervened to stop the conflict, an artificial intelligence frontier having been established on the 38th parallel, right across the country. Allied military forces had become established on this boundary, but there were frequent skirmishes along this line between North and South Korean forces. There were, of course, main railway and road supply lines coming from the north, and a number of military dumps and areas within our operational area.

On the 38th parallel, but about eight miles from the coast, i.e. outside territorial waters, were two islands called respectively Paengnyong-Do and Taecheong-Do, both uninhabited by Koreans. On the former was established an American Marine detachment. These were under the command of a U.S. Marine Major by the name of "Ehrghott". His detachment's task was to gather intelligence of North Korean Army formations and movements on the mainland in this area. In this context the code name for this officer was "Leopard", by which he was generally known in conversation or signals. One of the means by which this was achieved was by landing individual officers, perhaps accompanied by a South Korean interpreter, to make undercover reports on these matters, either by radio or by personal report on return.

One of our regular activities was to carry out frequent bombardments, with our 5 inch guns, up to ten miles inland from the light fleet carrier advised by "HMS Leopard", and using Fleet Air Arm aircraft from the light fleet carrier always on station about 30 miles to seaward of us. In fact there was no air opposition in our area, so we had no worries on that score.

However the rumour began to circulate among our sailors that we were just choosing village targets from the chart, and bombarding and killing unarmed families! In fact I had several sailors who believed this, who were members of turrets' crews or down in the magazines supplying the shells to the guns, and who refused duty for this reason. They were, of course, brought before me charged with refusing duty, a crime for which I should have considered drastic individual and unpleasant retribution. They were all young men, and I knew severe punishment would not stifle this rumour. On the other hand I could not tell them in detail about the underground system of intelligence I have described for fear that they might talk ashore in their cups and so endanger the lives of undercover men! And so I had to indicate that we had, from American secret intelligence sources, knowledge of real military targets, and asked them if they would be averse to being the crew of our 4 inch anti-aircraft guns, which we manned in case of attack on us! They all agreed gladly, and so it was arranged. But I warned them that any further spreading of the rumour would be regarded by me as a serious offence and dealt with "by the book". Luckily, about 10 days later, we were called upon to rush up by night well north of the 38th parallel, into the mouth of the Yalu River, to bring off one of these brave young men for whom the area was getting too hot to be healthy. And by the time we got back to South Korean waters and returned him to "Leopard" the story had gone round the ship, and my action with the "Doubting Thomas's" seemed to have been warmly approved by the lower deck as being wise and compassionate! We had no further trouble of this sort.

Then I did a very foolish thing! About 2 a.m. I went out alone onto the port waist to see if the quarterdeck awning, stowed overhead there, was secure. I had hardly arrived when a vast wave came crashing down onto the deck, picked me up and carried me over the side! I thought I was lost, for even if anyone had seen or heard my shout there was no chance of my being picked up. However, by some miracle the wave carried me aft and burst inboard over the quarterdeck, dumping me there up against the guard rails, from where, somewhat bruised and very wet, I managed to get back inside and find my way to my cabin! I ascribe this miracle to the fact that I had my son's "birth caul" with me, it being well known that such a talisman is a sure preventative against a ship sinking! I have it still.

At the beginning of October we had a change from our normal routine by going up the East Coast of Korea to join up with the American 7th Fleet. And again we had our Commander-in-Chief on board for the trip. En route there we carried out a dawn bombardment at 0600, to try and damage a vital railway supply line, and we had a spotter aircraft provided by a U.S. Carrier. All was going well when to our surprise we got a message from the spotter to say "Hang about a few minutes, there's a thing I've got to do!" And about ten minutes later he came up again with "Whoopee! I just saw a train coming out of a tunnel and went straight in to bomb it! It must have been an ammunition train, I guess, for it blew up with a giant explosion and brought down the tunnel entrance! Over to you again!" Our gunnery officer was angry at the improper conduct of his bombardment programme, but most of us felt the pilot had earned a few "Brownie Points" for his initiative and prompt action. And so on to Wonsan, which is about 70 miles north of the 38th parallel, where we joined up with the U.S. 7th Fleet. Wonsan is a very large bay about 12 miles across and some 5 miles deep. The main supply railway line runs along the coast here and not far away are a series of ammunition dumps and North Korean Army camps, so plenty of targets for our bombardments. These took place under way, in an operation known colloquially as the "Wonsan War Dance", where we all formed a circle and went round and round the bay bombarding as we went, and with our spotter aircraft working with us. It was not very exciting.

This War dance routine went on for three or four days, by which time we were heartily sick of it, and I felt sorry for the Americans who had to go on doing it over and over again!

Meanwhile we had a new Captain, Captain A.C.A.C. Duckworth RN (23 November 1951 – 26 November 1952) known, for some reason I never discovered, as "Bronnie". A very different proposition from Aubrey-Strawberry St. Clair-Ford, being reserved and serious most of the time, and it was a bit of a cultural shock to both officers and men to get used to him.

Only a few days later, still in Yokosuka, we had a visit by the Vice-President of the United States, Mr Alben W. Barkley, who was paying a flying visit to Japan, accompanied by two American Rear Admirals. He stayed with us only for a couple of hours and made no public appearance to the ship's company, but at least Admiral Scott-Moncrieff was able to tell him that the Royal Navy was pulling its weight in Korea!

So followed another trip up the West coast, which gave rise to an incident which woke us all up a bit. In the absence of an opposition from the enemy we had become rather casual about our habits when we were at Paengyong-Do, some six miles from the mainland, and on this occasion were at anchor, with two destroyers in line ahead, between the island and the coast. On these occasions it was our custom to be at a lower state of readiness, what we called "Cruising Stations", so we had only a couple of guns manned, and very reduced Damage Control parties on watch, but at instant notice for steam. It was a Sunday afternoon and I was in fact lying on my bunk resting when I heard the sound of gunfire followed by an explosion on our starboard side further forward, and then "Action Stations" sounded. I rushed forward to find one of our lower messdecks had a large hole in the ship's side, the messdeck was on fire and several bodies lying about. By the time I had the fire out we had slipped our anchor cable and were steaming out of range of the shore battery which had been firing on us, but sadly, although there were very few men on the messdeck, two of them, both Chinese, were killed outright. Needless to say we changed our habitat.

Not long after this we were summoned by radio to enter the Han River estuary, just a little north of the 38th parallel, where it was reported there had been a skirmish between North and South forces, and that there were quite a few wounded on each side. We anchored about 1½ miles up the river, and received on board some twenty-five sailors, some from each side, in a collection of motley uniforms with no identification buttons, and as we had not had enough room for them in our sick bay, we converted the torpedo space on the upper deck centre line as a first aid station, trying, with the aid of an English speaking Korean, to separate the South from the North armies by putting them on opposite sides of the compartment with a few of our sailors as sentries between them. Some were quite badly wounded, indeed two or three of them died. We found it difficult to distinguish between the sides, but not so the Koreans themselves, who knew which was which, and in spite of their wounds tried at every opportunity to scramble over and attack one of their enemies. The sentries were kept quite busy keeping them apart.

We arrived in Hong Kong early in December 1951 and it was at once as though we were back in peacetime. The ever faithful "Jenny" and her side party girls were waiting to take our headrope to the flagship buoy.

By now a really cold winter was upon us, and in February we went up the West Coast of Korea where we ran into pack ice which got progressively worse the further north we went until there was ice as far as the eye could see. And when it rained or snowed, and it did both, the capstan and anchor cable were frozen solid and the guardrails had a mass of icicles hanging from them. It was no fun for gun's crews, lookouts or the watchkeepers on the open bridge, and we had to set up a permanent team, armed with chipping hammers, to keep the ice clear, partly to ensure the anchors were free of ice and could be let go in emergency, and also for fear we got top heavy and became unstable. Luckily the sea did not freeze solid, and we were able to steam around with care not to damage our propeller on the small bergs.

We had in company with us the Dutch destroyer "Piet Hein" who took a bump on her starboard side while fuelling, making quite a hole in the side above the waterline. It seemed she had not got the equipment to repair herself, so we took her alongside, cut out a hole about six feet square, and welded in a new patch. I still have photographs which show it was rather a neat job, and it was much appreciated by the Dutch... Not long after this we had the news that we were to be relieved by HMS "Birmingham", and I began a correspondence with her Commander to persuade him to take on from us our Wardroom Messman and his Chinese staff, our Chinese "dhobey" firm and, by no means least, our faithful Jenny and her "side party" girls.

But many years later, when we handed over Hong Kong to the Chinese on termination of our 99 year lease of the New Territories in the summer of 1997, someone proposed that "Jenny" whose real name was Mrs Ng Muk-Kah! be gazetted in the Honours List with the reward of the British Empire Medal (B.E.M.), in recognition of her service to the Royal Navy of over 60 years! There must be thousands of naval officers and ratings who remember her with affection and who, like me, were delighted that she should be so honoured.

On our return home, after about half an hour, we found Jill, aged not quite 8, obviously rather cross about something, and it turned out she had found a photograph of me surrounded by Jenny and her side-party girls! She obviously did not really believe my explanation, and this had a sequel the next day at her school, for when her teacher asked her what I had been doing in Korea she replied "I don't know, but he had a party of girls on the side".

A final incident happened as I was leaving the ship by boat for the last time which gave me much pleasure. The sailor on the sternsheets of the boat said to me, apropos of nothing in particular, "You know Sir, when you joined us at Singapore we didn't know what to make of you, and we thought you might be a soft touch and pretty unpopular! But we found that you were not soft, but fair, and you learned our names and would talk to us when we met. May I tell you that you earned the respect and affection of most of us on the lower deck!" or words to that effect. This was probably the nicest moment of my time in "Belfast".

'Tiger' was Belfast's *mascot in the early 1950s.*

Alasdair Paton trained in HMS Belfast *as a Midshipman from 1 May 1951 to 7 May 1952, with three weeks' aircraft carrier experience in HMS* Glory *in early 1952. This extract sent by his wife, Joy Paton, is from his midshipman's journal and gives his impressions on joining one of the Royal Navy's 'big ships'; impressions from a different perspective from those recorded in the memoirs of his commander, Cdr Joseph Blackham.*

IMPORTANT NOTE.
This is a SECRET document during Hostilities. Instructions for the disposal of Journals are given in A.F.O 405/40 paragraph 2 and A.F.O. 1039/40.

S.519.— Revised, March , 1927

JOURNAL
FOR THE USE OF
MIDSHIPMEN.

Mr. ALASDAIR R. PATON

H.M.S. "BELFAST"	FROM 1ST MAY 1951	TO
CAPTAIN SIR AUBREY ST CLAIR-FORD	(left Friday 23rd November 1951)	
BART. DSO AND BAR, R.N.		
H.M.S. "BELFAST"	FROM	TO 21ST FEBRUARY 1952
CAPTAIN A.C.A.C. DUCKWORTH DSO, DSC, R.N.	(Joined Friday 23rd November 1951)	
H.M.S. "GLORY"	FROM 21ST FEBRUARY 1952 TO 4TH MARCH 1952	
CAPTAIN COLOQUHOUN. DSO, R.N.		
H.M.S. "BELFAST"	FROM 4th MARCH 1952	TO 7th MAY 1952

Tuesday 29 May
I arrived at Singapore late this evening on board the troopship "DILWARA". There were three other midshipmen bound for H.M.S. "BELFAST" as well, and it was not until this evening that we learned from her new commander – Commander Blackham, who travelled out in the "DILWARA" that she was undergoing a refit at the naval dockyards on Singapore island.

Wednesday 30 May
The following morning we joined the ship. We were met by the sub. of the gunroom, Sub Lieutenant Berger. He introduced us to our 'nurse', Lieutenant-Commander Ogilvie, who gave us until the end of the week to get to know the ship. Berger conducted the initial tour

and then we were left to ourselves to explore the ship. With the aid of a much tattered and out of date blue print of the ship we soon began to get our bearings. Compared with the spacious new H.M.S. "DEVONSHIRE", the ship seemed to be cramped, a maze of small compartments and narrow passages altogether bewildering. This impression was heightened by the chaotic state caused by the refit. The funnels were being dipped and repainted, the superstructure was also being dipped and coated with zinc chromate. The turrets and 4" mountings were being treated in the same way. The top of A turret had been removed to facilitate the dismantling of the barrels and the replacement by new ones. The ship swarmed with Chinese and Indians.

Thursday 31st May

We were told our divisions and various duties. Chandler and I found that we were in Forecastle division, and we went to our part of the ship where we found the second captain of top, P.O. Hack. He showed us round the various lockers and wire stowages. The arrangement was much simpler than on "DEVONSHIRE", all wires and hawsers being kept together as much as possible, mostly on 'B' gun deck.

In the morning we were introduced to the Captain, Captain Sir Aubrey St Clair Ford Bart., D.S.O and bar R.N. He told us that he was glad that, except for our time in an aircraft carrier, we would be serving continuously in the "BELFAST", as that would mean uninterrupted training.

The ship was going into the King George VI dock at 0720 next morning, so in the afternoon we went across to the dock to see the preparations. The blocks were laid ready, and on the floor of the dock was marked with the stem and stern positions of the "BELFAST". It was interesting to note that the stern position of the French warship "Duguay Troin" was also marked down. The dock is the largest one East of Suez, and is capable of docking the Queens.

The blocks were laid in three rows. A long one to support the keel, with a space near the bows to allow for the asdic dome, and a small row either side to support the ship's waist.

Pylon-like structures were placed at intervals along what was going to be the starboard side. These held the blocks which kept the ship upright. The blocks on the port side were supported by the dock wall itself.

Saturday 2nd June

We still kept exploring the ship. Viewed from the boatdeck, the converted hangars have given the back of the bridge the appearance of a sheer precipice. I was struck by the smallness of the actual bridge, but I suppose the gun direction platform can be used for normal lookouts etc. It was rather a surprise to find messdecks on the bridge superstructure. I was also rather bewildered by the different number of radar sets.

HMS Belfast *returning to Portsmouth after service in Korea.*
Photo courtesy Morgan-Giles family.

THE BATTLE OF CHANGNI-DO

An example of Belfast's role in the Korean War was demonstrated in this article abstracted from HMS Belfast's Commission Record in supporting the retaking of a strategically placed island off the west North Korean coast on 15 and 16 July 1952.

Maybe the title is a bit ambitious: maybe it won't rank in the history books with Trafalgar or Bannockburn or the Field of the Cloth of Gold. But nevertheless it was quite a do, as you may remember.

There we were on the morning of the 15th, steaming along from the Haeju area to Taechong-do and, for once, quietly minding our own business, which was to oil from *Brown Ranger*.

Then suddenly—out of the blue, as the authors say—came the news that the island of Changni-do had been invaded by the enemy during the night.

We, along with *Amethyst*, immediately closed Changni-do; and then it started.

As we came in, we sighted a small boat idling a mile or so off shore, and promptly lowered the L.C.P. to investigate. The boat, we found, contained three South Koreans who during the night before had gone off on a reconnaissance of the mainland. When they returned, they had known from their reception from the beaches that these were not their life-long friends whom they had left on the island the night before. Their luck changed when we arrived to pick them up.

Having brought the boat in, Lt. Morris and his merry men pushed off again on a reconnaissance towards the island along with *Amethyst's* boat. As they nosed inshore they were met with machine-gun fire, and Marine Coffin was wounded. They returned the fire themselves with interest; but this was more than impertinence and we began to bombard—ourselves on the South side and *Amethyst* on the North. By this time, the USS *Bataan's* strike aircraft were coming in under *Belfast's* control, and between us all we gave the enemy a hot time of it.

Towards evening a battery on the mainland to the North began firing on *Amethyst*. While we were observing this with more than a little interest—another battery to the East began firing at US!

Indignantly, taking advantage of our larger guns, we got out of their probable range, and let them have it.

The conditions, the Gunnery Officer said, were almost ideal. There was an obliging green slope up to where the flashes were coming from, and our first ranging shot made a nice brown mark, showing exactly where the shell had landed. So the G.O. merely stepped up his shots to the flashes. Anyway they stopped firing.

Early in the morning of the 16th, the island was reinvaded by friendly forces and at daylight the fun started in earnest. Strike aircraft kept coming in, and between them and our guns, the enemy had more to contend with than their immediate opponents ashore. Our gunfire was, of course, magnificent; and so also, the aircraft reported, was *Amethyst*'s. This is worth mentioning since *Amethyst* was not, after all, up some river or another at the time.

The communications—probably the most important single factor in such an operation—between shore and ship and aircraft were excellent throughout, and made a considerable contribution to the success.

Slowly the enemy was driven back, any grouping for counter-attack being dispersed by the aircraft. It was important that the island be retaken before dark, so that in the event of another night invasion, the friendly forces would not be pressed on two sides. This was accomplished. As the light began to fade, the last remnants, battered by gunfire and bombs, were being mopped up on a hill at the Northern end of the island.

As far as we were immediately concerned, the heroes were the Gunnery Officer and his guns' crews, Marine Coffin our single casualty—oh! and having read the Editorial—the *Belfast* herself.

TARCAP

Graham (Oggie) Swanson was a Sea Fury Fleet Air Arm fighter pilot based on board the aircraft carrier HMS Ocean working with HMS Belfast. His account, as this extract reveals, relates a mission incident that was focused around what was termed a 'Tarcap': an armed mission initially under the control of one of the fleet's vessels. They would spot for the ship's guns firing on their target – under and over, then bang on! Then they were released to find their own targets. But even flying on mission had its dangers.

Just 13 days later I too was shot down during a similar TARCAP. The drill for these was that the leader would dive bomb or rocket from a sixty-degree dive. As he turned away the other aircraft would attack on a ninety degree heading to the leader's. Our target was a gun emplacement on the coast of North West of 'Wales'. Bob Hallam had bombed in a southerly direction then I attacked on an easterly. Pulling up at some 300 knots after releasing my bombs the cockpit filled with red-hot 'smoke.' With canopy jettisoned I just could not get out because of the slip stream. To get rid of speed rapidly I heaved back on the stick and turned towards the sea although I could not see the instruments. Still I could not get out. Then suddenly the aircraft went into a violent spin and I was thrown out! Finger nails were lost frantically grabbing for the handle across my tummy. The 'chute opened just before my feet splashed down. Still blinded I detached and inflated the dinghy. To board, this had to be rocked to and fro to fill a balancing pocket with water. This done my feet touched bottom! Seated behind enemy lines hoping for rescue, machine gunfire made me jump back in. It was an American Corsair giving me cover. A helicopter eventually found and deposited me on HMS *Belfast*. Nurses found third-degree burns on all skin not protected by flying overalls, helmet and gloves. I can still make out the scars on wrists, ankles, face and those three right-hand glove fingers which wore out starting engines. A couple of days later I was transferred to *Ocean* by high-wire but I had missed those free drinks at follies night. Bob told me that my aircraft was on fire from nose to tail. The tail broke off and the fuselage span into the water as my 'chute opened. Probably the abnormal strain on a damaged fuselage by pulling up so violently caused this. It certainly gave me another life: more good thinking Oggie!

TALES FROM THE RECORD OF COMMISSION

Various members of Belfast*'s company wrote small essays of their experiences on board for her* Record of Commission 1950–1952. *This is a selection.*

The extent of the UK's help in the Korean War can be gauged by these impressive statistics achieved during her commission, although some are tongue in cheek!* To explain, 'Request Men' mentioned in the article are officially seen by the Captain standing at a desk usually in the Officer's Cabin Flat within the ship. The Rating, standing before him with cap removed, the Master-at-Arms and the Rating's Divisional Officer in attendance, can ask for welfare or leave considerations. A similar procedure is enacted for 'defaulters'; if a Rating is charged with disobeying orders.

We Steamed: 1950—10199 miles 1951—49534 miles 1952—37482 miles TOTAL—97035 miles

This represents an average speed of 5½ knots throughout the commission.

We ate and drank: Rum—56000 pints (½ million tots) Tea—10½ tons

Bread—250 tons Milk—208000 tins Potatoes—625 tons Meat—134 tons

We fired: 7816 rounds of 6-inch 538 rounds of 4-inch

No. of rounds fired at the radio controlled aircraft—Many.

We used: 1,000,000 sheets of signal paper: 150 miles of ticker-tape: 100 Ensigns: 200 Typewriter ribbons.

1 ocean of blood sweat and tears (The Communications Dept.)

We wrote: 8370 official letters.

The Captain saw: 1736 Request Men*.

We used 60000 tons of fuel and fuelled 96 times.

We had steam on main engines 455 days (1 yr. 3 mths. in 2 yrs. including Singapore).

An unknown voice said "P.C.O., telephone please!" 1936 times.

No. of aspirins consumed by the Captain's Secretary is confidential.

The Instructor Officer started 573 arguments and won 3.

Weather reports

The ship had her own meteorological officer, who was a 'Schoolie' or instructor officer, not just trained in education, but also in oceanography and meteorology. Weather reports were, of course, vital in war planning, but of interest to note is that a copy of the 'Climate Table of Korea, Climatological Standard Normals Part 1', published by the Central Meteorological Office, Seoul, Republic of Korea, 1968 and held by the

*Meteorological Office, Exeter contains very little data for 1950–52, and
also stated in the preface that no data from Pyongyang had been received
since 1949.*

*The barometric pressure dropped to 924 millibars when Typhoon Ruth,
category 4 with winds of up to 220km/h (140mph) hit Japan on 15
October, killing 1,294 people and destroying 34,000 buildings. The
Australian aircraft carrier HMAS Sydney lost four Sea Fury aircraft
overboard. This account gives an idea of the Belfast's experience.*

Typhoon Ruth

On Saturday 13th October, while in Sasebo, we first became anxious
about the lady called Ruth; and the Met Officer looked worried – all
of him. By early Sunday morning it looked as if she was going to
pass unpleasantly close, and along with the other ships we weighed
anchor and made for the broad open spaces. On that morning, we
sailed out in as gentle a wind and sea as ever was seen. But by the
time we were only a little way out there was already a fresh breeze,
and in little over an hour later almost a full gale and steep seas.
That's the way it seems typhoons work – suddenly and if you're
not on watch, unexpectedly: just like any other woman. We wanted
to get as far west as possible, but just before 1600 we had to heave
to so that 6-inch shells which had broken loose could be secured. I
had wondered about certain rumblings and clankings coming from
below me; but I was extremely grateful that I never knew what they
were until afterwards.

The barometer kept on falling and the wind refused to back.
That was ominous: it could mean that Ruth had changed to a more
northerly course; making a dead set at us in other words. However
at last the wind did back, and we breathed again. During the night
Belfast and *Unicorn* remained within four miles of each other, with
Athabaskan (Royal Canadian Navy tribal class destroyer) twelve
miles to the north.

That night of the 14th October was quite a thing. The best solution
was to heave to and ride it out, keeping the wind about 20 degrees
on the starboard bow. An official document – always a masterpiece
of understatement – refers to the seas as 'terrific'. The ship rolled up

to 35 degrees and the seas filled all the waists (on the upper deck, amidships) to a depth of three to four feet. Certainly to stand at the level of our Flag Deck and look at wave-crests higher than you are is a situation in which no one of God's children should ever want to find himself.

And the wind! If the wind in John Masefield's poem was, as he says, like a "whetted knife", this particular wind was all the swords, scimitars, daggers and stilettos that have ever been forged, cast, tempered and sharpened.

It struck me, and no doubt many others, just what a weak, puny and impotent thing we were in the face of this comparatively slight phenomenon of Nature.

The speed with which the typhoon hit us was only equalled in surprise by the speed with which it disappeared. Monday morning was warm and sunny; and the sea with no more than a medium swell. And the funnels were still there and the masts and the Bridge. I was quietly and secretly surprised.

We lost seven Carley floats and supports, and the Starboard Lower Boom. There were extensive electrical defects and the Capstan motor and Controller were flooded out. There was too a lot of damage to upper-deck fittings.

Of course a point for sober consideration is that we were never nearer than 100 miles to the centre of the typhoon. Now supposing Ruth had continued north towards us...

The Action Information Organisation (AIO)

The AIO is the nerve centre of the ship into which passes all the electronic information from radar, radio and other sources and where the tactical situation is presented to the Command on plotting tables and screens for them to make decisions as to how to conduct the battle. This extract from the Commission Book gives a typical idea of what happened.

To many people onboard, the Action Information Organisation (A.I.O.) was merely a voice blaring through a loudspeaker, to others it was just three letters; without their knowing what they stood for or what the organisation involved.

In many ways, it was one of the most important departments in the ship. Without it, we could never have operated quite so successfully in the confined waters off the West Coast of Korea nor could we have had the co-operation of the spotting aircraft, which made our bombardments so effective. Every ship that operated on the West Coast was either plotted or had some dealing with the A.I.O. Numerous aircraft were plotted, often as many as a hundred a day. On one occasion, even geese were plotted, but it was never established definitely whether they were friendly or enemy, although they were reported to be showing the correct identification code!

It may not have been realised by many that whilst the ship was operating in the Yellow Sea, we were constantly within the range of enemy bombers operating from the airfields in Northern Korea and Manchuria. For this reason, a Target Area Combat Air Patrol (Tarcap) was always supplied when the ship was in the Chodo area. Usually these aircraft came from the British or American Carrier operating off the West Coast, but frequently we had aircraft from the Fifth United States Airforce, the United States Marine Airwing and the South African Fighter/Bomber Squadron. The primary purpose of these aircraft was to provide air cover for the ships in the Chodo area, but they were also used to attack gun positions and enemy troops on the mainland and though you could not always see them, they were always in radio touch with the A.D.R. and available should enemy aircraft be detected.

All this work more often than not, was performed in semidarkness, often under trying conditions, so that if the R.P. ratings look like troglodytes after two years of continual operating, one must not he surprised.

Let it not be forgotten that a great deal of credit should go to the Electrical Department, who were responsible for keeping the radar and radio sets operating for lengthy periods under extremely difficult and trying conditions. Let us also remember that other departments contributed much towards helping the A.I.O. fulfil its role.

The Royals

The Royal Marines have been the Royal Navy's soldiers since 1755. They man one of the main 6in. guns on board and form the Royal Marine band to perform on ceremonial occasions such as the Monarch's birthday or 'Beat the Retreat' at formal 'Sunset', and provide a guard of honour for visiting dignitaries.

The ship has been very fortunate in having a very much alive and go-ahead R.M. Detachment throughout the commission. At top strength it consisted of 118, including officers and N.C.Os. The "Beating Retreat" ceremony has been performed on four occasions: at Singapore, Kure, Chinhae and Kobe; and the standard of arms drill and marching that one expects from the Corps was certainly maintained. There have been too, numerous Guards of Honour for visiting V.I.Ps. and senior officers.

Mention must be made of the Band which, under the able direction of Bandmaster Woods, has performed nobly: and not only the official military variety, but also the dance-band which "made" one or two functions.

In sport the detachment's record has been impressive. The Birmingham Cup (the Inter-R.M. Shooting Competition) has been won twice. The Inter-Part Soccer Cup has been won three times; and *"Belfast's"* tug-o'-war team, which won the Naval Championship at Singapore, contained eight Marines.

In spite of naval nattering, which is an ancient Service custom, they've been a bunch worth having.

The Sick Bay

The Sick Bay on board was always busy and had more than just broken bones or venereal disease among their own ship's company to cope with, as there were injured from smaller ships and serious war injuries too. This account explains, with some humour, how they managed.

On one occasion early in the Commission, when the heat and the huge consumption of drinking water had driven the Engineers to turn off the supply, a dishevelled and sweaty face appeared around the Sick Bay door and asked for two aspirin. With the usual Sick Bay courtesy he was given these but was refused a glass of water to swallow them with. He left the aspirin and departed, still thirsty. During the "Battle of Chang-ni do", when, the Sick Bay was strewn with stretchers and blood lay thick, a brave sailor penetrated past the notices on the Sick Bay door and again requested two aspirin. It is said that he avoids the Sick Bay these days.

Since the beginning of the Commission, eighteen thousand aspirin and eleven thousand codeine tablets have been issued; but besides the doling out of these, which takes place on almost all occasions and for many different reasons, the Sick Bay carries on the whole time with its other routine work. Queues for treatments, inoculations, vaccinations and examinations are a regular part of the life of the Ship and from time to time call forth caustic comments from the Heads of Departments. Working off the Korean Coast, away from any Hospital facilities, we have had to deal with both our own emergencies and those of smaller ships and the Islands. Signals to the Senior Medical Officer or the Dental Officer became quite common-place. Patients would come off to see us at odd times and for odd reasons. They would sneak across quietly from an oiler, be carried across to us in motor-boats or in sampans, and even on occasion be landed with great bally-hoo on the Quarter Deck in the helicopter.

The cases that came off seldom appeared to have much relation to the signals about them. The first case who arrived after an urgent signal and a difficult boat journey, turned out to have caught his finger in a door. Another case with a 'confirmed' diagnosis of acute appendicitis was seen at the first look to have an old appendix scar.

On the other hand there were also the ones who were carried on board with Death already at their elbows. One or two of them did die, but others with amazing toughness and stoicism struggled back to life: One of these was the Korean soldier who was brought off with wounds in his belly. For some reason that we never discovered he had tried toasting a grenade in a bonfire. In an operation that took two and a half hours, eight holes in his intestines were repaired and later he was shipped off to Inchon considerably the worse for wear.

However we heard a month after that he had recovered both from the grenade and the knife.

In all (including the Chang-ni do casualties, which kept the Sick Bay going continuously for twenty-four hours) we have had to deal with about thirty casualties from shore-side as well as doing five other emergency abdominal operations.

However no confusion did occur and from these sources we have managed to get through thirty-five and a half miles of bandage and five hundred and ninety-four pounds of cotton wool and lint. For those who like figures we have used 49,500 sulpha-tablets and 1,373,000,000 Units of penicillin.

Ode to the Oggin

The sailor's word for the sea is the 'oggin' and to demonstrate they are sensitive and poetical, and can be creative when off-watch at sea, here is a poem written by a member of the ship's company.

Have you seen the gray dark oggin just around The Nore?
    Or the vivid violet oggin outside Singapore?
Have you seen the shot-silk oggin when the sun sinks in the Bay?
    That's Kipling's flipping oggin where the flying fishes play.
Well, don't believe it, sailor! It's all a ruddy game.
    It's all just ruddy oggin, and it's all the ruddy same!
You read about them hardy blokes who've nothing else to do
    But sail the flipping oggin in a dinghy or canoe.
All around the world they'll go, and oggin all the way,
    It's stupendous, it's terrific, it's adventure—so they say.
Well, don't believe it, sailor! Them blokes is flipping mad,
    Oggin's ruddy oggin, and there's nothing quite as bad.
And then there are the Scientists—they shoot a pretty line
    'Bout oggin rich as Croesus, like a flipping diamond mine.
"There's gold in that thar oggin, and pearls in the deep below."
    Now that's a lie, if I ever heard, pearls come from Sasebo.
So don't believe it, sailor! Just keep on saying, "No!
    Oggin's ruddy oggin, even when it's H_2O."
Pion.

Simple Japanese

R Adm Scott-Moncrieff hauled down his flag in Belfast *on 26 September when the Korean War ended, and* Belfast *was relieved on station by HMS* Birmingham, *and by* Newcastle *on patrol. As she set sail for the UK to pay off and end this commission, a helpful 'Simple Japanese' guide was produced for HMS* Birmingham's *benefit!*

Japanese	English
Wassamattayou	Eager as I am to co-operate I do not quite understand.
Beero?	Is there but a remote possibility of alcoholic refreshment within these gracious portals?
Anone	Now look here, you listen to me and I don't want any god-damned argument.
	Note: Prefixes most Japanese statements.
Chotto matte	Take it easy, Navy boy.
Nevvahappen	You have definitely and decidedly been misinformed.
Scoshisodanoice	I am an Englishman.
Me sell fo' treefeetee nie ?	I'll really let you have it for a hundred.

Last words

HMS Belfast *paid off in Chatham on 4 November 1952 and entered reserve at Devonport on 1 December.*

If you look in the shipwrights' workshop on board HMS *Belfast* you'll see a toolbox with the initials C. J. W. on it. These are for Colin Jack White, my father. He served as the 'Chief Chippy' during the Korean

War. Sadly, my dad died in 2004 but before he did we assembled some of his HMS *Belfast* memorabilia and passed them on to the Association for posterity. Of note is dad's photo album, which contains some unique pictures taken in the Far East, including those of HMS *Amethyst* following the 'Yangtse Incident'.

Andy White BSc (Hons) MIET CENG MAPM

CHAPTER 4

Final commissions in the Far East

After some six years in reserve with an extensive refit incorporating the following changes, Belfast *recommissioned in Devonport on 12 May 1959 under the command of Capt J. V. Wilkinson DSO*, DSC, RN.*

New twin MK5 40 mm and twin 4-inch mount with individual MRS8 directors

4-inch guns training and elevation speed increased

Protection for key parts of the ship against nuclear, biological or chemical attack

Enlarging and enclosing her bridge with a two-tiered, five-sided superstructure (giving a striking change to her profile)

Improved accommodation and smaller crew

Tripod masts replaced with lattice masts

Timber decking replaced with steel throughout (apart from the quarterdeck)

HA armament - 6 twin Bofors guns and close-range fire direction linked to 8 close-range blind fire directors working with type 262 radar

Type 274 radar main armament direction

Type 277Q and 293Q radars (height-finding and surface warning)

Type 960M Radar (air warning)

Type 974 Radar (surface warning)

Torpedoes and associated gear taken out to save weight

HMS Belfast *arrived in Singapore on 16 December 1959, and spent most of 1960 at sea on exercise, although calling at ports in Hong Kong, Borneo, India, Ceylon (now Sri Lanka), Australia, the Philippines and Japan.*

You look familiar—who are you? (W. R. Beard Contest, 1959)

Belfast *had often to embark a flag officer as the Far East Fleet Flagship. From 1958 to 1960 the commodore-in-charge, Hong Kong Naval Base, was Cdre David Gregory, a notable wartime submariner. His flag lieutenant was Tim Reeder. During this time* Belfast *would wear the flag of FO2, Far East Fleet, R Adm Varyl Begg. Writing today, Tim gives a strategic view looking back at his navy time in Hong Kong, albeit from the perspective of junior staff, with a flavour of life as a flag lieutenant in the colony, the formalities in vogue at that time, and his association with HMS* Belfast.

By the late 1950s the process of withdrawing from Empire to become the Commonwealth was well under way. The trade routes from Britain to the Far East had been marked by a string of Naval bases from Gibraltar, to Malta, Bombay (now Indian Navy), Trincomalee, Singapore and Hong Kong; or turning south to Sydney (RAN), and Wellington (RNZN). Hong Kong was a full dockyard with a "battleship-sized" dry dock able to handle repairs and refits to any ship in the fleet. The dockyard was being run down over several years. In 1959 the dry dock was filled in and many buildings were demolished. The naval base was named HMS

Tamar continuing the name of a venerable depot ship moored in HK harbour until she was sunk by the Japanese in 1941. HK was described by some as "a last cradle of colonial privilege" with pomp, protocol and ceremony for the civil, business and military administrations of the Crown Colony. It was a favourite "run ashore" for RN ships and a sought after R&R (Rest & Recreation) visit for American ships serving off Vietnam. *Belfast* led fleet visits, or her own single ship visits to Hong Kong. Gun salutes were fired, where appropriate, and formal calls were exchanged between ships and Commodore HK. Hospitality was offered to visiting senior naval officers and if required to any wives who needed to live ashore. Protocol demanded proper precedence at formal dinners and events. Flag Officers, whether ashore or afloat, had retinues led by a Flag Lieutenant, who took care of diaries, accommodation and messing for their Flag Officer.

Belfast made a visit to Hong Kong over Christmas 1959 wearing the flag of Rear Admiral Varyl Begg, who was entertained both formally and informally at Commodore House by the generous hosts David and Eve Gregory. Admiral Begg's family in UK had illness to deal with in his absence. The Gregorys gave all the help they could, as they did for many other visitors. Hospitality was returned by dinner on board *Belfast* for the Gregorys and their Flag Lieutenant.

ACCOMMODATING A FLAG OFFICER ON BOARD
While on the Far East Station, HMS Belfast *was the flagship for various flag officers. With an admiral embarked, the captain moved into smaller quarters and the admiral's staff needed their own bridge and use of the ship's operations room to conduct the affairs of the fleet. Below is an example of the duty staff officer's orders when R Adm Michael Le Fanu was Flag Officer Far East Fleet. He was to become First Sea Lord and Chief of the Naval Staff in August 1968 and appointed as Chief of Defence Staff, but died in 1968 before taking up the position. This example of the flag officer's orders for the duty staff officer at sea demonstrate the need for tact between the flag, who was commanding the*

fleet, and the captain, who commanded the ship, and that the one should not interfere (cross the bows) with the other.

Onboard H.M.S BELFAST   Office of the Flag Officer
at Singapore   Second-in-Command
                                Far East Station
                                23rd July, 1960

<u>ORDERS FOR THE DUTY STAFF OFFICER</u>
<u>AT SEA</u>

WHEN REQUIRED

1. At all times when the Flag is in company with two or more ships, a duty staff officer is required between sunset and 0800.

DUTIES

2. <u>General</u>. He is responsible to me <u>through the Flag Captain</u> for the safety of the forces as a whole both navigationally and for normal alterations to avoid shipping, bearing in mind the width of front covered by the Fleet and hazards to wing ships.

3. <u>Place of Duty</u>. He is free to move between the bridge, Admiral's bridge and Operations Room as circumstances dictate.

4. <u>Calls</u>. In addition to the orders the Captain may have in force, I wish to be called on the following occasions:-

    (a) For any alterations of course.
    (b) A change in the weather.
    (c) Any unusual occurrence.
    (d) Meeting of Foreign warships.
    (e) Ships joining or leaving the force.

5. I would far rather be called several times unnecessarily than miss some important occurrence.

6. When calling me always use the Admiral's voice pipe.

7. <u>Signals</u>. Although the S.O.(O) and Flag Lieutenant will be shaken for important signals, the duty staff officer, as the man on the spot, must initiate action on any immediate signals, consulting the Flag Captain and me, as appropriate. He is to

ensure that the S.O.(O) is informed as soon as circumstances permit.

8. He should decide whether signals should be shown to me, asking the S.O.(O) if in doubt.

IN HARBOUR

9. In harbour the Duty Commanding Officer assumes the duties of Duty Staff Officer and when the S.O.(O) or Flag Lieutenant are ashore initiates any action he thinks necessary through the Flag Captain and me as appropriate.

10. I wish to be informed whenever H.M. Ships leave or enter harbour.

GENERAL

11. <u>Taking over Duty</u>. The Duty Staff Officer is to inform the M.S.O when he takes over duty and be absolutely certain he is on the distribution of all operational signals.

12. Should the O.O.W. at sea or in harbour not be able to get in touch with either the S.O.(O). or the duty staff officer, he should make sure I am informed as in paragraph 4 above.

Signed M. le Fanu
REAR ADMIRAL

Distribution:
H.M.S. BELFAST
Flag Captain, Commander All D.C.O.'s All O.O.W.'s Flag Lieutenant S.O.(O). (10 Copies)
The Commanding Officer, H.M.S. ALBION. (20 Copies).
The Commanding Officer, H.M.S. BULWARK.(20 Copies)

CAPT MORGAN MORGAN-GILES' COMMISSION: 31 JANUARY 1961 TO 19 JUNE 1962

HMS Belfast's 1961 commission was officially begun with the commissioning warrant that was read out to the ship's company in Singapore by her new commanding officer, Capt Morgan-Giles, to formally mark the start of this commission, which included hoisting the White Ensign and a church service to bless the ship. This was the opportunity to lay out his strategy for what could be up to a two-and-a-half-year assignment.

> *By SIR JOHN DAVID LUCE Knight Commander of the Most Honourable Order of the Bath, Companion in the Distinguished Service Order, Officer of the Most Excellent Order of the British Empire, Admiral in Her Majesty's Fleet and Commander-in-Chief of Her Majesty's Ships and Vessels employed and to be employed on the Far East Station.*

H.M.S BELFAST – Recommissioning Order

The Lords Commissioners of the Admiralty having directed that Her Majesty's Ship *Belfast* recommission at Singapore on 31st January, 1961, you are to proceed to recommission her accordingly and to prepare her for a Foreign Service Commission.

Until further notice Her Majesty's Ship *Belfast* will be administered by the Flag Officer Second-in-Command, Far East Station. You are to bring to the immediate notice of the Flag Officer Second-in-Command Far East Station any reason you may have for dissatisfaction with the state of training, discipline or welfare of the ship's company or with the general state of her material or any part of her.

May God's blessing be upon the ship and company hereby entrusted to your command, and may your joint endeavours to uphold the highest traditions of the Royal Navy in the service of Her Majesty the Queen be crowned with success and happiness.

Given under my hand at Her Majesty's Naval Base, Singapore, this 25th day of January, 1961.

J D Luce
Admiral

Captain M. C. Giles, D.S.O., O.B.E., G.M., Royal Navy
Her Majesty's Ship, *Belfast*

Copy to: The Flag Office, Second-in-Command, Far East Station

Frank Donald took this photograph of the ship in the King George VI dry dock in Singapore in October/November 1960. He was then a sub-lieutenant in the coastal minesweeper HMS Chawton. He remembers watching her going astern out of the Stores Basin, which, because of her length, seemed to go on forever. His first visit to the ship, and introduction to the triple 6in. turrets, was at Devonport in September 1953 when she was being refitted to go into reserve. His godfather, Cdr J. C. Richards, DSC, RN, was then in command and had had a dual career as a pilot in the early Fleet Air Arm, and in minesweeping. On D-Day he was senior officer of the 6th Minesweeping Flotilla.

Capt Morgan Morgan-Giles was Belfast's Captain for her final foreign commission of 1961 and 1962. He was to retire as a rear admiral after a distinguished naval career during and after the war and to be elected as MP for Winchester. His full title was R Adm Sir Morgan Morgan-Giles DSO, OBE, GM and his family have kindly consented

to the reprint of various excerpts that relate to his command of HMS
Belfast *from his privately published book* The Unforgiving Minute *for*
circulation principally to his grandchildren and family. These anecdotes
give an intriguing personal perspective into the life of those who served
in her during this commission, and they typify the experiences of her
various crews across the ship's 25-year sea-going life. They cover his
captaincy of HMS Belfast *and, in chapter 5, his steadfast achievement*
in getting her preserved as a Museum Ship for the Nation, moored in
the Pool of London.

So we now began an intensive work-up programme. A big exercise
called "Jet 61" was due shortly and we had just three weeks in which
to become a fully worked up and operational ship. I think it was
actually on the first day we went to sea that there was an unscheduled
piece of excitement when a Sea Vixen of the Fleet Air Arm was seen
to crash into the sea about 10 miles away. As we increased to full
speed the upper deck was crowded with anxious, staring eyes. An oil
slick was spotted and a whaler was launched to pick up any available
wreckage. There was no sign of the pilot and observer, but we were
shortly joined by an RAF Shackleton and a naval helicopter and they
were the first to spot the survivors. The observer was picked up by
the helicopter and landed on our Quarterdeck. In the meantime we
had reached the pilot who lay nonchalantly back in his rubber dinghy
smoking his pipe. A sea boat was lowered to pick him up and both
proved to be little worse for their ordeal. As they left the ship later
that evening a cheerful voice was heard to say "Nice of you to have
dropped in".

There were two aspects of life at sea which occupied much of
our time and our thinking. The first was what was called "RAS",
short for refuelling at sea. In the Pacific war with its long distances
the US Navy had become expert at transfer of fuel from big ships
to small ships. The way it was done was that the bigger ship, or an
Auxiliary tanker, would steer a steady course and steady speed, while
the receiving ship would come up alongside and take exact station
about 100 ft on the beam of the supplying ship. Then lines would
be shot across and oil hoses hauled in and connected so that the fuel

could be pumped across. Pumping took a long time, often an hour or two, so was a rather nerve-wracking experience for the Captain of the ship which had to keep exact station. If he steered too far out, even slightly so, or too far ahead he would break the hoses. If he steered too far in – bump! Getting into the exact position was tricky because there is an area on the quarter of any big ship which tends to suck you in – so the technique was to take station quite far out and then edge in. The steering and the endless minor changes of speed also called for great attention by the helmsman and in the Engine Room.

Once in position it is possible to transfer other things besides fuel. Heavy ropes as jackstays are put across, through a leading block and then manned by several dozen sailors (rather like a tug of war) so that the lines can be kept taut. Thus it becomes possible to sling across even heavy loads like ammunition and stores of every sort. Mail, written orders, fresh bread etc are also transferred and personnel including perhaps sick men who need to see a medical officer. This RAS operation was very frequently undertaken, either as an exercise or for necessity – and I have a note that it was done 283 times during our commission.

Incidentally this led to a custom which we adopted as a speciality for HMS *Belfast*. From Japan we bought 1,000 baseball caps with "HMS BELFAST" embroidered on them. The idea was that these would be convenient to wear during RAS exercises as they would not blow off like a sailor's ordinary round cap so easily does, and they gave some protection from the glare of the tropical sun. They were dark blue and rather smart and were also known as "RAS caps". This, as a special HMS *Belfast* gimmick, was a great success with the ship's company and eventually we always wore them at sea when not in company with the Fleet. But being strictly non-uniform, they were frowned on by one of our Admirals.

Another HMS *Belfast* speciality was a bathing net. We bought in Japan a large quantity of nylon fishing net. This was sewn up by the Petty Officer Sailmaker into the shape of a very large swimming pool. Lead weights were on the bottom corners, and corks along the top edge. Two large booms were rigged up, about 30 ft long, hinged at the inner inboard end so they lay snugly along the ship's gunwale when not in use. During the dog-watches whenever possible we would stop for half an hour, push out the booms and the net – then one blast on the bugle and all sailors off duty could dive over the side and have a swim. At the same time we would lower a whaler with a man with a rifle in her as an additional shark patrol. Of course the swimming pool net had a bottom, so there was no real danger from sharks – although one has to take every precaution because it is a fact that whenever the sea temperature is 70 degrees or over there may be sharks.

This swimming net was an enormous advantage because conditions on board in the tropics could be extremely uncomfortable – especially for the Engine Room and Boiler Room crews. When the ship was modernised in 1955 only half the accommodation had been air-conditioned and not the other half. I must say that this net idea did a great deal for the health and morale of the ship's company.

HMS Belfast *leaving Singapore, 1961. Photo courtesy of Morgan-Giles family.*

At the end of 1961 Belfast, after a refit in dry dock in Singapore, sailed to the Coral Sea area north-west of Queensland on 5 August to exercise with the Royal Australian Navy. Belfast was accompanied by RFA Wave Master in which Capt Morgan-Giles' eldest daughter Penelope and the wife of Belfast's commander, Cdr David Loram, took passage. The RFA captain over-rode instructions of the C-in-C Far East Fleet, as is recounted in this excerpt.

There was a domestic incident because when my wife Pamela had flown back to Sydney she had to leave behind Penelope, aged 14, who had a severe cold and was not allowed to fly. With great difficulty I obtained from the C-in-C permission for her to take passage in the Royal Fleet Auxiliary *Wave Master* (a fleet support tanker), together with Fiona Loram, the delightful young wife of Commander Loram, but the C-in-C insisted that these girls were not to appear on deck during the voyage. However this restriction did not hamper Captain "Muddy" Waters of the *Wave Master*. As soon as we were clear of territorial waters he said "I give the orders in this ship. These girls can go on deck for sun and fresh air as much as they want". Every few days we would go close alongside *Wave Master* to exercise "refuelling at sea". When we did this we were able to haul across a telephone wire and have a chat with the girls.

Pamela Bushell was born in Sydney and had married Capt Morgan-Giles in 1946. When Belfast visited Sydney in 1952 she was able to arrange a party for the entire ship's company, and this is described by her husband. It was extraordinarily generous of her and very much appreciated by those present.

In Sydney, Australia Pamela had done a wonderful thing. She had arranged a ball at the Trocadero to which the whole ship's company had been invited. The ship's magazine said afterwards "We were greeted at Trocadero by an equal number of the belles of Sydney. A delicious hot chicken supper was served to everybody and altogether the evening was a triumphant success." Unknown to us the ship's company had bought a silver tea and coffee set and the tray was inscribed with the words "Presented to Mrs Morgan-Giles by the ship's company of HMS *Belfast*, Sydney, Australia, September 1961". The youngest seaman on board (Ordinary Seaman Lambert) made the presentation. It happened that earlier in the day Admiral Frewen had arrived in Sydney by air and joined the ship. So the first event which occurred was this huge party, to which he was invited. He was a most austere man and seemed rather astonished by all this. One good moment was when Pamela was presented also with a RAS cap, which suited her very well on top of her evening dress. We took the opportunity, too, to present a specially embroidered RAS cap to the Admiral. I knew that he disapproved of them but nevertheless, for sheer politeness, he had to put it on!

HMS Belfast *sailed to Dar-es-Salaam for Tanganyika's (now Tanzania) Independence Ceremony on 19 December 1961, where the Duke of Edinburgh, representing the UK, attended.*

Two frigates, HMS *Rhyl* and HMS *Lock Alvie* sailed with us from Mombasa and we entered the harbour at Dar-es-Salaam at 0600 in the morning. Even at that early hour we were welcomed by crowds of Africans and Europeans.

During the morning of our arrival the Governor of Tanganyika, Sir Richard Turnbull, visited the ship and inspected a Royal Marine guard of honour. The Governor arrived in his full Diplomatic Corps uniform, very tight trousers and one of those white helmets with plumes of feathers on the top of it. Before following the Admiral down the steep ladder from the Quarterdeck he took off his helmet and put it on top of one of the ventilator outlets. A few minutes later I was pacing up and down the Quarterdeck, with my telescope under my arm, when out of the corner of my eye I spied Lt Robin Nelson, a cheerful but irreverent character, advancing with an egg in his hand to put under the feather helmet. I was just in time. Years later, Robin married a charming girl introduced to him by Pamela, and settled in Melbourne.

An example of how the Royal Navy gave positive help while on 'showing the flag' visits round the world was when David Watson (now 80 years old) was serving as an able seaman in HMS Belfast *at the time of Tanganyika's Independence. The Duke of Edinburgh came on board prior to the ceremony and attended the celebrations as the Queen's representative. David was asked to prepare and paint the new flag design on to a Zulu shield, which was made by the ship's 'chippy' (shipwright). The British Embassy had sent a cutting from the local newspaper, which formed the basis of the design, and, as noted on Daily Orders below for 15 June 1961 the shield was later presented to Burton Street Primary School in Dar-es-Salaam.*

We sailed from Pearl Harbour [sic] on Easter Sunday 22nd April and set off on the 2,100 mile passage to San Francisco. It was on this passage that one of the more difficult moments of the commission arose. We received information from Singapore and Hong Kong that we were probably being used to transport large quantities of heroin and opium from the Far East to America, and perhaps to England as well. From my previous experience in the Far East I had warned the ship's company that this might happen and told them to hand in to the Regulating Office (ship' police) anything that they had been asked to take to America or to England. This led to the discovery of a suitcase containing a massive quantity of heroin. This confirmed in no uncertain manner that we had drugs on board and we instituted a huge search. Searching a warship the size of *Belfast* is a formidable task. Smaller amounts of various drugs were found hidden in different places around the ship. Our main concern was that no illicit drugs whatsoever should be landed in the USA. Our second concern was that our leave should not be stopped during our time in San Francisco. Of course the ship might be put into isolation if the US authorities wanted to search her for themselves.

So I decided to send a signal to the Admiralty and request them to inform the United States authorities. This was done, and thus fortunately we avoided any criticism from the Americans. After all we had found the drugs for ourselves and we had made a clean breast of it, so to speak.

The head of the Federal Narcotics Bureau came on board and in my cabin he said "Say, Captain, I've been in this Department all

I can assure you Admiral, Belfast is a very happy ship!

my life and you have got a <u>really</u> big haul". Commander Loram had found that three Chinese cooks and stewards had been responsible for bringing the drugs on board and these three were already locked up in the ship's cells. In due course there was quite a lot of comment in the British newspapers about "drugs in British warship", but there was no adverse comment in the US press at all, as far as I am aware.

FIGURES FOR SPEECH

Capt Morgan Morgan-Giles believed very much in keeping his ship's company informed, and his supply commander on joining was, to his surprise, also appointed ship's information officer and told to produce regular bulletins about what was happening – to be broadcast to the sailors on board.

The Morgan-Giles family, looking through his papers, found this memo produced by the supply commander (responsible for victuals, spare-part stores, the captain's office and paperwork) for their captain's mid-commission speech to the ship's company; interesting figures today.

MINUTE SHEET
Subject:- FIGURES FOR CAPTAIN'S SPEECH
To: Captain
By: Cdr (S)

1. The following facts may be useful for your speech to the ship's
    company:-
    (a) Monthly wage bill – officers and men = £20,000
    (b) Monthly food allowance = £4,000
    (c) Cost of one ton of fuel = £7-1s-6d [old money = 7 pounds,
         1 shilling and 6 pence]
    (d) One hour's consumption FFO = 5 tons at economical
         speed (4 boilers, 4 shafts)
    (e) Cost of a day's steaming = £849–0s–0d at economical
         speed

2. Regret I cannot calculate the consumption in monetary terms
    of stores nor the cost of maintenance which is allied to it, but
    these items may be worth mentioning.

27 June '61   (Signature)

RADIO AND RADAR-OPERATING REFERENCE LIST

*In response to the increasing complexity of electromagnetic waves, this
simple guide, found among the papers of Morgan-Giles, was prepared by
the comms department for the officer of the watch on the bridge.*

	Band	Freq	Wave length	Use Radio Radar
Infra-red		3000 G^c/s	0.1mm	
		900 G^c/s	0.3mm	No radio or radar on these freqs
		3000 G^c/s	1mm	"V" may be used in future for secure comms over a precise short range

	Band	Freq	Wave length	Use Radio Radar
EHF	V	75 G^c/s		
		60 G^c/s	5mm	
		50 G^c/s		
		40 G^c/s		Note 1 G^c/s (gigacycle) = 1,000 M^c/s
	Q	30 G^c/s	1cm	
		25 G^c/s	1.25cm	
SHF	K	18 G^c/s	1.65cm	Splash spotting - Radar
	J	11.5 G^c/s	2.6cm	
	X	10 G^c/s	3cm	High definition close range radar - Airborne radar
				GW radar 262. 978
	C	7.1 G^c/s		Submarine surface radar - USN surface search radar
		4.1 G^c/s	7cm	
UHF	S	3 G^c/s	10cm	Gunnery radar 274 277 293
		2.5 G^c/s		(984) AEW radar W.S. and air directory sets
	L1	1 G^c/s	25cm	USN and Dutch air warning
			30cm	sets
			50cm	Point to point tropospheric scatter
				Obsolescent gunnery radars Probable band for Colour Television

	Band	Freq	Wave length	Use Radio Radar
	L2	300 M ^{c}/s	1m	New freqs for close range tactical comms
VHF		214 M ^{c}/s		Small ships air radar warning Old freqs for close range tactical comms
		100 M ^{c}/s		Band 11 FM
		60 M ^{c}/s		
		50 M ^{c}/s		This band will be used for long range point to point comms using ionospheric scatter
		30 M ^{c}/s	10m	Long range naval communications including point to point ie fixed services
HF		3 M ^{c}/s	100m	
MF		300 K ^{c}/s	1km	Medium range "port or local" circuits Long and medium range navigational aids
LF		30 K ^{c}/s	10km	Submarine broadcasts Rugby
VLF		3 K ^{c}/s	100km	

MAINTAINING MORALE

Ship's company morale is a very high priority for any commanding officer, particularly in a 'big ship' with a complement of more than 800, and, as noted elsewhere, Belfast was a very happy ship – and a happy ship is an efficient ship. Capt Morgan-Giles understood very well the need to keep wives, sweethearts and families at home supporting their menfolk while

away overseas for long periods, and vice versa. His Christmas message
shown here and sent to everyone reveals his concern.

From:- Captain Morgan Giles, D.S.O, O.B.E, G.M., Royal Navy

H.M.S BELFAST,

At sea

1st December 1961

This letter is intended as a Christmas message to the families and
friends of the present Ship's Company of H.M.S. BELFAST. I hope
that it will help to bridge the 9,000 mile gap between every man in
the ship and his home when we are in Singapore on Christmas Day;
and also help to explain to you something of the doings of H.M.S.
BELFAST during her present commission in the Far East.

After only a couple of weeks to find out all about the different
tasks onboard – "how the wheels go round", in fact – we took part in
a large scale exercise called JET, held in the Indian Ocean. This is an
annual affair in which all available British ships go off to do practices
and manoeuvres with the Commonwealth Navies – in this case ships
from Australia and New Zealand, Pakistan, Indian and Ceylon.

Ships are often at sea for several weeks at a time. This frequently
makes it difficult to receive and despatch mail, although of course
every opportunity is taken to send mail ashore by any ship which
has to proceed into harbour for any reason. After spending Easter
at Singapore, we went off for another large scale exercise with the
American Navy, off the coast of North Borneo. Next came our first
trip to Hong Kong – the 'Pearl of the Orient' – which is always the
most popular visit of all.

The climate in Hong Kong, except in mid-summer, is cool and
enjoyable. And this is of course a very pleasant change for the 700
men who live onboard in conditions which are usually terribly hot
and sticky. Any warship is always crowded and difficult to ventilate;
when H.M.S. BELFAST was modernised three years ago, a huge
air-conditioning plant was installed, but even this is not powerful
enough to look after more than a small proportion of the living
accommodation.

Well, after Hong Kong the ship made a long cruise up to Japan, then back to Singapore for docking. During this time at Singapore anybody who wanted to go on leave for a week was able to do so. Due to this docking we missed being sent to KUWAIT – but it was a very near miss! Then afterwards we went "down under" to Australia – through the Great Barrier Reef, a week's exercising in the Coral Sea, and on to Melbourne and Sydney. Everybody onboard agreed that this Australian cruise was the highlight of the whole commission. It was certainly worth every day of the five weeks at sea (11,595 miles) to steam there and back. Also it was cool enough for us to have to change into blue uniform.

After returning from Australia, an exercise called FOTEX brought us sharply back to our senses. The guns were firing day and night, and every department in the ship was really flat out.

There followed a second visit to Hong Kong, the whole fleet being there to welcome Princess Alexandra during the Royal Visit to the Colony. Now we are on our way to represent the Royal Navy at the Tanganyika Independence Celebrations – which will be attended by the Duke of Edinburgh.

During these comparatively long trips at sea there is always a lot of work onboard, particularly for the Engine Room people, who are on watch at least eight hours every day. All departments are very busy cleaning and painting and generally smartening up the ship before the next port of call. I need hardly tell you that H.M.S. BELFAST is a most beautiful looking ship – perhaps the best looking ship in the Navy today. Being flagship of the Far East Fleet, our biggest fleet, she has to be outstandingly clean and smart.

At sea after working hours there are all sorts of games and competitions to keep people from getting bored! Deck hockey played on the quarter-deck; Rifle shooting; Radio quizzes; Nightly film shows; Concerts by the Royal Marine Band whenever they are with us; Bathing in a net over the side. The Chaplain holds regular services in the tiny ship's chapel, and there will be a carol service on Christmas Day. Perhaps the three most popular pursuits are (a) sleeping (b) eating (c) sunbathing. The facilities onboard for all these three things are quite excellent.

I think it is fair to say that BELFAST has an absolutely outstandingly good Ships Company this time – perhaps the best I have ever known. A sense of community soon builds up onboard if the Ships Company is a good one. A Welfare Committee is elected, and many worthwhile things are done by them. For example, the Ships Company have already subscribed £250 and bought a cottage for the resettlement of a refugee family (Chinese man and woman and eight children) from the poorest part of Hong Kong. Also a regular Raffle provides a guide dog for the Blind.

May I end with a personal request? It is natural that wives and families sometimes get down in the dumps when their menfolk are overseas. So of course do the menfolk. The greatest thing that you can all do from home to help us out here is to write cheerful and regular letters. "Mail ready for distribution" are the most exciting words heard over the ship's loudspeakers: please write cheerfully and look on the bright side of things – such as "Only six months to go!"

With best wishes for Christmas and the New Year,
Yours sincerely
Morgan Giles
Captain RN

PERSONAL IMPRESSIONS OF THE COMMISSION

These two amusing anecdotes, one sent in by Charles Nixon-Eckersall, a retired submariner, and another by James Milne, a retired Royal Navy observer, demonstrate that junior officers found the then commander, David Loram, a stickler for cleanliness and a tiddly ship.

However, Loram's captain, later to become R Adm Sir Morgan Morgan-Giles, wrote very highly of his commander, so one must assume Loram's efficiency overcame his regard for protocol!

Submariner Charles Nixon-Eckersall recalls how HMS Belfast was also a 'mother hen' for submarines in Singapore. This included HMS Tactician, who of necessity, being without her own ship's boat, needed a depot ship to berth alongside.

In the early 60s HMS *Belfast* was the Far East Fleet flagship. *Tactician*, in which I was the 3rd hand, was one of the oldest submarines in the navy, un-air-conditioned and totally unsuited to service in the Far East. *Belfast* was known with great affection to the local Singapore submariners as 'Wave Belfast' because in the provision of victuals, stores, human support, etc, she was the best RFA/depot ship of all. Submarines, being boatless, used to tie up alongside her at fleet anchorages like Pulau Tioman for weekends of R&R. We were always very welcome with those in *Belfast*, with the possible exception of the Commander who disliked these ugly black things mooring bow-to-stern alongside his pristine quarterdeck. One evening after dinner in the cruiser's wardroom and enjoying coffee plus on the quarterdeck with some 'skimmer' mates, I was approached by said Commander who asked me what the boat's ship's company were doing. To my reply of not knowing, he invited me to the starboard after accommodation ladder platform from which one had a clear view of the submarine's fore-casing, on which were sat some 20 plus ratings. Oh, said I, they are watching a movie. He asked what they used as a screen and when I said his ship's side, he remarked that a grey ship side was unlikely to make a good screen. I assured him it was excellent as our guys would have painted a large white rectangle over the grey to act as the screen. I am afraid he lost it, demanding that the film was stopped and his ship's side repainted immediately. Subsequently, everyone except one thought that this spoof was well-meant and very poorly received. Our friendship with *Belfast* was not damaged at all.

Charles Nixon-Eckersall

In September/October 1961 I was serving in 825 Naval Air Squadron (Whirlwind 7s) onboard HMS VICTORIOUS.

However, my crewman was tasked to winch mail down to HMS *Belfast*, who was operating to the East of Singapore. I remember the transfer of mail went well, a friendly wave and we were off back to the Royal Naval Air Station, RNAS *Sembawang*, on Singapore Island. On arrival we were greeted by one of the Squadron 'wheels', who said that a signal had been received from

HMS BELFAST that stated we had managed to drop oil on the Quarterdeck during the mail transfer, and would the crew kindly help in removing said oil. Or words to that effect! I do not know what reply, if any, was sent.

Consequently when I visited the *Belfast* some years ago to see The White Ensign Association, I looked for oil patches on the Quarterdeck. Needless to say I was unable to find any trace!

James (Jim) Milne MBE
Lt Cdr RN (Rtd) former Observer

Peter Waddington was a newly promoted lieutenant when he joined HMS Belfast *in Singapore in January 1961. He recalls his impressions of the commission up to June 1962, partly reproduced here with his kind permission, as they give a vivid insight to the idiosyncrasies and unexpected demands of life on board. On Capt Morgan-Giles' recommendation Peter was selected to train as an RN clearance diving officer, i.e. a full-time diver.*

General Background.
The first of the Pre-Joining Training was a Shallow Water Diving Officer course at HMS *Vernon*. Shallow Water Breathing Apparatus (SWBA) was the oxygen only version of Clearance Diving Breathing Apparatus, this being marginally before the introduction of the Ships Diver qualification and the introduction of a compressed air set.

Gun training
The next course was the main one, at HMS *Excellent*, for training of *Belfast's* 6" turret and 4" mounting crews. There I met up with some of the other officers and many of the gunnery ratings, and learned that as well as Diving Officer I was to be Quarterdeck Officer, X Turret Quarters Officer and Quarters Officer for the Port After 4" mounting, and therefore joined up with the future Quarterdeck Petty Officer and GI, Joe Lines, and many of my future Quarterdeck ratings for 6" and 4" gun drill.

Joining the ship
During January 1961 we were all flown out in batches to join the ship and settle in to our duties in preparation for the recommissioning ceremony, which took place at Singapore on 31 January. Daily work on the Quarterdeck consisted of keeping the ceremonial "Holy of Holies" looking pristine; i.e. polishing the brightwork, scrubbing the wooden deck and touching up paintwork, sloping the awning in inclement weather and re-spreading it when dry etc. Awning, stanchions, ridgeropes and backbone had to be stowed prior to going to sea, and re-rigged prior to entering harbour, and the ceremonial awning had also to be spread for special functions on the Quarterdeck. Towing aft, towing splash targets and preparing for helicopter landings were additional periodic evolutions for our part of ship, and, particularly prior to helicopter transfers or landings, required special precautions for protecting the deck.

For Diving, it being before the general introduction of wet suits, and too hot for our dry suits, we took to using our dark blue undersuits in order to present a dark profile. It was part of our diving training to be discouraged from splashing around on the surface, so that was not a problem. We were provided with shark repellent, in the form of small pouches of black dye to attach to the diving sets, but this stuff was extremely messy, and was soon abandoned. In the event we never encountered any sharks.

We dived at least once almost every time we stopped, either in harbour or at anchor, carrying out ship's bottom searches or other training or recreational dives everywhere between Dar es Salaam and Mombasa in the West to Japan, Australia and all points East on our homeward passage via the United States.

The Flag Officers. During our time on station, we were flagship to two successive Flag Officers Second in Command of the Far East Station (FO2FES). The first of these was the then Rear Admiral Michael Le Fanu (later to become FOME, and finally First Sea Lord).

He was, on the face of it, the more affable and less severe of the two. Amongst his apparent "peculiarities", he had the habit, presumably carried over from old routine at BRNC Dartmouth, of taking a 15-minute daily nap on his bunk after lunch. In harbour in Singapore he would take off in his staff car in the afternoon, and go for a walk in South Johore, taking with him an apparently randomly selected junior rating as a walking companion. I can remember, if the rating was from one's own division, wondering what said rating was telling the Admiral about his Divisional Officer.

Admiral Le Fanu C-in-C Far East Fleet

The only other incident I can remember distinctly regarding Admiral Le Fanu involved me personally, on the Quarterdeck. We were getting ready for a ceremonial arrival in Hong Kong, and preparations had been held up by bad weather, so the Commander, David Loram, appeared on the Quarterdeck and instructed me to carry on working my hands during their dinner hour, to complete the rigging and spreading of the awning. This was received reasonably cheerfully, and the hands carried on working, but one of them came to me and pointed out that the rum ration had been issued, and that if their grog was not consumed in 20 minutes or so it would have gone flat and become undrinkable. He therefore asked if it could be brought up and drunk on deck while they were working. I thought this was a reasonable request, and gave permission. However, no sooner had the grog been produced than the Admiral appeared to take his lunchtime exercise. While pacing the Quarterdeck, he noticed the rum and asked me what was going on. I explained the circumstances, and was given a relatively mild telling off for allowing drinking on deck. The Admiral then sent for the Commander, and somewhat to my embarrassment gave him a considerable and audible "roasting" in front of my ratings, not about the rum, but for keeping the hands working through their meal time. Admiral Le Fanu was, of course, later instrumental, as First Sea Lord, in abolishing the rum ration as being an anachronism and incompatible with the requirement for personnel to handle modern weapons and machinery. I have sometimes wondered whether this incident had any bearing on his subsequent action.

Rear Admiral Le Fanu's successor, Rear Admiral John (aka "Black Jack") Frewen, was a completely different character. Severe in expression and thin to the point of appearing gaunt, we were given early in his time with us to understand that he had ulcer problems. Indeed, not long after he joined us he visited the US Navy, and they made the mistake of catapulting him off a carrier deck, by way of giving him a "show". This severely aggravated his medical problem. We bridge watchkeepers were told to virtually tiptoe past his cabin door on the way on and off watch to avoid disturbing him. I only once witnessed him actually venting his wrath. This was on the Quarterdeck. The booms and ladders went out as required, but the electricians in the Port waist mistook the bugler sounding the 'G' for the "Carry on" signalling the end of the ceremonial, flung a screen door open and charged down the deck, bearing their floodlighting booms like lances, and narrowly missing "Black Jack", who instantly illustrated the background to his nickname by calling for the Commander, standing inches in front of his face and bawling in front of everyone words to the effect of "If I ever witness anything like this again I will personally ensure that you go no further in the service".

Most of my bridge watches and my Quarterdeck watches in harbour were reasonably uneventful. The harbour watch incident was again a middle watch. We were alongside in the US naval base at Subic Bay, and had given shore leave to Olongapo, a notorious night spot where leave to the US sailors expired at 0200, and it had been decided that we, as visitors, would have to follow suit. Our sailors, however, were accustomed to having all night leave, and many of them, with a few drinks inside them, had either forgotten the expiry time or decided to ignore it, so at 0200 there were something like 100 ratings still ashore. For a short while I decided to turn a blind eye, as ratings were drifting back a few at a time. By about 0215, when there were still about 30 people missing, I started retaining Station Cards.

I had already put returning drunks in the two cells under supervision, and used the ship's handcuffs to shackle others to various parts of the forepeak outside the cells when I considered they were too far gone to be allowed on the messdecks. I had also sent ashore to the US Shore Patrol to borrow more handcuffs. At about 0230, one junior rating from my own division, whose card had been retained because he was adrift but whom I had sent below, having not recognised him as being drunk, appeared on deck in his underpants and came after me with a large galley knife. He was intercepted by the gangway staff and locked up with the others, happily not having harmed anyone. The upshot of this was that I spent several hours on each of several days attending Commander's defaulters and then Captain's defaulters. My Able Seaman came and apologised profusely the next day, but was sentenced to detention, and despite his apology and my statement that I was willing to let him back, the Captain deemed it wise to move him to a different division.

Gunnery.
We carried out a number of 6" and 4" firings, but the only firing of note that I remember was the single occasion on which we fired a 12 gun 6" broadside. We had usually fired salvoes, one barrel at a time, which had little noticeable effect on the ship, but on this occasion, firing 12 barrels simultaneously and more-or-less on the beam, the ship appeared to take a considerable leap sideways, and I seem to remember the electricians spending many hours replacing virtually every lightbulb in the ship.

Torpedo and Anti-Submarine duties. My sonar duties were limited to ensuring that the limited number of sonar ratings on board operated the sonar periodically with identification and classification tapes running, so that they could practise properly detecting and classifying submarine-like contacts. With that in mind, I remember on one occasion making a broadcast saying "UCs muster in the ACR for IDCT", knowing full well that the ratings concerned would understand the instruction.

However, the Commander had a thing about people using acronyms and sent for me, asked "What the hell was that all about?" He then told me to spell things out in future.

The Commander. While on the subject, I will mention that Commander David Anning Loram MVO, Royal Navy was not popular as the ship's

Commander. He was a hard taskmaster, but I think the main reason for his unpopularity, particularly amongst the Part of Ship officers, was that he appeared not to be able or willing to let people get on with their job without perpetual interference. On the other hand, socially and when off duty, he was friendly and charming. I took a few days' local leave on one occasion when the ship was in Singapore, and went up to Kuala Lumpur to stay with some friends. I had a full beard when I joined the ship, but while ashore I decided to become clean shaven. On my return, walking up the gangway in civilian clothes and saluting, I was greeted by the Commander, who happened to be on the Quarterdeck, and was treated like a welcome visitor (until I pointed out that I was one of his officers and had been so for half a year or so).

The Passage Home.
The passage, via Guam, Honolulu, San Francisco, Seattle, Vancouver, Victoria, Panama Canal, and Trinidad, combined with our time on station between Dar es Salaam and Mombasa in the West and Ceylon (now Sri Lanka), India, the Maldives, Singapore,

HMS Belfast *coming alongside in Portsmouth Harbour on completion of her 1961–62 commission. Families are waiting on board the bow of an RN aircraft carrier.*

Hong Kong, Borneo, the Philippines, Japan in the North and Australia in the South turned the 18 month commission as a whole into a magnificent world tour. Our reception on the way home, particularly on the West coasts of the USA and Canada, was quite extraordinary, with people travelling many miles to attend receptions on board, and many hundreds queuing to invite British sailors to visit their homes, and to attend dinners, dances and parties ashore. In San Francisco, Seattle and Vancouver there was a "Lurk List" in the wardroom, requiring off-duty officers to attend one or more reception/dinner/dance ashore per night until they had a duty night on board or reached the bottom of the list, having attended a specified "quota" of events. It became a relief to get to sea for the relatively short passages between ports.

The last twelve gun salvo from a Royal Navy warship
I served as a Helicopter Pilot in the Fleet Air Arm in the 1960s. On the 18th September 1962 I was tasked to fly an HAS Whirlwind Mk VII of 771 Squadron (No:- 753) with a Naval Photographer to photograph the last 12 Gun Salvo fired by HMS *Belfast* just south of Portland. I believe that this was the last 12 gun salvo fired by the Royal Navy, quite a sight and I am glad they were blanks!

Lieutenant Don Macdonald RN

CHAPTER 5

Life in the Reserve Fleet

In July 1963 HMS Belfast was called out of the Reserve Fleet to conduct a Royal Naval Reserve minesweeping exercise involving 16 RNR minesweepers and manned with a Royal Naval Reserve crew and sea cadets embarked. This was called Exercise Rockhaul.

Capt Sir Norman Lloyd-Edwards KCVO, GCStJ, JP, RNR, serving in the RNR, was captain's secretary to the admiral commanding reserves and he remembers an experience.

In 1963 Rear (later Vice) Admiral Hugh Martell, as Admiral Commanding Reserves, had the brilliant idea to take HMS *Belfast* out of the Reserve Fleet to act as "mother hen" to the eleven Minesweepers attached to the RNR Divisions throughout UK on an expedition to Gibraltar. The purpose was to give an added impulse and excitement to the RNR when carrying out their 14 day annual training.

The Ship's Company consisted of RN officers and ratings with a good smattering of RNR and I was lucky as a two ringer RNR to be selected as Captain's Secretary. It meant joining her a week earlier than the rest to help establish a working ship. My cabin was just below the Bridge and is now designated that of a Royal Marine Officer. To add to the excitement 100 Sea Cadets were to be borne.

We sailed from Portsmouth in August with the MS's in line ahead into a heavy swell. I felt very smug standing on BELFAST's Quarter Deck watching the others pitching and rolling. On the way, there were the usual manoeuvres and trials. One evening I was on the Quarter Deck taking my post-prandial coffee when suddenly the deck dropped from under me and the ship's propellers zipped our speed from 8 knots to her fullest of 30 knots. The lookout had spotted a blaze on the horizon. We tore through the lane of MS, who pitched in her wake and got to a Spanish fishing vessel on fire. All the crew were rescued but their ship sank.

On arrival at Gib, the cadets were put to work with pulling races and runs to the top of the Rock to make them too tired to get up to any mischief. The rest enjoyed being in tropical rig for the first time with runs ashore, where they were able to sample delicacies like swordfish and buy Arabic souvenirs to take home. Many had never been abroad before so it was a case of "Join the Navy to see the World".

One evening I was Officer of the Day and on watch during the Middle. The Admiral had gone ashore with some of his Staff and on his return he handed me a piece of paper with the order to deliver it immediately to his Chief of Staff. His bright eyes and unsteady walk caused me to read the note. It said "get stuffed". I therefore decided to postpone its delivery as I knew the COS had retired. The next morning during breakfast I heard the pipe: "Captain's Secretary to the Admiral's Cabin at the rush." I was asked why I had not delivered the message. I handed it to the COS who promptly said "you did the right thing" to the huge amusement of the rest of the Staff.

Hugh Martell's obituary in the *Independent* referred to this Exercise as being one which amazed our NATO allies that it had been carried out by Reservists in the main.

The voyage home was uneventful but the success of the venture was deemed so effective that there were a number of other Rockhauls in later years but sadly without the comforting presence of BELFAST.

In 1971 HMS Belfast *was saved for the Nation as a Museum Ship. R Adm Sir Morgan Morgan-Giles wrote how this was achieved.*

HMS *Belfast* had been lying in Portsmouth for seven or eight years as the Headquarters ship and "living ship" for the Reserve Fleet. In this capacity she was permanently at anchor and not in full commission. The threat of scrapping this famous old ship and the proposal to save her attracted a lot of attention, both in the Navy and in the National Press.

An "early day motion" was tabled in the House of Commons proposing that the ship should be saved from scrapping and preserved as part of the Nation's Maritime heritage.

A couple of days later, Mr John Smith, the MP for Westminster and the City of London, spoke to me about it. He had been in the Navy during the war, a pilot in the Fleet Air Arm and was very keen on the project. He promised to make a very large sum of money available to Prince Philip's Maritime Trust, specifically earmarked for HMS *Belfast*.

My fellow Trustees were:

> Dr Noble Frankland, CB, CBE, DFC
> Sir Peter Masefield
> Lord Dalkeith MP (now the Duke of Buccleuch)
> Mr Gordon Strang, a skilled Accountant
> Mr Aubrey Bowden
> Sir Arthur Drew, KCB (of the Standing Commission in Museums and Galleries.

As Executive Director of the Trust we had recruited the recently retired Admiral Sir Donald Gibson.

On 15th October 1971 she was towed up from Tilbury, under Tower Bridge, and into her berth.

Finally, HMS *Belfast* was opened to visitors on Trafalgar Day, 21st October, 1971.We found that the public was particularly interested in the conditions under which the ship's companies lived on board in wartime.

At this stage the ship was a private enterprise venture entirely run by the HMS Belfast Trust. We received a great deal of help and encouragement. The First Sea Lord of the day, with some misgivings (!) handed over a White Ensign which we were allowed to use. To commemorate the ship's part in the Normandy Landings on D-Day, the ship was visited by HRH The Duke of Edinburgh.

HMS *Belfast* has always been a good ship for a party... The proceeds of catering were very profitable for the Trust. HMS *Belfast* remained under the control of the original Trustees until 1978. Our income was sufficient to pay the salary of the Director and his staff, the wages of the Wardens, and to keep the ship clean. However it became apparent that we would not be able to put enough money into reserve for the eventual dry-docking.

So, in March 1978, the ownership of HMS *Belfast* was transferred to the Imperial War Museum.

HMS *Belfast* is now one of the three out-stations of the Imperial War Museum, the others being the airfield at Duxford (near Cambridge) and the War Cabinet Room.

In the Coronation Jubilee Year, the Lord Mayor of London, Alderman Sir Robin Gillet, had arranged an exhibition of marine paintings in the library of the Guildhall. The Lord Mayor was also a Commander RNR and the pictures had all been painted by John Hamilton, a famous marine artist [who] agreed to sell them to the HMS Belfast Trust for £30,000 if we kept them on permanent display on the ship.

As part of the original arrangements with the Port of London Authority, HMS *Belfast* is the berth used for visiting Warships or Cruise Liners to lie alongside when they visit the Pool of London.

The then Lord Mayor of Belfast, Councillor James Stewart, with Rear Admiral Sir Morgan Morgan-Giles at the ceremony for the handing back of the bell aboard HMS Belfast *on 21 October 1977.*

NEW MASTS FOR HMS *BELFAST*

Richard Thorne wrote this article to explain how Belfast's original rusting masts were replaced. He retired from the Royal Navy in 1989 as a commander (marine engineering), having served on board her in 1961 as a sub-lieutenant under training. He is now a committee member of the HMS Belfast Association.

It was the 15th August 2005. Two men, one of them Brad King, the then Imperial War Museum's Director of HMS *Belfast*, the other, one of three HMS Belfast Association's Vice Presidents – Tim Lewin – were discussing the parlous state of the ship's masts.

It was Tim who suggested that an approach should be made to the Russians asking them to sponsor the supply of new masts. At that time the Russian steel industry was prospering and Tim was fully aware of the great fund of goodwill that exists on the Russian side for the one remaining ship to have taken part in the Arctic convoys in the 2nd Word War. Tim also has close links with people in very high places in Russia and so he agreed to make the necessary initial contacts!

Thus was born the "Last Witness Project", the aim of which was to replace the two badly corroded masts with new ones.

Lattice Mast Corrosion 2005

As an aside: over the course of the period 1941 to 1945 some 78 convoys ran the gauntlet to Archangel, or Murmansk, in northern Russia carrying, in all, four million tons of supplies, which included some 7,000 aircraft and 5,000 tanks. The convoy route passed between the Arctic ice pack and the coast of Norway and was very, very dangerous because of the proximity of German submarines and aircraft from their bases in occupied Norway; this was especially the case in winter when the ice came further south, indeed, more ships were lost to the ice than to the enemy. The price was heavy with some 100 merchant and 19 RN ships sunk and the loss of almost 3,000 seamen.

The Arctic convoys were absolutely critical to the Russian fight against the invading Germans and their eventual victory and, among the RN ships defending the convoys, was HMS *Belfast* whose Battle Honours include: "Arctic 1943" and "North Cape 1943".

As a further aside: although a ship's masts certainly add to the aesthetic appearance of a warship, such as HMS *Belfast*, they also carry, among other fittings, an array of radar aerials as high as possible in the ship. The new long range search radar fitted during her 26 month refit in Devonport, which completed in November 1942, proved to be crucially effective in locating, shadowing and, subsequently, the sinking of the "Scharnhorst" in the Battle of North Cape in December 1943. Through the Russian Federation, around £1,000,000 was donated by Russian companies for *Belfast's* new masts. The masts were dedicated in the presence of HRH the Duke of Edinburgh and Russian representatives on 19 October 2019.

Finally a tribute to R Adm Sir Morgan C. Morgan-Giles DSO, OBE, GM, who did so much to preserve HMS Belfast as a Museum Ship and who chaired HMS Belfast Trust. It was placed in the summer 2013 edition of HMS Belfast Association's newsletter The Sea Horse.

Members of the Association, particularly those who served in HMS BELFAST during the 1961–62 Commission when Captain Morgan-Giles was in command, will be saddened to learn that our Patron crossed the bar on Saturday 4 May 2013, aged 98 years. There are many tributes to Sir Morgan-Giles where he is described as "a highly decorated naval officer who became a colourful Conservative MP for Winchester".

He took his seat on the Commons back benches in 1964 and very quickly earned a reputation for his forthright approach to parliamentary business and was frequently greeted by affectionate Labour cries of "send a gunboat" as the genial Morgan-Giles duly steamed into action with all guns blazing on behalf of his beloved service. It was from the floor of the House of Commons that Sir Morgan-Giles proposed to save HMS BELFAST for the nation. He was successful in his bid to have the ship taken off the Disposal List and, having raised a considerable sum of money, became the Chairman of the HMS BELFAST Trust. He was on the bridge when the ship passed under Tower Bridge and moored at her current berth on the River Thames.

Rear Admiral Sir Morgan-Giles was born on 19th June 1914. He joined the Royal Navy in 1932 and while serving in the training cruiser

Frobisher, visited the West Indies and the Baltic. He then served in a number of ships on the China Station before qualifying as a TAS Officer at HMS VERNON, where later in his career he commanded the establishment in the rank of Captain. Early in the Second World War, Lieutenant Morgan-Giles coordinated mine disposal work in the Suez Canal, and during the six months siege of Tobruk, he laid mines and landed troops to undertake fighting patrols. During this period, he received the George Medal.

While in Cairo, Lieutenant Morgan-Giles met Brigadier Fitzroy MacLean who was liaising with Tito and his partisans in Yugoslavia. Following this meeting, Lieutenant Morgan-Giles delivered arms and supplies to the partisans from Bari in Italy to the island of Vis in the Adriatic, as well as coordinating the commando raids carried out by coastal forces along the Dalmatian coast. After the war, he served in staff appointments in the Far East, in Trieste, then as the CO of HMS CHIEFTAIN of the Dartmouth Training Squadron, and then as Captain of HMS BELFAST. On promotion to Rear Admiral, he became Admiral President of the Royal Naval College at Greenwich, before retiring from the Royal Navy. His career as an MP was equally challenging, but that is another story!

However the honours and awards earned by him during his lifetime are:

   The George Medal – 2nd September 1941
   Member of the British Empire – 1st January 1944
   Officer of the British Empire – 11th July 1944
   Distinguished Service Order – 24th April 1945
   Knight Bachelor – 1975

Rear Admiral Sir Morgan C. Morgan-Giles DSO OBE GM 19 June 1914 to 4 May 2013 age 98

Acknowledgements

My grateful thanks to these individuals and organisations that have contributed, given information or advice, or helped me find people who did.

HMS *Belfast* Association: Wally Filby, David Gibbon, Hon. Tim Lewin, Fred Wooding MBE, Richard Thorne; Mike Smith, HMS *Belfast* guide ARNO (Association of Royal Navy Officers); Jane Harrold – Archivist, BRNC Dartmouth; The Britannia Association; Royal Navy Association; Bill Emery, British Library; Angus Menzies, The Clerk, Honourable Company of Master Mariners; Forces Pension Society; Anne Cowan, Lloyd's Register Foundation; William Spencer, The National Archives; Paul Johnson, The National Archives, Image Library Manager; The Naval Review; Explosion Museum, Gosport; Fleet Air Arm Museum, Yeovilton; Navy News; Fiona Byrne: William Blair, Head of Human History, National Museums Northern Ireland; Desmond McCabe, Public Services, Public Record, Office Northern Ireland (PRONI); Belfast Central Library; Royal Naval Amateur Radio Society (RNARS); Royal Institute of Navigation; Peter Tilley, Archivist, Gieves & Hawkes Outfitters; Ian Killick, Archive Research Manager UKHO; Mrs Heather Johnson Curator (Archives), RN Museum Portsmouth; National Maritime Museum; Ngaire Bushell, IWM; Duncan Ball, Information Specialist, Met Office, Exeter; Jenny Wraight, Admiralty Librarian Royal Navy, Naval Historical Branch, Portsmouth; Andy Curran Conservation & Facilities Manager, HMS Belfast; Clive Kidd, Hon Curator, HMS Collingwood Heritage Collection; Ken Sutton, Hon. Curator, Communications Branch Museum, HMS Collingwood; Jeremy Michell, MA, Historic Photographs and Ships Plans Curator & Manager, National Maritime Museum; Penelope Cartwright and Alexandra Bolitho, family of Rear Admiral Sir Morgan Morgan-Giles; Mike Allen; Kim Bellamy; Admiral Sir Jeremy Blackham; Peter Brands; Don Cam; Captain Peter Grindal CBE RN; Rear Admiral Conrad Jenkin; Rear Admiral Robin Musson; Lt Cdr Bob Jezzard RN; R Adm Terance Loughran CB Lt Cdr; Lt Cdr James (Jim) Milne MBE RN; Captain Sir Norman Lloyd-Edwards KCVO GCStJ JP RNR; Lt Don Macdonald RN; Commodore Jamie Miller CBE; Robin Mills (Lt Cdr); Charles Nixon-Eckersall; Alec Paddy; Joy Paton, wife of Lt Cdr Alasdair Paton RN; Tim Reeder; James Townson; Simon Tosswill; Cdr Edward Thring RN; Peter Waddington; David Watson; Roger Welby-Everard; Andy White BSc (Hons).

Further reading

Men of the Sea: HMS Belfast Association, Ernest E Smith, Melrose Books
Firing on Fortress Europe: HMS Belfast at D-Day Nick Hewitt, IWM
HMS Belfast Cruiser 1939, Richard Johnstone-Bryden, Seaforth Historic Ships
In Trust for the Nation HMS Belfast, John Wingate DSC, Profile Publications Ltd
The Last Big Gun, Brian Lavery, Pool of London
The Unforgiving Minute, Rear Admiral Sir Morgan Morgan-Giles, Published privately
HMS Belfast Guide Book, IWM
Anatomy of the Ship: The Cruiser HMS Belfast, Ross Watton, Conway
Commission Books 1950-1952, 1959-1961, 1960-1962
Death of the Scharnhorst, John Winton, Cassell Military Paperbacks.
The King's Cruisers, Gordon Holman, Hodder & Stoughton
The War at Sea, 1939-1945 (Three volumes), Captain S W Roskill CBE, DSC FBA, DLitt HMSO
HMS Belfast – An Illustrated Tour of the Machinery Spaces, John J. Hole.

Glossary of Abbreviations

PERSONNEL

AB	Able Seaman
AF	Admiral of the Fleet
AS	Admiral Superintendent (of Rosyth Naval Base)
CD	Captain of the Dockyard
C-in-C Rosyth	Commander-in-Chief, Rosyth Naval Base (1939 – 1943 Rear-Admiral)
D4	Captain of 4th Destroyer Squadron
DCO	Duty Commanding Officer
DNC	Director Naval Construction
GO	Gunnery Officer
MS	Minesweeper
OOW	Officer of the Watch
PCO	Principal Control Officer
PO	Petty Officer
RN	Royal Navy
RNR	Royal Naval Reserve
RP Rating	Radar Plotter
Snotty	Midshipman
S.O.(O).	Staff Officer (Operations)
V Adm	Vice Admiral

ORDERS, DECORATIONS AND MEDALS

CB	Companion, The Most Honourable Order of the Bath
CBE	Commander of The Order of the British Empire
DSO	Distinguished Service Order
DSC	Distinguished Service Cross
DL	Deputy Lieutenant (of a county)
GCB	Knight Grand Cross, The Most Honourable Order of the Bath
GCStJ	Bailiff Grand Cross of the Order of St John
JP	Justice of the Peace
KCVO	Knight Commander of the Royal Victorian Order
KG	Knight of The Most Noble Order of the Garter
LVO	Lieutenant of the Royal Victorian Order
OBE	Officer of The Order of the British Empire

FUNCTIONS/DEPARTMENTS

ADR — Aircraft Direction Room
AIO — Action Information Organisation
Cwt — Hundredweight (long or imperial hundredweight of 8 stone (112 lb or 50.802345 kg): 20 hundredweight = 1 ton, a long (UK/Imperial) ton of 2240 lb.
ER — Engine Room
FFO — Furnace Fuel Oil
MSO — Main Signal Office
r.p.m. — Revolutions per Minute

SIGNALS

PL — Plain Language (in regard to signalling lamp messages)
TOD — Time of Despatch (for signal)
TOR — Time of Receipt

UPPER DECK

Boat's Falls — Ropes to hoist boats inboard the ship
Capstan — Machinery to wind in the anchor cable
Carley Floats — Life-saving equipment
Gunwale — The top edge along the boat or ship's side
Paravane — a towed, winged (hydrofoiled) underwater object; like a water kite
RAS — Replenishment at Sea
RFA — Royal Fleet Auxiliary
RNSA — Royal Naval Sailing Association
Scupper — Gutters to take sea water down ship's side

NAVIGATION & SURFACE/AIR DEFENCE

AA — Anti-aircraft
Arctic Convoys — JW – Outward from Iceland, usually off Hvalfjörður north of Jan Mayen Island to Arkhangelsk or Murmansk. From February 1942 from Loch Ewe, Scotland
RA – Inward back to Iceland and then Loch Ewe
ARL table — Admiralty Research laboratory to compute position etc
AWL — Above the Waterline
DCT — Director Control Tower
D/F — Direction Finding
GDP — Gun Direction Platform
HA — High Altitude
IFF — Identification Friend or Foe
MLA — In navigation; Mean Line of Advance
W/T — Wireless Telegraphy

Index

HMS *BELFAST* TIMELINE

21 September 1936	Contracts placed for HMS *Edinburgh* (Swan Hunter) and HMS *Belfast* (Harland and Wolff, Yard No.1000)
10 December 1936	Keel laid down
17 March 1938	Launched by Mrs Neville Chamberlain
17 March to 3 August 1939	Fitting out and trials
5 August 1939	Commissioned
3 September 1939	Northern patrol – joined 18th Cruiser Squadron
9 October 1939	Capture of Cap Norte
21 November 1939	Struck German mine in Firth of Forth
28 June 1940	Sailed Rosyth to Devonport
4 July 1940 to 31 October 1942	Repairs and update in Devonport
3 November 1942	Recommissioned under Captain FR Parham RN. Sailed to Scapa Flow: flag ship to V Adm Robert Burnett, 10th Cruiser Squadron, Home Fleet
December 1942 to August 1945	Involved with Arctic Convoys, Northern Blockade patrol
26 December 1943	Battle of North Cape (sinking of *Scharnhorst*)
3 April 1944	With Home Fleet during strike against *Tirpitz* – Operation Tungsten
6 June to 12 July 1944	D-Day Landings – Operation Neptune – HQ ship of Bombardment Group Eastern Task Force, Juno Beach
July 1944 to 18 April 1945	Refit in Sunderland for Far East deployment
17 June 1945	Sailed for the Far East
August 1945	Short refit Sydney, Australia
9 September to 30 December 1945	R Adm RM Servaes hoisted flag – involved in rehabilitating POWs and imprisoned civilians Shanghai
16 May to 15 July 1946	Refit in Singapore
29 July 1946	Flagship of V Adm Sir Denis Boyd – visits to Japan and Hong Kong
1947	Malayan Emergency
15 Oct 1947 to 15 Oct 1948	Paid off into reserve in Portsmouth. Long refit
20 October 1948	Official visit to city of Belfast
December 1949	Hong Kong as Flagship of 5th Cruiser Squadron under V Adm ACC Madden